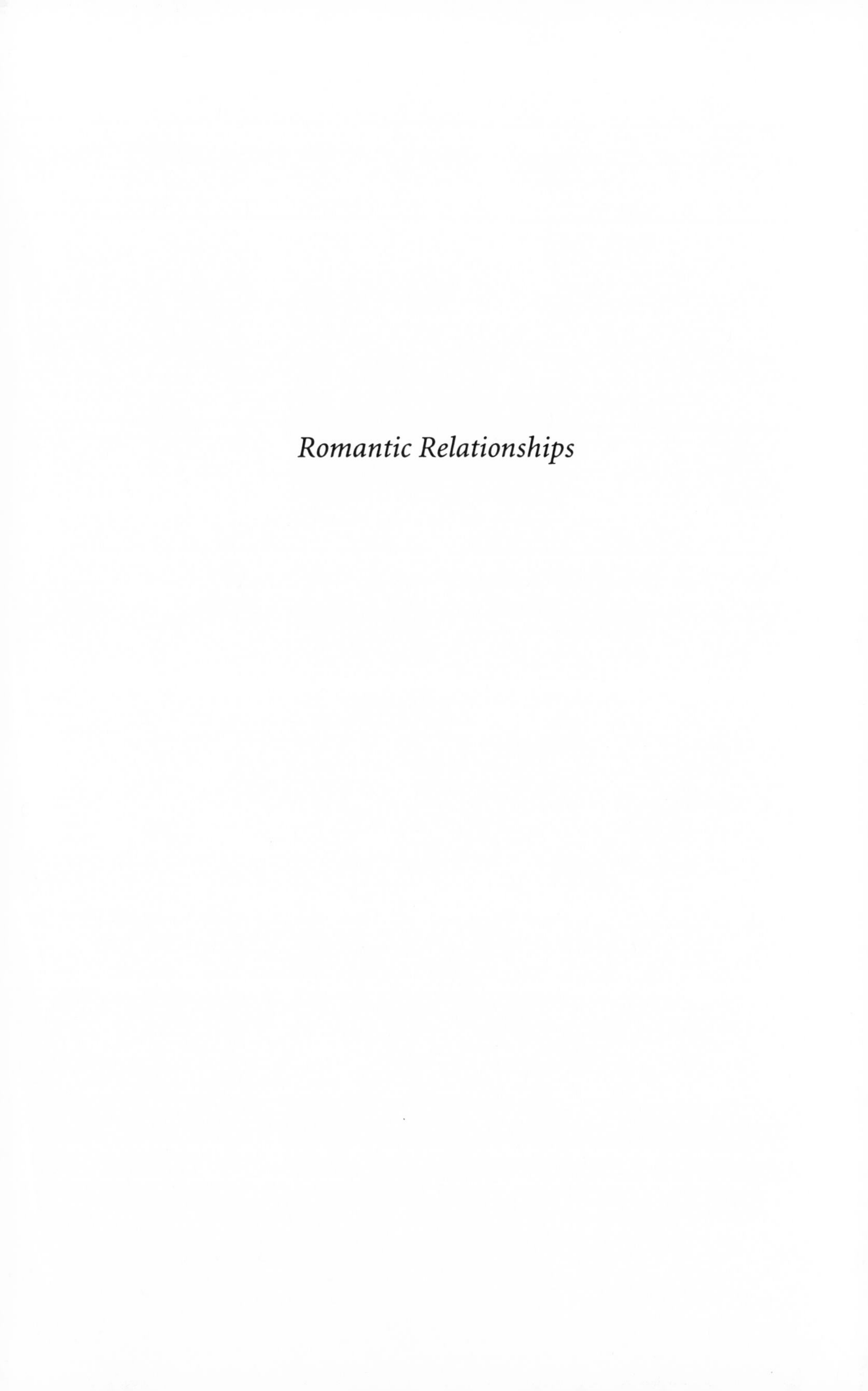

Romantic Relationships

Romantic Relationships

A Psychologist Answers Frequently Asked Questions

by

Paul R. Robbins

McFarland & Company, Inc., Publishers
Jefferson, North Carolina, and London

Front cover photo: Courtesy of Jared and Tressa Wayman.
Back cover photo: Courtesy of Allen and Helen Miller.

British Library Cataloguing-in-Publication data are available

Library of Congress Cataloguing-in-Publication Data

Robbins, Paul R. (Paul Richard)
Romantic relationships : a psychologist answers frequently asked questions / by Paul R. Robbins.
p. cm.
Includes bibliographical references (p.) and index.
ISBN 0-7864-0192-3 (sewn softcover : 50# alk. paper) ♾
1. Intimacy (Psychology) 2. Love. 3. Interpersonal relations. I. Title.
BF575.I5R63 1996
306.7—dc20 96-24583
CIP

Manufactured in the United States of America

McFarland & Company, Inc., Publishers
Box 611, Jefferson, North Carolina 28640

To Sharon,
my brothers, and their wives

Acknowledgments

The author would like to thank Sharon Hauge, Martha Weaver, and Miriam Yarmolinsky for their help in preparing the manuscript.

Grateful acknowledgment is also made to the following for granting permission to reprint from their copyrighted materials: Sage Publications for C. Hendrick et al., "Do Men and Women Love Differently?" *Journal of Social and Personal Relationships,* 1 (1984): 177–195, and J.H. Harvey et al., "Vivid Memories of Vivid Loves Gone By," *Journal of Social and Personal Relationships,* 3 (1986): 359–373; Sussex Publications for P. Salovey and J. Rodin, "The Heart of Jealousy," *Psychology Today,* September 1985, J. Lauer and R. Lauer, "Marriages Are Made to Last," *Psychology Today,* June 1985, and T. P. Cash et al., "The Great American Shape-Up," *Psychology Today,* April 1986; the American Orthopsychiatric Association for A.W. Burgess and L.L. Holmstrom, "Rape, Sexual Disruption and Recovery," *American Journal of Orthopsychiatry,* 49 (1989): 648–657; the American Psychiatric Association for *Diagnostic and Statistical Manual of Mental Disorders Third Edition, Revised,* Washington, D.C., 1987; *Psychotherapy* for R.M. Bergner and L.L. Bergner, "Sexual Misunderstanding: A Descriptive and Pragmatic Formulation," *Psychotherapy,* 27 (1990): 464–467; Baywood Publishing Company for A.F. Campagna, "Fantasy and Sexual Arousal in College Men: Normative and Functional Aspects," *Imagination, Cognition and Personality,* 5 (1985–1986): 3–20.

The author also wishes to thank the following individuals for granting permission to quote from their materials: Leo P. Hennigan, *A Conspiracy of Silence: Alcoholism* (Bethesda, MD: Gannel, 1989); Etiony Aldarondo, "Cessation and Persistence of Wife Assault: A Longitudinal Analysis," presented at the annual meeting of the American Psychological Association (1992); Ed Long, *Self Dyadic Perspective-Taking Scale* (1990); Mauricio Gaborit et al., *Codependency and Self-Monitoring;* and Mary P. Koss for her August 29, 1990, testimony before the Senate Judiciary Committee, "Rape Incidence: A Review and Assessment of the Data."

Table of Contents

4 ❤ Male and Female Expectations

5 ❤ Meeting the Opposite Sex

6 ❤ Rape

7 ❤ Relationships

8 ❤ Understanding Your Partner

9 ❤ Conflict Resolution

10 ❤ Sexual Activity

11 ❤ Drugs and AIDS

12 ❤ Sexual Fantasies

13 ❤ Relationships and Marriage

Preface

I have been practicing psychotherapy for many years in a suburb of Washington, D.C. My consulting office is in my home. It is a pleasant setting; the office overlooks a wooded area fronted with large oak trees and populated by small wild creatures: birds, squirrels, tortoises, raccoons and an occasional cottontail. I find it a congenial place to work, and the setting seems to have a relaxing effect on my clients, which is helpful, for therapy can be serious business when people are feeling agitated or very depressed.

Some of the people who have come to see me over the years have had phobias. Other clients have had drug or alcohol problems. On one occasion, a young woman came to see me and stated that she had 26 distinct personalities, a story reminiscent of the movie *Three Faces of Eve.* Still, by and large, the people who come to see me are not at all unusual. They are indistinguishable from one's friends, neighbors and coworkers. They may be feeling upset, and their morale may have taken a temporary tumble. In trying to discover the source of their problems, I have found that often my clients are experiencing difficulties with interpersonal relationships. Things are just not working out well with people who are important in their lives. And very often, the trouble is with a romantic partner — husband, wife, boyfriend or girlfriend.

In the seclusion of my office my clients and I often discuss romantic relationships. They ask such questions as the following: "I'm lonely, how do I meet someone?" "We've been going together for over a year. I love him, but he doesn't want to make a commitment. What should I do?" "My wife and I fight all the time. It's wrecking our marriage. What can we do?" "Since we broke up, I've been depressed. I can't get her off my mind. How do I get over her?"

I try not to offer pat answers to such questions, because I'm not sure there are any hard and fast answers that work for everybody. That doesn't mean, however, that there are not useful things to talk about and valuable information to share. Like most therapists, I draw on my own personal experience, on what I have learned while working with patients, and on the research reported in the psychological literature. While researchers have much yet to discover about the subtleties of human relationships, they have found out a good deal. Some of the findings reported from research on romantic relationships confirm what our common sense tells us. Other findings are surprising. Most of what research has revealed is interesting and much of it is useful.

While research about romantic relationships produces valuable information, the information is not always easy for most people to access. Research is reported in scholarly journals and written in technical language. I wondered if one could take the main findings of these reports, translate them into everyday language, and organize them into an easily accessible form. I believed so and set out to accomplish the task. I have used the question and answer format because it keeps the discussion focused and to the point. While the questions follow each other in an organized manner there is no need to start at the beginning of the book. One can start with any question of particular interest. This work contains a number of anecdotes and brief stories about people in order to illustrate the points being considered. While the stories that I present are based on real people, they have been substantially altered to protect the identities of the people involved.

Paul R. Robbins, Ph.D.
July 1, 1996

1. Romantic Love

What is romantic love?

Every year on Valentine's Day, a large metropolitan newspaper prints a special section of love notes. Hundreds of these notes are penned by men for the women in their lives, and by women for the men in their lives. If you peruse these notes, you will encounter sentimentality, passion, and lavish praise for loved ones: "I adore you." "You are always in my thoughts." "You are my dreams come true." "You're perfect—never, never change." "You have filled the emptiness in my heart with happiness." When we inquire about the nature of romantic love, it is hard to escape the feeling that the answer lies in such notes, that the essence of romantic love is scattered among these messages, waiting to be distilled and defined.

In reading through these love notes, however, it soon becomes clear that the writers are expressing a number of different ideas. A few of the messages have erotic overtones, stating, for example, how wonderful it was to sleep together the night before. Other messages speak of activities shared together—that special trip to the mountains, those walks in the park. Still others speak of long years of devotion, of being a wonderful husband and father: "Thank you for twelve years of being a wonderful mate to me and a loving father for Julie and Karen." Even the most romantic of people, when voicing their thoughts beyond a simple declaration of love, give different meanings to the word.

"Love Is a Many-Splendored Thing" is the title of a popular song of many years ago. It is a lovely, evocative title, based on a book entitled *A Many-Splendored Thing* by the Eurasian writer Suyim Han. The title suggests that love is both beautiful and multifaceted. Research, too, suggests that love is multifaceted with different meanings for different people. Two Canadian psychologists, Beverly Fehr and James Russell, asked a group of college students to list "as many types of love as come to mind."[1] The students wrote down over 200 types of love. The list included parental love, brotherly love, patriotic love, and love of God, art, nature, pets, beauty, work, and self. Interestingly, the researchers observed that the students did not see sharp boundaries between love and related experiences. Many of the college students said "passion" was a type of love, but many did not. The same was true for "tenderness." And the students were split about evenly on whether they felt "desire" was a form of love or something else.

While most of us share a central or core understanding of the word "love," the meaning of the word can become blurred around the edges. When a man and a woman talk about loving each other, they many not be talking about precisely the same thing. He may mean one thing; she may mean something else. As we shall see later in this book, such differences may have a multitude of consequences.

Since the time of Freud, psychologists have theorized about the nature of love. Freud had quite a lot to say about the subject in his three essays "Contributions to the Psychology of Love," as did those who followed him in the psychoanalytic tradition. Theodore Reik, for example, wrote a book called *A Psychologist Looks at Love,* and Eric Fromm contributed *The Art of Loving.* There is a growing list of people coming from the ranks of academic psychology who have contributed both research and fresh ideas to our understanding of love. Some of these theories about love are intriguing For example, it has been proposed that the kinds of romantic attachments that adults form with each other are similar to the early attachments they had with their parents, particularly their mothers. The idea is that children who have had secure early attachments are more likely to have secure relationships with their romantic partners, and children who have had insecure early attachments will have predictable kinds of difficulties in their adult romantic relationships. We will examine the evidence for this theory later.

Robert Sternberg of Yale University has proposed a way of looking at love that I find particularly useful. He views love as having three major components. The first is intimacy: "those feelings in a relationship that promote closeness, bondedness, and connectedness."[2] Think of such behavior as sharing conversations about the day's events and disclosing confidences. A good example would be "pillow talk," those intimate conversations between a husband and wife before going to sleep. The second component is passion. Sternberg views passion as a mix of biological and psychological needs. With passion, there is longing for another person, often heightened by strong sexual desires. Passion has an intensity that contrasts with the quiet of intimacy. One thinks of the passions of romantic novels. Finally, there is the component called decision/commitment. Decision is simply a recognition: "Yes, it's true — I love him." Commitment, in contrast, is long term: "I'm going to stay with him."

Try looking at these components two at a time as pairs and asking yourself what it would be like in a relationship to have both present or to have one without the other. Consider, for example, an intimate relationship without passion. Doesn't that sound like platonic friendship? Or how about passion without intimacy? Sternberg sees this as infatuation. Passion without commitment sounds like another name for a one-night stand. Sternberg views romantic love as a relationship with both passion and intimacy. When you add commitment to these two, then you might expect to have the most encompassing and possibly the most fulfilling of male-female relationships.

Sternberg's model of love is a useful way of organizing one's thinking, but may fall short of capturing the subtleties of romantic love. Think, for example, of the feeling of being in love, the sense of excitement, magic, bewilderment, the ups and downs, the preoccupation with the object of affection. When one is in love, life transcends the routine and acquires a specialness. It is difficult to do justice to these feelings in an abstract psychological model. The language of poets with its metaphors and similes has advantages in communicating the range of feelings and experiences involved.

Psychologists are far from poets. They are trained in a scientific tradition and try to define things as precisely as they can so they can do research which allows other investigators to confirm and replicate what they have found. And we must state that the study of romantic relationships is still in an early stage. The language psychologists use in describing romantic love is by no means settled, and there are still uncertainties about fundamental questions. It is not entirely clear how romantic love differs from other types of love or to what extent love overlaps with or differs from what we call liking. But we have no wish to begin this inquiry by becoming bogged down in semantics. Instead, let us simply recognize that the meanings of love can be varied and that the shades of differences that we have in our understandings of love may complicate our relationships.

How do friends behave toward friends and how do lovers behave toward lovers?

Bill and Julie have been very good friends for a number of years. They both teach at a suburban high school. She teaches English and creative writing, and he teaches mathematics. They talk to each other every day at school and often call each other on the telephone to discuss events at the school as well as things that happen to them in their daily lives. They have a high regard for each other, but have never dated. Their relationship is an example of what Robert Sternberg called intimacy without passion. In contrast,

John and Karen met in a singles bar. On their third date, they became sexually intimate. Their romance has maintained a high intensity level featuring two knock down, drag-out fights. Putting these aside, Karen is planning on moving in with John.

Sexual intimacy and passion color the relationship of John and Karen and seem to be totally lacking in the relationship of Bill and Julie. Are these elements the keys to distinguishing romantic love and friendship? Or is there more? Keith Davis of the University of South Carolina with his colleague Michael Todd has been carrying out research comparing the reactions of lovers and best friends. They have reported some interesting and surprising results.

First, male-female "best-friends" relationships (without any romantic elements) occur more often than one might suppose. Friendships like Bill and Julie's are not that unusual. Twenty-seven percent of the subjects in the study reported that their best friend was of the opposite sex.[3] When the researchers compared the relationships of lovers to the relationships of friends, they found higher levels of fascination, exclusiveness, and enjoyment among the lovers. But, lovers also displayed higher levels of ambivalence and conflict and less acceptance of each other than was the case with friends. And perhaps most importantly, there was less stability among lovers. Lovers were more concerned that the relationship might break up.

For friends and lovers, there was about the same level of trust, confiding and respect. So for the quieter moments of human interaction, it doesn't seem to matter that much whether one's partner is a friend or lover. The differences emerge in the higher voltage aspects of male-female interactions that one sees with John and Karen. Here one is more likely to find both passion and volatility. Do we wish to make lovers of friends? Is that the way to go? As we shall see, many women find this an attractive idea. It offers prospects of long-term stability. But love can be like a powder keg that when ignited doesn't follow neat rules.

How high a value do we place on romantic relationships?

While it would be presumptuous to place numerical values on romantic relationships, a few statistics might be instructive. In 1992, U.S. sales of cosmetics and related products totaled 19.5 billion dollars.[4] In a book prepared by the American Academy of Facial, Plastic, and Reconstructive Surgery, it was stated that over 500,000 people a year contact facial plastic surgeons concerning surgery that would give them a more aesthetically pleasing nose.[5] In 1994, circulation of *Glamour* magazine was listed at 2.3 million.[6] Obviously, people want to look good for a variety of reasons besides increasing their attractiveness for romantic relationships, but a good deal of the money spent for such items as perfumes, colognes, false eyelashes, and lipsticks is targeted toward attracting the opposite sex.

There are singles clubs in churches and singles clubs which are businesses. There are even some businesses which have gone nationwide, franchising the opportunity of meeting someone for a romantic relationship. And the costs of participating are not inexpensive. Our preoccupation with romantic relationships is also evidenced by coverage in the mass media. Supermarket tabloids make a living publishing stories about sex and celebrities. Daytime television on the networks is largely given over to soap operas, saturated with romantic passions. One of the best selling genres of paperback books is the romantic novel. And the songs recorded by our favorite artists that have sold in the millions are often about love. How many country-western songs have been written about hearts—broken, busted, or cheating?

While it is hard to put an exact value on what romantic relationships mean in our lives, judging from the time and effort we put into pursuing such relationships, it is obvious that they mean a great deal. Romantic relationships even seep into our fantasies. I have been carrying out research about the daydreams of college students. Do students daydream about being successful writers, artists, or entrepreneurs? Do they dream of chucking it all and going to a South Seas island? A few do, but most of the students in my sample fantasize about their boyfriends and girlfriends.

If we look at romantic relationships from the vantage point of the sadness and grief of failed relationships, it is evident that these relationships can be at the very top of the list of what is compelling in our lives. One can see this clearly in psychotherapy where we often work with people who are experiencing despair that is a result of unrequited, conflicted and dissolving romantic relationships. Michele is a good illustration. A flight attendant in her mid-twenties, Michele entered therapy because she was feeling depressed about breaking up with a man she had been seeing for several years. She said, "I still think about him a lot. I wish he were here. He promises to telephone me, but he doesn't. Sometimes I think about calling him. I go to the phone and just stand there. I don't even dial. Then I panic. I go to his apartment and see him. He tells me he's sorry. He apologizes for not calling. But, I know he's not going to. It's just so hard. He meant so much to me."

Relationships are very important. Studies show that people who are married are generally happier, healthier and live longer than people who are not.[7] The alternative to a romantic relationship is not necessarily loneliness. There are other relationships in life which offer companionship and support. Still people who do not have someone who is special and exclusive in their lives may feel left out. They may have a lingering sense of frustration that they are missing some of the best things that life can offer.

The problem can be particularly troublesome for people who are not in relationships and feel conflict about developing the level of intimacy one experiences in romantic relationships. In studying a group of sorority women, Nancy Cantor of Princeton University and her colleagues found that women who experienced such conflicts and had no relationship spent as much time thinking about relationships as their sorority sisters who had relationships. The difference was that these conflicted women "experienced the task as more difficult, challenging and stressful than did their peers who were in relationships."[8] One senses here a combination of preoccupation, uncertainty, and dissatisfaction.

Are you a romantic?

A dictionary provided a variety of meanings for the word "romantic." A romantic was described as visionary, impractical, quixotic, passionate, adventurous, and preoccupied with idealized courting and lovemaking. These words bring to mind a picture of an empty-headed swashbuckler, a caricature of the Three Musketeers. This is not exactly what I have in mind when I think of a romantic. If we confine the meaning more narrowly to relationships, my idea of a romantic is a person who responds warmly to the idea of love, a person who is receptive to being in love and feels empathy with others who are in love. Does this describe you? If you're not sure, consider how you respond to romantic ideas.

Do you ever watch the late-night show or a channel that features old movies? If you do, on rare occasions you might run across such films as *The Student Prince* or *The Desert Song* or perhaps even *New Moon* or *Maytime*, all of these being operettas of Sigmund Romberg. Or perhaps you might watch a showing of Victor Herbert's *Naughty Marietta*, Franz Lehar's *Merry Widow* or Rudolf Friml's *Rose Marie* or *Vagabond King*. These vintage operettas with their soaring melodies and lyrics of strongly felt love are long out of fashion. But when operettas were in vogue, audiences thrilled to beautiful voices singing beautiful songs — men and women singing of their love for each other to each other. If you like this kind of music, I would say that you're an unabashed romantic.

Musical styles change. In America, we have gone from the operetta, which was a European import, to the Broadway musical and to Tin Pan Alley, jazz, country-western, rock 'n' roll, and new musical forms beyond. Romantic love songs have been composed in almost all of these musical genres. Think of George and Ira Gershwin's "Embraceable You," Rodgers and

Hammerstein's "If I Loved You," Meredith Willson's "Till There Was You," Cole Porter's "So in Love Am I," and Lerner and Lowe's "If Ever I Would Leave You?" to name a few songs from the brilliant array of musicals that played on Broadway. Or consider the songs of Duke Ellington or contemporary country or rock. Are there special songs in your life? How do you respond when you hear them? Do they bring back memories of special moments and special people? Do they put you in a mood for love? If they do, you have a romantic streak.

Romantic love poems may be as out-of-style as operettas. Many of us have not opened a book of poetry since our last high school or college class in English. Do you remember having to analyze poems in terms of meters and poetic devices? Remember tetrameters, pentameters, and hexameters and such dreadful terms as "onomatopoeia"? How did you respond to poems of deeply felt love such as this classic statement of Elizabeth Barrett Browning?

> How do I love thee? Let me count the ways.
> I love thee to the depth and breadth and height
> My soul can reach, when feeling out of sight
> For the ends of Being and ideal Grace.
> I love thee to the level of everyday's
> Most quiet need, by sun and candle-light.
> I love thee freely, as men strive for Right;
> I love thee purely, as they turn from Praise.
> I love thee with the passion put to use
> In my old griefs, and with my childhood's faith.
> I love thee with a love I seemed to lose
> With my lost saints — I love thee with the breath,
> Smiles, tears, of all my life! — and, if God choose,
> I shall but love thee better after death.[9]

Does this poem move you? If so, are you also touched by the recognition of love in Shakespeare's beautiful balcony scene in Romeo and Juliet? Can you recall some of the tender phrases that Shakespeare put into the mouths of his young lovers?

> But, soft! what light through yonder window breaks?
> It is the east, and Juliet is the sun.
>
> What's in a name? That which we call a rose
> By any other word would smell as sweet;
> So Romeo would, were he not Romeo call'd,
> Retain that dear perfection which he owes
> Without that title.
>
> My bounty is as boundless as the sea,
> My love as deep; the more I give to thee,
> The more I have, for both are infinite.

> Good-night, good night! Parting is such sweet sorrow,
> That I shall say good-night till it be morrow.[10]

Do these lines bring back the scene? If the awakening of young love gives you a warm feeling, there is more than a little of the romantic in you. Chances are that you also enjoy that touching scene in the opera *La Bohème* where Rudolpho and Mimi discover their feelings for each other on a wintry evening in the garrets of Paris.

How do you respond to scenes in which lovers are parted forever by circumstances beyond their control? Remember the sad ending of Erich Segal's *Love Story* or the final scenes of the operas *La Traviata* or *La Bohème* where the heroines die after lingering illnesses? Or do you recall the real tragedy of Crown Prince Rudolph, heir to the Austrian throne, who in a deserted hunting lodge near the village of Mayerling died in an apparent suicide with his lover Baroness Vetssera, because the nineteenth century world they knew would not permit them to be together.

Or finally, think about one of Hollywood's most memorable movies, *Casablanca.* Wouldn't it be nice if every pair of lovers had a pianist like Sam to play "As Time Goes By" while they sat and sipped champagne in a romantic cafe? Do you recall the last scenes in the film where Rick (Humphrey Bogart) was faced with the wrenching decision to give up Ilsa (Ingrid Bergman), because what she had to do was recognized as more important than their feelings for each other? I have heard it stated, though I don't know whether it is true, that the decision of how to end the film — whether Ilsa would stay with Rick — was so tough that even the people who made the movie were not certain what to do until shooting was almost finished.

As a romantic, one would have to say that the decision, sad and inspirational as it was, had to be made the way it was. But how unsatisfying. Isn't there some way that true lovers Rick and Ilsa could get together without upsetting the constraints of geopolitics? Alas, not in that war-time movie. But, how about a sequel? Couldn't there be a *Casablanca II*? Why not? They wrote a sequel for *Gone with the Wind.* If you are a romantic, you should be able to imagine your own sequel. For example, can you picture Rick successfully completing the hazardous missions for the free French which he was on the verge of joining as the film ended? Perhaps, Rick could become an attaché with Patton's invading army as it rolled through North Africa, and when the war is finally over (it might take *Casablanca III* or *IV* to get this far) is reunited with Ilsa who is given her freedom by understanding husband Victor Lazlo who, recognizing the sacrifice Ilsa made, does the right things. If you're a true romantic, why not?

2. *Childhood Influences*

How do our attachments in childhood influence our ability to experience love as adults?

Some people who come to see me about relationship problems not only present their own diagnosis, "I'm co-dependent," but also have already formulated an explanation of how they got that way. The most popular explanation offered is deficiencies in the way they were reared as children. The following are typical complaints: "There was no affection in my house." "My mother was cold — remote." "My father was critical — it didn't pay to argue with him." "Neither of my parents was affectionate. I didn't know what affection was until I met Joan." "My father was never there." The culprits in these cases are sometimes the father, more often the mother, and sometimes both parents. What mother did or failed to do has been blamed for everything that has gone wrong or could go wrong. Is this fair? Probably not. Is there any truth to the charge? Probably yes. The relationship between mother and child has an impact which appears to be far reaching even into adult romantic relationships.

This is an assertion which needs documenting. The documentation I will offer is a brief description of some of the research that led to this conclusion. My story begins in England around the time of the Second World War. A psychiatrist, John Bowlby, was observing very young children who had been separated from their parents. Bowlby noted that the effects of a prolonged separation were sometimes profound. The child reacted initially with angry protest, which in time subsided, giving way to despair. Finally, the child seemed detached, with diminished interest in relating to adults.[1] Bowlby concluded that a secure early attachment between the young child and his primary caregiver seemed vital for the child's normal development. Severe neglect of children can result in serious emotional problems.

Now Bowlby's observations were of young children raised under unusual conditions. What happens when we look within the normal range of mother-child interactions? Does the quality of the attachment the child develops with his mother influence his ability to form relationships with others? And if so, how far-reaching is the effect?

To examine these questions, let's turn next to the work of a Canadian psychologist, Mary Ainsworth, who developed an experimental procedure for studying the effects of separating mother and child called the "strange situation."[2] In the procedure, infants are left by their mothers in an unfamiliar room—at times all alone, and at times with an unfamiliar person. The behavior of the infant is carefully observed, both in these unfamiliar circumstances and when the infant is reunited with his mother. After watching the infants, observers characterize them as being secure in the strange situation or as showing either of two patterns of insecure behavior. The secure infant is easily comforted by his mother when she returns and is quick to resume normal activities. The two patterns of insecure attachment observers look for have been called "avoidant" (the child avoids and ignores the mother during much of the experiment) and "anxious/ambivalent" (the child both seeks his mother and acts resistant to her).

The behavior of young children in the strange situation is a fairly good indicator of how they behave in the real world. Very young children who appear securely attached to their mothers in the strange situation seem more competent in the way they explore the world in which they live, and they are more comfortable in the way they interact with others. Trust and confidence in his mother seem to promote increased confidence in the child in developing secure relationships with other people.

This does not mean, of course, that a poor early relationship with his mother inevitably produces a child and eventually an adult who cannot develop secure relationships with others. Too many things happen in life's myriad of experiences to allow one to make an accurate prediction for any given individual. Through the course of the years, some children with poor early parenting turn out well, and some with excellent early parenting develop lots of problems. Still there is tentative evidence that the reach of early development can be a long one, even influencing the comfort level and closeness of adult romantic relationships.

Following Ainsworth's research with the strange situation, psychologists were intrigued by similarities in the way she described children's attachments to their mothers and the kind of romantic attachments adult men and women form with each other. Some adult romantic relationships are secure; others are insecure in ways that resemble Ainsworth's categories. Researchers Cindy Hazan and Philip Shaver translated Ainsworth's descriptions into three adult analogues. Romantic attachments were characterized as follows: (1) "secure" (you feel it's easy to get close to others, you're comfortable depending on others, and you're not worried about being abandoned or someone's getting too close to you); (2) "avoidant" (you're uncomfortable being close to others, you find it difficult to trust another completely, you get nervous when someone gets too close to you, and romantic partners want you to be more intimate than you are comfortable about); (3) "anxious/ambivalent" (you feel your partner is not as close as you would like, you wonder whether your partner really loves you, you have a desire to get very close to the other person which can scare him or her away, and you worry about being abandoned).

You might pause for a moment and ask yourself which of these categories comes closest to describing your own pattern of attachment in a romantic relationship. Hazan and Shaver reported that slightly over half of their subjects described themselves as secure, about one-quarter as avoidant, and about one-fifth as anxious/ambivalent. Interestingly, researchers who have carried our similar studies in other countries (Australia and Israel) have reported very similar figures.

Hazan and Shaver then studied the attitudes that people with these three patterns of romantic attachment had about love. They found that people who reported that their attachments were secure were more likely to endorse such statements as "Romantic feelings wax and wane over the course of a relationship, but at times they can be an intense as they were at the start." People with avoidant attachments were more likely to endorse such statements as "It's rare to find someone you can really fall in love with," while those with anxious/ambivalent attachments were more likely to endorse statements such as "It's easy to fall in love. I feel myself beginning to fall in love often."[3]

The researchers then took the step of linking adult romantic attachment styles with the subjects' memories of the kind of attachments they had with their parents. Here is what they reported: "These results can be summarized by saying that secure subjects, in comparison with insecure subjects, reported warmer relationships with both parents and between their two parents. Avoidant subjects, in comparison with anxious/ambivalent subjects, described their mothers as cold and rejecting. Anxious/ambivalent subjects saw their fathers as unfair."[4]

In a follow-up study, Nancy Collins and Stephen Read of the University of Southern California confirmed some of these results finding that students with more secure attachment styles tended to report that their parents had "been warm and not rejecting," while students with anxious attachment styles indicated that their parents had been "cold or inconsistent."[5] The researchers also reported that the level of trust the students currently placed in the dependability of others was related to their memories of their parents. A recollection of "warm and responsive" parents was related to more trust, while a memory of "rejecting and inconsistent parenting" was related to less trust.[6]

I would like to stress that these studies are retrospective, utilizing memories of how one's parents behaved during one's early years. Because such memories can be biased in various ways, we have to be cautious in accepting the results at face value. However if the conclusions prove to be valid, then it would appear that the reach of early parent-child interactions may extend to the comfort level we experience in our most intimate adult relationships.

What can go wrong in childhood that can diminish our capacity for love?

There are many things that happen during our childhoods which influence the way we relate to other people and our capacities to give and experience love. Sometimes these events enhance our capacities, like growing up amongst warm and wonderful people. Sometimes we experience childhood events which create anger and lingering distrust. Childhood experiences influence us in both profound and subtle ways; and in the latter instances we may be only dimly aware of what is happening to us. I would like to spend some time discussing three types of profound experiences that happen to many people during childhood which often have long-term implications for the way they relate to others. These experiences are child abuse, breakup of the family, and peer rejection.

Kathy is an outpatient at a community mental health clinic. She came to the clinic because she felt lonely and depressed, and because she has been unable to form close relationships with people. She reported that she has never had a sustained, satisfactory relationship with a man. She said she didn't trust people and often felt very angry. In the initial interview, Kathy described her father as an alcoholic who sometimes became violent when drunk, and her mother as being both verbally and physically abusive to her. At the age of fourteen, after a knockdown, drag-out fight with her father, she ran away. She lived in a succession of foster homes, took up with several men, had an abortion, then found herself alone and isolated. She entered therapy in the hope of turning her life around.

Kathy's story is not very different from the stories of thousands of other men and women. In all too many homes, parent-child relationships are destructive; children are emotionally and physically abused. We are talking about impatient, frustrated, angry and alcoholic parents who often scream at their children, berate and humiliate them and use them as punching bags.

Parents who physically and emotionally abuse their children are not as a rule crazy or weird or profoundly disturbed. They do tend to be "stressed out" by parenting, and often lack the patience and equanimity needed to cope with the constant demands of a young child. They react too often to these demands with angry outbursts and physical beatings.

The psychological effects of such child abuse have been studied by researchers. In a 1989 special issue of *American Psychologist* devoted to children, Robert Emery summarized some of these effects.

> A listing of difficulties that have been found in empirical research on abused children illustrates the point that the outcomes of abuse are diverse. These include increased aggression ... troubled peer relationships ... impaired social cognitions ... lack of empathy ... depression ... and lower performance on cognitive tasks.[7]

Troubled peer relationships, lack of empathy and increased aggression are outcomes which do not augur well for future adult relationships. Increased aggression, in particular, is worrisome, for there is evidence that children who are abused have a higher risk of becoming abusive themselves when they become husbands and wives, and parents. (I shall have more to say about angry men in relationships later in the book.) Even if a child is not the direct target of family violence, just growing up in a household which is prone to discord and conflict can engender emotional damage in the child. Watching parents quarrel incessantly, or witnessing violence between spouses is distressing to children. This discord can even affect infants. In his article, Emery noted, "children as young as 12 months old have been found to respond to episodes of anger *not directed at them* with signs of distress ranging from crying to increased aggression."[8]

The psychological effects of a breakup of the family, particularly through divorce, are diverse. Boys and girls tend to react somewhat differently to the divorce of their parents, with girls often making the better initial adjustments. Still, many children of both sexes feel anxious, lonely and depressed, and have angry feelings towards one or both parents. These children may also have problems, both in and out of school. Shattered family ties take a toll which requires time to heal. Researcher E. Mavis Hetherington compared girls whose mothers were divorced with girls whose mothers were widowed, and observed an interesting difference: girls of divorced parents were more likely to begin dating earlier and to become sexually involved earlier than girls whose mothers were widowed. [9] For some of these girls, there seemed to be a compelling need to become reinvolved with a man after the father had left the home.

Tina, who grew up with her single mother, Caroline, provides a clear example of such a precocious sexual interest. Caroline's husband of three years, Tommy, left her when Tina was a baby, and disappeared from their lives. Caroline carved out a new life for herself, holding a variety of jobs, and taking college courses in computer programming. She began dating again and went through a series of unstable and unsatisfying relationships. As Tina grew into a pre-teen, she began to compete with her mother for her boyfriends' attention. When a boyfriend said good-night, Tina would slip out of her bedroom and kiss him on the lips the same way her mother did. She left her mother's home as a teenager and was repeatedly pregnant. It was as if Tina was saying to her mother "I'll do as you do."

Rejection by one's peers during childhood may have long-term implications for later relationships. We are not talking about children who tend to be ignored—kids who quietly fade into the background and to whom nobody pays much attention. These children are usually not disliked, just unnoticed. While they may be shy or have problems in being assertive, their difficulties pale in comparison to the children who are actively disliked and are at the bottom of the popularity poll. Sometimes children may be rejected for completely arbitrary reasons, such as the way they look or speak, or because of their ethnic background. Sometimes it is because of a lack of social skills or because of personal habits which lead to ridicule. Often it is because these children tend to be their own worst enemies; they may be aggressive and disruptive. Whatever the reasons for peer rejection, the rejected child may feel very lonely, even alienated, and is at risk for a variety of short-term and maybe long-range adjustment problems. The symptoms of impending difficulties—avoidance of school and poor school performance—may be observed as early as kindergarten.

In each of these three situations, there is a potential for a serious dislocation in the development of healthy interpersonal relationships. It seems prudent to watch such children for problems as they grow up. If problems emerge, it makes sense to deal with them quickly rather than to wait. Redirection in childhood may head off long term difficulties.

What are the chances of experiencing sexual abuse as a child and what are its long-term effects?

Some time ago, I was asked to respond to a questionnaire survey of psychologists which inquired about our views regarding childhood sexual abuse. One of the questions asked was to estimate the percentage of the population which has experienced such abuse. At the time, I had no idea, and wrote in a rather low figure. Since that time, I have seen estimates published in psychological journals which are a good deal higher than I suspected. For example, in a survey of over 1,000 women students at Memphis State University, 13 percent reported sexual abuse by a family member, and 10 percent by a non–family member.[10] In a study carried out in Los Angeles County, the reports of sexual abuse were even higher: 62 percent of the women surveyed had experienced at least one incident of such abuse.[11] Now if this figure seems astonishing, and I must admit it does to me, it should be pointed out that the researchers included not only incidents involving small children, but those involving adolescents as well. The definitions the researchers used were for children through 17 years of age, so long as the incident was initiated by persons at least five years older than the subject, or involved coercion. I have trouble with this definition, because a relationship between a 17 year old and a 22 year old is not what I think of when I think of child abuse.

Despite my reservations about some of these figures, I have no doubt that childhood sexual abuse is widespread. Sometimes such abuse is an isolated, non-recurring incident; sometimes it is a repeated pattern. In the worse instances, these sexual contacts, including intercourse, occur on a daily basis. Until recently, childhood sexual abuse was one of those "closet conditions"—everyone knew it was happening but few people talked about it. Now there is both increasing discussion of child abuse and research on the problem. The emotional effects of sexual abuse of children are varied. Studies indicate that many of the children will experience symptoms of anxiety and depression. Nightmares are also commonly experienced. About one-third of the children studied show inappropriate sexual behaviors such as making sexual overtures towards other children.[12]

The degree of harm engendered by childhood sexual abuse ranges from relatively slight—a large number of children have no observable problems—to severe, and the more serious problems often persist into adulthood. Adults who were sexually abused as children have reported anxiety, nightmares, and suicidal thoughts. The likelihood of experiencing serious psychological consequences in adulthood seems greater if the incidents were frequent, occurred over an extended period, and generated strong emotional reactions such as guilt, anger and disgust. In considering the impact of childhood sexual abuse on the capacity of women to enter into satisfying adult romantic relationships, one should note that many women have gone through these experiences without reporting serious difficulties in their later relationships. These women apparently weathered the childhood incidents and seem to be doing all right. In some cases, the incidents have only marginal effects. In other cases, the women were able to work through the experience by themselves or with the help of others.

A study by Mavis Tsai and her colleagues at the University of Washington sheds some light on recovery from childhood sexual abuse. The researchers asked women who had been sexually abused as children but had adjusted well to the experience as adults what had happened in their own lives that had made this adjustment possible. These researchers reported the following:

> Two factors were suggested more frequently than all others: (a) support from friends and family members in the form of assurance that the woman had not been at fault, had no reason to feel guilty, and was still a worthwhile person; and (b) sympathetic and understanding sexual partners who helped the woman discontinue generalizing to all men her feelings of "hatred and disgust" for the man who had molested her.[13]

While it is clear that many women are able to substantially recover from childhood sexual abuse and develop satisfying relationships with men, it is equally clear that for many women, this abuse has lingering destructive effects on their ability to relate to men. The abuse has not only damaged their relationships to men, it has negatively impacted their interpersonal relations in general. These women often feel isolated. Frequently, they find it difficult to trust other people. Having been betrayed in childhood, they find it difficult to regain trust in others as adults. Incest victims, in particular, may have difficulties in forming close relationships. Incest is an act which is not likely to be disclosed and may be a secret trauma for years. In one study of incest victims under treatment, nearly two-thirds of the women said they had conflicts with, or fear of, their husbands or romantic partners.[14]

A frequent problem reported by women who experienced childhood sexual abuse is making a sexual adjustment. Many women who were sexually abused as children have anxiety about sex, are unreceptive to sexual invitations, feel guilty about sex, and are dissatisfied when they have sex. Victims of childhood sexual abuse tend to have more negative attitudes about sex.

There are curious cross-currents in the sexual behavior of sexually abused women. While their attitudes towards sex are often negative, research carried out at the University of Rhode Island suggests that they often become sexually active earlier in life, and have more sexual partners than women who did not experience childhood sexual abuse.[15] Paradoxically, rather than avoid sex, some victims of sexual abuse become promiscuous. One theory advanced to explain this behavior is that these victims have learned in their childhood experiences that being sexually available for a man will get them attention and affection; they continue to use sex as the means to fulfill these needs. Perhaps the saddest commentary on the tendency of some abused women to become promiscuous is studies of prostitutes which find a large number of the prostitutes studied were sexually abused as children.

Does growing up with older siblings of the opposite sex help one to interact with members of the opposite sex?

With the exception of his mother, a modest, retiring woman, Fred grew up in an all-male household. There was his father, an older brother and a younger brother. Fred grew up in an environment of baseball bats, footballs, ship models, and toy guns. There were no dolls in the house, no jump ropes, no books written for girls, and the presence of girls in the house was a rarity. Except for casual contacts with classmates at school, to Fred, girls might as well have been an alien species from another planet. When Fred entered adolescence, he became very attracted to a girl in his high school English class. He was entranced by the way she looked, walked, talked and smiled. As the weeks went by, he developed a king-sized crush on her. Fred's problem arose when he tried to talk to her. He felt shy and awkward, and seemed all at sea. He had never really interacted with girls, and had no idea what to say. He was both smitten and miserable.

Fred probably would have had an easier time of it had he had a sister, particularly an older one. For it is a truism that we learn to relate by relating. And what better way is there of developing a feeling of ease in relating to the opposite sex than having an opposite sex sibling growing up in the same household. If that sibling is older, so much the better. One can learn a great deal from an older brother or sister, for she knows more, is more skilled in just about everything, and can help and teach life experiences.

If this analysis is correct, we would expect that people who have grown up with opposite sex siblings would be more at ease as adults in relating to the opposite sex. They would have an advantage over adults who didn't have this formative experience. And in an experiment carried out by William Ickes and Marilyn Turner at the University of Missouri in St. Louis, that is what they found. In the experiment, pairs of male and female university students were left alone in a room ostensibly waiting for a research assistant to fetch some questionnaires that she "had just run out of." While the students were alone, their interactions were videotaped, and their voices recorded. The data were analyzed for both verbal and nonverbal behaviors (e.g., smiles, directed gazes, the physical distance they maintained from each other). The researchers also obtained information later from the two students about what they thought of each other. The researchers used only first-born and last-born individuals in the study. Here is what the researchers reported:

> The data provide strong, converging evidence that individuals with older, opposite-sex siblings are particularly likely to have "successful" (i.e., involving and rewarding) initial interactions with strangers of the opposite sex. This ... was most clearly evident in the case of male dyad members. When compared to firstborn men with younger sisters, last born men with older sisters talked nearly twice as long, tended to ask more questions, and evoked significantly more gazes, verbal reinforcers, and self-reported liking from their female partners.[16]

For their part, "Last-born women with older brothers were perceived as more likeable and were more likely to initiate the interaction."[17] This experiment suggests that if you grew up with an opposite sex older sibling, chances are you will tend to be less shy of and more comfortable with the opposite sex. While that older brother or sister of yours might have seemed a bit bossy at times, there were distinct advantages in having him or her around.

Just how sexually active are today's teenagers?

A well-dressed man who looked between 60 and 70 years of age was having his thinning hair carefully trimmed by his barber. Several other men sat in chairs along the far wall of the room reading sports and auto magazines while patiently waiting their turns for the barber. Strong scents of hair oil and facial cologne filled the air. The man in the chair had been talking for a while, rather derisively, about today's teenagers. "They lack discipline," he said. "They don't appreciate the value of money; they aren't learning anything in school; they spend too much time playing video games; they use drugs; and the amount of sex—" he shrugged his shoulders, "—it's incredible." He shook his head judgmentally, and continued, "We didn't do things like that. Why, we hardly dated in high school, and we respected girls. To get a girl in trouble would have been disgraceful!"

Railing against the excesses of the younger generation is nothing new. Quotations have come down to us from ancient times which sound very similar to the sentiments expressed in the barber shop. Still, the gentleman in the barber chair has a point. There have been pronounced changes in the dating behavior of teenagers in the post–Second World War generations.

In considering teenage dating, it is important to recognize that young people are reaching puberty at an earlier age. Consider these statistics: records indicate that in eighteenth century Germany, the boys in Johann Sebastian Bach's choir gave up their soprano singing roles because of voice changes around age eighteen. Change of voice now occurs around age thirteen. At the beginning of this century, the age of first menstruation for girls was about age eighteen; now the age is about twelve. With hormonal changes coming earlier, children appear more physically mature at an earlier age. Looking mature, many children expect more freedom from their parents in terms of what they can do and how long they can stay out, and they often get this freedom. Children date at an earlier age than in past generations, and with earlier dating, there is an increased likelihood of earlier sexual behavior.

Whether and when teenagers become sexually active depends in large part on their beliefs about what their peers are doing. Writing in the *American Psychologist*, Jeanne Brooks-Gunn and Frank Furstenberg note that perceptions of what others are doing might be more strongly associated with initiation of sexual behavior than the actual behavior of one's peers. Statistical information about the percentage of adolescents who are sexually active was not as accurate in the past as it is today, so one must be cautious in interpreting trends over the years. Nonetheless, there is little question that the numbers have been increasing. Brooks-Gunn and Furstenberg have summarized these trends:

> Dramatic increases in the number of teenage girls having intercourse have taken place in the last 50 years. In 1938 to 1950, approximately 7 percent of white females had intercourse by age 16. ... By 1971, one third of never-married white girls 16 years of age had had intercourse with the figure rising to 44 percent by 1982.[18]

The percentages for African-American girls tends to be even higher. In regard to the sexual activity of boys, the writers observed: "Historically, boys were much more likely to make their sexual debut as teenagers than girls."[19] The figures were consistently higher for boys, and are currently of the order of three boys out of four in some cities. While the high rates of teenage sex are most pronounced in the big cities, the trend also extends to America's heartland. Melody Graham surveyed over 1,300 students in school districts in Cedar Rapids, Iowa. This is an area where there was low unemployment; the large majority of the students were white, and some students lived in rural areas. The survey revealed that over 40 percent of the students in grades seven through twelve had had sexual intercourse. Seventeen percent of the boys reported having had sex by age twelve.[20]

Statistics show that the percentage of young people having intercourse rises steadily with age. By age 20, according to a recent congressional report entitled *A Decade of Denial*, 68 percent of adolescent females and 86 percent of adolescent males were sexually active. Something like a quarter of sexually experienced teenagers ages 18–19 have had a history of six or more partners.[21] Statistics on the use of contraceptives reveal that a substantial number of sexually active teenagers are not using contraceptives consistently or at all. Contraceptive use is generally lower in the lower socioeconomic classes and among the less educated. The pregnancy rate of unmarried teenagers, particularly in the urban centers, is high. In some major American cities, more births are occurring outside of wedlock than among married women.

According to research findings, most teenage girls report being very surprised when they find themselves pregnant. Brooks-Gunn and Furstenberg list some of the reasons for this astonishment. Some adolescent girls believed they couldn't become pregnant because of the timing of intercourse in the monthly cycle. Parenthetically, many teenage girls were unable to identify the time in their menstrual cycle when ovulation occurs. Some girls believed they did not have sex often enough to become pregnant. Many girls had a sense of invulnerability, feeling it could not happen to them. And for some, it was simply a matter of procrastination or indifference in getting and using birth control devices.

3. *Physical Attractiveness*

How important is physical attractiveness?

The answer in brief is that physical attractiveness can be quite important. First, how you look influences the impressions people form about you. Second, whether or not you think you're physically attractive can influence your own behavior and even your mental health. These conclusions are based upon scores of studies which one may find reviewed in an article by Alan Feingold in *The Psychological Bulletin.*[1]

Let's look at some of the more interesting findings that emerge from these studies. To begin with, the way you think you look — how physically attractive you believe you are — may be quite different from what other people think. While there is some correspondence between how attractive others perceive one as being and how one perceives oneself, the relation is smaller than one might think. Try looking into a mirror with a less demanding version of the question Snow White's stepmother posed: "Mirror, mirror on the wall — Who is fairest of them all?" What the mirror tells you may be quite different from what other people believe.

June, a woman in her late twenties, is a good example. June has always been convinced that she is unattractive. Sometimes she says she looks "ugly." The people who know her, however, describe her very differently. They say she has a pretty face with a pleasant smile, and a trim figure. She has no shortage of male admirers. As is the case for many people, June's self-evaluation and the perceptions of others are very different.

Second, if you are judged to be attractive by most other people you encounter, you are likely to have significant advantages. The perception that you are physically attractive influences other kinds of judgments which are made about you, and these judgments are likely to be biased in your favor. Physically attractive people are likely to be viewed as more socially skilled, sexually warm, mentally healthy and more intelligent. What a help that would be when you were interviewing for a job or looking for a new romantic interest. The favorable aura that is cast onto the physically attractive holds for both men and women. Now this favorable perceptual bias does not extend to evaluations of "character." Physically attractive people are no more likely to be seen as having good character than other people, but I guess those who are blessed with good looks can't have everything in their favor. And in the realities of the world, they do have a lot going for them. Physically attractive people tend to be more popular with the opposite sex, and have more friends of the same sex and report less loneliness.

The third point that comes through in these studies is that people who believe they are physically attractive (whether they are or not) seem to enjoy a positive boost in their lifestyles. They tend to be more extroverted, more comfortable with others, and more popular with the opposite sex, and they have relatively high levels of self-esteem. While one cannot be entirely sure what is happening here, it may be that feeling good about the way one looks helps to instill the confidence needed to successfully engage the challenges of life, particularly in the chancy arena of romantic relationships.

Is it true that men place a higher value on physical attractiveness when choosing a romantic partner than women do?

If you believe the answer is true, the odds are very high that you are right. Our supporting data come from responses to "date selection" and "mate selection" questionnaires. These are questionnaires which present people with a list of qualities such as "intelligent," "kind-understanding," and "good looks" and ask how important the quality would be in selecting a date. In some studies, the question asks about selecting a mate. Researchers used these questionnaires in a number of studies in the United States, and the results are clear. In choosing both dates and mates, men place a higher value on physical attractiveness in women than women do in men.[2]

If you think you might find a more equitable situation abroad, think again. Using a mate selection questionnaire, David Buss of the University of Michigan studied people in different areas of the globe, in countries as disparate as Australia and Zambia, and found the same pattern almost everywhere he looked. In 34 of 37 samples studied, men placed more value on physical attractiveness in women than women did in men.[3] The three places studied in which there were no gender differences were Sweden, India, and Poland.

Consider another approach to the question. Psychologists have studied the advertisements people have placed in the personal columns of magazines. You probably have seen such ads: "Single, White male, 32 years old, college graduate. Likes outdoor activities, camping, biking, tennis, boating, waterfront restaurants. Would like to meet like-minded woman to share these experiences."

Now, if you look through a bunch of these ads, taking out your marker and putting a circle around those which specifically state that the writer is looking for someone who is physically attractive, you will find that men make this point more often than women do. Judging from a review of this research once again carried out by Alan Feingold, men bring up physical attractiveness more than twice as often as women.[4]

Do very attractive people scare off potential dates?

A movie star once remarked that she was lonely because men simply figured she wouldn't be available, and therefore didn't even attempt to ask her out. And she was probably right, in the sense that a man might look at a glamorous woman and conclude that she wouldn't be interested in him because she could have anyone she wanted. Many people feel intimidated about approaching someone for a date who they feel is a lot more attractive on that mythical one-to-ten scale than they are. Instead of pursuing the most attractive possibility, the decision is often made to temper one's desire with what one believes is a dose of reality; the dose of reality being a kind of probability statement of how likely it is that the person would accept the invitation to go out.

Imagine that you are presented with pairs of photographs of potential dates. One potential date in each pair is clearly more attractive than the other. For each pair of photographs you are asked to select the person you would try to make a date with. Psychologists posed such choices to female students at Kansas State University and found that while some women almost always opted for the most attractive of the male photographs, the majority of the women did not do so. Instead, they avoided both the most attractive and least attractive candidates and chose dates of intermediate attractiveness. The researchers, James Shanteau and Geraldine Nagy, concluded that both the potential dates' physical attractiveness and the probabilities that the invitation will be accepted are part of the equation in pursuing a romantic partner.[5]

A neat illustration of this tendency towards caution was provided in a study carried out in singles bars in Rochester, New York. Male researchers in their twenties were stationed in the bars with instructions to unobtrusively observe unattached women. The observers found that the most attractive women were not approached by men any more than other women. To see whether the women observed would in fact be standoffish, the observer walked over and began a conversation. Most of the women (63 percent) responded positively to the initiative.[6]

If there are any morals to this story, they are the following: (1) Be aware of the fear others might have that if they approach you, you might reject them. If you sense this and want to break down such barriers, you may have to communicate your interest by making the first move. (2) Don't be intimidated by the fact that a prospective partner is attractive. All she or he can do is say "no," and who knows, she or he might not!

Can one become too concerned with body image?

You are waiting in a doctor's office. As you thumb through the pages of a magazine, you stop at a full-page advertisement. You see a woman in a chic black evening gown, standing in an elegantly furnished apartment. She is wearing large golden earrings which, set against her black dress, make her look altogether stunning. You flip through the pages and look at another ad. This time, it is a woman dressed in a summer frock, her feet clad in sandals. She sits on the edge of a marble table in the midst of a spacious, flower-bedecked patio. The scene is one of summer elegance. You put down the magazine, and pick up another. As you browse through the pages, another ad catches you eye. It is a woman standing in an open field. The atmosphere is country, but she looks sophisticated in an off-the-shoulder dress. All three fashion models are pretty. All are tall. And above all, all are thin. Call it what you will — slim, sleek, slender — these women are thin.

Contemporary Western culture promotes an ideal of a thin body, particularly for women. To be thin is to be beautiful, sexy, and healthy. The problem is that to stay in this happy state requires persistent care in eating the right foods and often forces one to eat less than one wants. It is not surprising, then, that a very large number of both men and women are unable to keep as slender as they feel they should be. As a consequence, many people are dissatisfied with the way they look. One particularly finds concern about being overweight among women. A 1986 survey of satisfaction with "body image" reported in *Psychology Today* found that 38 percent of the female respondents disagreed with the statement "I like my looks just the way they are." The principal problems cited were weight-related. Fifty-five percent of the women were unhappy with their weight, and 63 percent said that they were afraid of becoming fat.[7]

Feeling unhappy about the way one looks is frequently accompanied by a less than positive self-image and lowered morale. Feeling down-in-the-dumps, in turn, can spill over into other areas of one's life, such as job performance and relationships. You can see the makings of a real trap here, if one buys into the idea that thinness is an imperative and it turns out to be an imperative one cannot meet. There are other problems relating to preoccupation with thinness that may have very serious consequences. Concern about body image is closely linked to the eating disorders, anorexia nervosa and bulimia. Anorexia nervosa is a form of self-starvation characterized by a pronounced loss of body weight (at least 25 percent) and a preoccupation with food and the way one looks. The disorder may lead to serious medical complications. If left untreated, anorexia can be very dangerous. Bulimia is a pattern of binge eating often followed by purging or vomiting. Bulimia may also be associated with significant medical problems. The vast majority of persons experiencing such eating disorders are women. The highest risk group is adolescent girls between the ages of 12 and 20. The disorders appear most concentrated in the middle- and upper-socioeconomic classes.

It would be a misstatement and an oversimplification to say that these eating disorders are solely caused by an obsession to become thinner. There may be a variety of physiological and psychological causes for these conditions. Still, it is hard to escape from the idea that our preoccupation with thinness is a significant part of the problem. And research does show that women with eating disorders have attitudes which emphasize the importance of thinness.

In seeking an explanation for the fact that eating disorders seem to be concentrated among middle- and upper-class women, Ruth Striegel-Moore and her colleagues at Yale University point to the influence of the culture in which these women live.

> One source of influence is the subculture within which they live. Although attitudes about thinness and obesity pervade our entire society, they also are intensified within certain strata. Women of higher socioeconomic status are most likely to emulate closely the trendsetters of beauty and fashion ... and therefore not surprisingly, they exhibit greater weight preoccupation.[8]

In looking for an explanation for gender differences in the prevalence of anorexia and bulimia, the writers point to attitudes that are fostered by society beginning in early childhood.

> From their families, little girls learn that one of their functions is to "pretty up" the environment, to serve as aesthetic adornment. ... Young girls learn that being attractive is intricately interwoven with pleasing and serving others and, in turn, will secure their love.[9]

This message is further reinforced in the books children read. A 1972 study of children's readers revealed "that girls in these primers were constantly concerned about how they look, whereas boys never were."[10] It would fly in the face of reality to dismiss the importance of physical appearance in the world we live in. However, it is one thing to recognize its importance and to try to look as attractive as you can, and quite another to become obsessed with your appearance, letting this drive you to behaviors which are self-destructive.

4. *Male and Female Expectations*

Do men and women want the same things from a relationship?

Raymond and Laurie Bergner wrote an interesting article published in *Psychotherapy* which suggests that in the long run, some of the important psychological needs that men and women look to fulfill in a romantic relationship are more similar than one might suspect.[1] The Bergners suggest that both men and women are looking for closeness with their partner and affirmation from their partner. The Bergners view closeness as overcoming uncomfortable feelings of isolation and alienation, and affirmation as receiving communications — verbal and nonverbal — that one is special, loved, appreciated, and accepted.

There are differences, however, in the way men and women go about satisfying these needs. The Bergners theorize that sexual intimacy provides a vehicle for many men to realize these feelings. When a woman consents to sexual intercourse, this physical acceptance of the man communicates an affirmation that she loves and accepts him. In contrast, for many women, sex is not the means to establish closeness and affirmation; rather sex seems to deepen feelings which have been previously established by essentially nonsexual interactions. These feelings develop through doing things together and, perhaps most importantly, through conversation. And the kind of conversation that promotes these feelings is the sharing of experiences and concerns. The Bergners do not claim that this difference between men and women in their approach to developing relationships is invariable; they claim only that it is a common pattern.

Drawing on these ideas, we would expect that the desires that men and women have in the early stages of a relationship would be different. For many men, there would be a quicker and more compelling interest in establishing a sexual relationship. For many women, there would be more interest in just developing conversational intimacy and companionship. The evidence we have from studies bears this out. To cite an example, Clyde Hendrick and his colleagues administered scales dealing with attitudes toward love to hundreds of students at the University of Miami. They found that men were more likely to endorse items dealing with the erotic aspects of relationships; men were attracted by physical appearance and desired to kiss soon after becoming acquainted. In contrast, women were more likely to endorse items stating that "love came slowly and quietly," "required caring first," and "was best when based on friendship."[2] In general, research shows that men are more interested in casual sex, while women tend to believe that sex is appropriate in loving committed relationships.

In dating, women enjoy sharing confidences, entertainment, cultural activities, companionship, and physical affection not necessarily leading to sex. It isn't simply the number of shared activities that makes the differences. It is the perception of the quality of the relationship. Women tend to feel positive about their relationships with men who themselves are comfortable about being close. In commenting on their research on students at Eastern Illinois University, Marge Davis and Alan Oathout reported that the woman's perception that her partner was a good listener and willing discloser was very important to her. They reported that "female satisfaction was more strongly influenced by this perception than by any other."[3]

While there are gender differences in expectations about romantic relationships, it would be a mistake to overdo the idea and to react to members of the opposite sex in terms of a stereotype. This caveat was expressed by Roy Eidelson and Norman Epstein in an article on dysfunctional relationship beliefs. They write, "Finally, the belief that men and women differ dramatically in their personalities and relationship needs is likely to encourage stereotyped perceptions of one's partner and diminish sensitivity to his or her idiosyncratic desires and characteristics."[4] As always, you have to understand the needs and expectations of your partner who is a unique individual.

What are some of the potential problems that can arise from the different expectations of men and women about romantic relationships?

Research has documented what most of us suspect. Men are typically more interested in sex than women, while women are typically more interested in companionship and in conversation—particularly conversation in which people share experiences and confidences. I use the qualifier "typically" because the world is full of exceptions to this rule. But when we observe these typical patterns in a couple, we can anticipate problems arising from their different expectations in both the early and subsequent stages of a romantic relationship.

Consider gender differences in eagerness for sexual intimacy in the early stages of a relationship. Does this vignette have a familiar ring to it? Jim met Sandy at an office party during the Christmas season. Two nights after the party, he called her, and on the following evening they went out to dinner to a very nice Italian restaurant. They both had a pleasant time. When Jim asked Sandy out for a second date, she agreed, and they went to a movie in the mall. After the movie, they returned to Sandy's apartment. She invited him in for a cup of coffee. Picture the scene. They sit together on the couch. A coffee table stands in front of the couch, half covered with magazines. Jim's cup rests on the table. Sandy holds her cup in her hand, occasionally sipping from it while she talks in an animated voice about the movie. She smiles as she talks. Jim looks at her and listens. Her words begin to blur as he studies her face and looks into her eyes. His desire mounts. He edges closer to her, touches her and kisses her. She permits this, but is not overly responsive. He pulls her close and begins stroking her hair. She stays in his arms but is not relaxed. When he begins to fondle her breasts, she quickly removes his hand. He kisses her again, more intensely. Suddenly she pulls away. She shakes her head. Now there is a chill in the room. Jim feels stupid, embarrassed. Sandy feels uncomfortable and disconcerted. Jim had come on too strong, too fast, and Sandy wasn't ready for it. While the situation is retrievable, Jim's sensitivities were not acute, his timing was poor, and the incident was not helpful.

Judging from surveys of college women, many if not most of the respondents believe that sex is acceptable in dating couples, but only in a loving, committed relationship.[5] When a relationship provides a woman with the kind of emotional intimacy she needs, the man's needs for sexual intimacy are much less likely to pose a problem. In Sandy's case, the relationship wasn't there yet, and she wasn't ready to respond to Jim's advances.

Now let's consider long-term relationships, particularly those which are in trouble where the quality of the relationship is deteriorating. If the woman feels she is not experiencing the emotional closeness she needs in the relationship, the man's sexual advances may be seen not so much as affection but as exploitation. The Bergners describe a possible emerging conflict.

> When the state of the relationship is less than positive, the male partner often will continue to pursue sexual involvement with his partner. From his perspective, pursuing such involvement is a way to reconnect or make-up, a way to re-establish missing closeness and affirmation between himself and his partner. Of course, he will typically have further reasons, such as physical pleasure, for desiring sexuality. For his partner, however, his

> pursuit of sexuality at such a time will seem impersonal and exploitive. For her, sexuality is supposed to express an existent intimacy, but no such intimacy exists. Her partner's sexual initiations will therefore appear to her to be a case of his merely seeking physical satisfaction and of using her to achieve this. They will not be seen, since she does not understand his perspective, as cases of him trying to establish missing closeness and affirmation. Further, if he also avoids participation in verbal and other nonsexual means of establishing closeness and affirmation — avoids the very things that will most compellingly tell her of his *personal* interest and connectedness to her — he will seem to her to be personally rejecting or uninterested. When such events occur repeatedly over time, the woman will evolve a general view of her partner as someone who does not really care about her as a person, but uses her to achieve his own sexual gratification.[6]

In the Bergners' scenario, the man may feel rejected — the woman used. A misunderstanding if not rejection of each other's needs becomes a large part of the problem. Let's probe a little further into such conflicts, looking at them from the perspective of the woman's need for emotional intimacy. As the Bergners suggest, the vehicle for achieving such intimacy is often conversation. Many women enjoy talking in detail about their daily experiences — what happened during the day, the things they did, the conversations they had, what their family and friends are doing, their feelings about important events — and they enjoy relating and discussing them. What they are looking for is a good receptive listener, a person who is sympathetic and understanding, and can in turn share experiences with them.

Before becoming involved with the man in her life, the woman most likely had female friends as confidantes. Now she turns to the man that she increasingly spends her time with, and thinks about and focuses on, and wants to share her experiences with him. And as she gets to know him better, she may find that he's uncomfortable in this role. He's not used to talking about people and relationships. He is not only not psychologically attuned to these nuances of everyday life, he may also seem uninterested if not indifferent to them. He may think about his job, and prefer to talk about sports or politics. He listens for a while when she talks, but it may be only with half an ear. His eyes are focused on the television set or the newspaper, and his mind is not on what she is saying. It is as if he has tuned out. She is left with the conclusion that what is important to her seems trivial to him. And she becomes turned off.

In the kind of "socialization experiences" that boys traditionally go through as they grow up, they are not trained to be receptive listeners or to focus on the nuances of human interactions. Instead, they learn to focus on activities — sports, hobbies. The traditional male model was to be self-reliant, competitive, tough, to be a doer and a problem-solver. For many years, one of the movie images of the male hero was a strong, silent type —

hardly a model for becoming an intimate conversationalist. The tendency also extends to self-disclosure. With this kind of programming, many men are uncomfortable, even unwilling to talk about their problems and their feelings. They keep things to themselves. So the frustrations for the woman looking for emotional intimacy mount. She cannot adequately share her experiences with him because he isn't really listening, and to compound the problem, he doesn't share with her. The kinds of conversation that would bring her close to him are not happening. She becomes more uptight, more aloof, and less receptive to him sexually. And he doesn't understand why.

5. Meeting the Opposite Sex

How can shyness in approaching the opposite sex be overcome?

Jim is one of the shyest persons one would ever be likely to encounter. He is an extremely intelligent man. Holding advanced degrees in biology from a prestigious West Coast university, Jim works on basic research problems in a biotechnology firm. Jim is much more comfortable in the recesses of the laboratory inoculating mice than he is talking with people in the "real world" outside. He feels ill-at-ease meeting new people and is nearly petrified at the thought of asking a woman out for a date. While he finds women very attractive, he has never been out on a date. Jim is now approaching thirty and would like to become involved with a woman, but when he seriously thinks about the idea, fear overwhelms him, and he lapses back into a long-standing pattern of avoidance.

While Jim's shyness is extreme, there are countless people who experience shyness in lesser degrees. They may feel anxious and self-conscious when encountering someone of the opposite sex, and find making conversation difficult. They may not know what to say or even how to begin a conversation. If a social encounter proves particularly awkward and uncomfortable, they may react like Jim by avoiding similar situations in the future. Shyness can be described as a form of social anxiety. Chances are that you cannot overcome shyness by avoidance anymore than you can cure a phobia by avoiding what makes you afraid. For some phobias it doesn't make much difference whether you overcome them or not. For example, if you have a fear of spiders and react by avoiding them, your loss is negligible. But missing a romantic relationship is another thing altogether. It is a high price to pay for having a problem of social anxiety. Avoidance won't cure the problem and you stand to lose a great deal.

If avoidance is not the answer, then what is? When a shyness problem is severe, therapy is probably your best bet. If the problem is not severe, you still might find some of the techniques used by therapists of interest, and you might be able to adapt them to your own situation. With this possibility in mind, I will describe two types of therapeutic approaches that might be helpful. The first used by cognitive therapists is a process in which you look critically at the thought patterns that are associated with your shyness. The second used by behavioral therapists is a teaching approach which attempts to directly improve your social skills by observing people with effective social skills, by coaching and by practice.

In considering the cognitive approach, imagine for a moment that there is a very attractive person of the opposite sex in your workplace or classroom. You see him often, but you hardly know him. He is now standing alone. You have an opportunity to talk to him and get to know him better. You would really like to ask him to have some coffee with you in the snack bar down the hall. You begin to approach him. As you draw near, you begin to experience those old uncomfortable feelings — your pulse speeds up, your stomach feels like it is on an elevator ride, and you feel like you need to clear your throat. In rapid succession, the following thoughts sweep through your mind: "Why am I doing this? How will he react? I'll look like a fool. He'll notice how nervous I am. He'll say no. I'll feel rejected. I'll feel awful." Let's consider these thought patterns the way a cognitive therapist might. What you are really saying is, "I'm scared. He'll notice that I'm scared. He could reject me. If I'm rejected, it would be terrible."

How valid are these ideas? How much sense do they make? The first idea that you're scared is perfectly valid. If you're scared, you're scared. About all that one can offer in the way of solace is the knowledge that you're not alone. At one time or another, almost everyone feels anxious about something. Try making up a list of experiences that can elicit anxiety, and you might find it would get pretty long. You might begin with giving a speech, taking a test in school, going to the dentist or doctor, competing in sports, driving a car on a crowded freeway, getting married or having sex. While anxiety can make a person very uncomfortable, it is important to note that anxiety often diminishes as the experience progresses. If you can tolerate the uncomfortable feelings, chances are they should subside and let you continue with what you are trying to do. If you are able to master the situation and experience success, you may feel less uncomfortable the next time out.

The second idea, that he'll notice the butterflies you're experiencing, is probably not true. It is difficult to gauge what another person is feeling inside. Even a polygraph test isn't foolproof. So don't worry about the sensations you're experiencing — you're probably the only person who's fully aware of them.

The next concern is possible rejection — that he might say, "No. There's no interest in having a cup of coffee with you." Does this mean he is rejecting you? Perhaps yes, perhaps not; one should not jump to conclusions. There may be valid reasons for saying no, which have nothing to do with you. For example, he may be pressed for time or already have other plans. Suppose you then say, "Could I call you sometime? I'd like to get to know you better." If he says yes, light up with a happy smile. You may be in business. If the answer is no, it's clear enough that he is not interested in you.

A cognitive therapist would tell you that it is very important how you interpret this rejection. The therapist would stress that you should not blow the incident out of proportion. It means simply that this particular individual is not for you. It does not mean that someone else would not be interested in you. The mistake many people make is to overgeneralize from an unsuccessful experience and conclude that it's always going to turn out that way — or worse, that you are not worthwhile enough for someone to bother with. If you don't overgeneralize from the incident and "catastrophize" the unsuccessful outcome, you're unlikely to feel that bad. Instead of feeling dismal, why not look at what happened in a more positive light. You could say to yourself, "Hey, I did it! I overcame my fears. It's time to go forward and try again." The approach of the cognitive therapist, then, would include taking a critical look at the assumptions you are making about the way others might react to your overtures. Doing this may help you cast the situation in a less threatening light.

The approach of the behavioral therapist is to help people improve their social skills. To illustrate the techniques used by behavioral therapists, let's look at a social skills training program developed by Craig Twentyman and Richard McFall at the University of Wisconsin.[1] The procedures included modeling (observing someone with effective social skills), coaching, and practice with a member of the opposite sex. The training might go something like this: As one of your starting assignments, you are asked to imagine you are about to call up a woman you are slightly acquainted with and ask her out on a date. You are first asked to think about what you would say. Then before you verbalize this, you listen to tape recorded conversations in which the people talking very skillfully make telephone dates. You think about what these skilled models said and sharpen your own approach. You also receive some coaching. When you think that your approach is finely honed, you're ready for some real live simulation. You call on the intercom pretending it's a telephone and talk to an opposite sex member of the team. If the conversation goes well, you're given the telephone number of another member of the team to call at home. Then, you graduate to face-to-face practice. Does this behavioral training work? Twentyman and McFall presented some evidence that it does. After male students were given this training, they appeared less anxious when interacting with women. Improved competence and practice help in making dates as they do in most other situations that arouse anxiety.

Charlene Muehlenhard and her colleagues at Texas A&M University have gone a step further in working out a system for helping women overcome shyness. They have gone high-tech, developing a computer program to guide women in starting conversations with men. The program, written in Apple SuperPILOT, has been tested and appears to be effective. Muehlenhard reported that women who used it dated more often than a control group of women who did not use the program.[2]

You might find in universities or mental health settings training programs for overcoming shyness which bring together men and women in small groups where, with good coaching and socially skilled models, they practice together to improve their skills. If you do not have such opportunities available, you can still draw on some of these ideas. Try rehearsing your approach in front of a mirror. If you are lucky, you might find a friend who will serve as a friendly critic. But most of all, keep in mind the precept that a failure is not a catastrophe, and success should increase your confidence.

What are the nonverbal signals that communicate interest?

Before you have spoken a word to that attractive stranger sitting on the bar stool, is it possible to communicate the message that you would like to meet him or her? And when you do begin to converse, is it possible to convey additional messages over and beyond what you say in words? The answer, of course, is yes, and the telegraphing that is employed is "nonverbal" signals.

We all send out nonverbal signals even when we try not to. If you try to keep your body still and your face expressionless, you may convey a message of indifference in doing so. In the more likely situation where we want to communicate a message or impression, we use our face, body, clothes, tone of voice, proximity to others, and touch to help us. Think of the impressions of alertness, congeniality, and professionalism one tries to communicate when interviewing for a job. Do you recall your last job interview? Remember your choice of clothes, the extra care you took in grooming, the way you sat in the chair, the eye contact you maintained with the interviewer, the attentiveness you showed, the tone of your voice and the way you smiled at the appropriate times. While these signals may not have spoken directly about your skills and knowledge to do the job, they did communicate an impression about you that was important to the employer in making his or her decision to hire you.

One of the virtues of nonverbal communication is that the message is sent and received almost instantaneously. It takes time to convey a thought in words, but a look or smile is quick and appears spontaneous. One of the disadvantages of nonverbal signals is that the message you send may not be precise. You may not be fully aware of what you are sending out. In an article in the *Psychological Bulletin*, Bella DePaulo noted that "People never see their own facial expressions exactly as others do," and that "The tone of a person's voice also sounds different to her or him than it does to others."[3] DePaulo concluded that "In interpersonal interactions ... people never know as much about their own nonverbal behaviors as do the people with whom they are interacting."[4]

Facial expressions are an example of nonverbal signals that can be complex and difficult to read. Expressions of basic emotions such as fear, happiness, and anger are usually obvious and interestingly appear to be the same throughout the world — as if these reactions are wired-in to our human programming. But facial expressions are also rapidly changing conveyors of information, much of which escapes the casual observer. If you watch a videotape of conversations, you might be astonished at the complexity of the signals conveyed. Researcher William J. Rinn noted that for many people, "The face and head are almost constantly generating expressions and gestures."[5] Nonverbal signs are important in romantic relationships; they may communicate initial availability, continued interest, understanding, affection, and togetherness.

How does a woman signal "I'm available"? Researcher Monica Moore and her co-workers spent a lot of time frequenting singles bars watching women who were unaccompanied by a man. They recorded nonverbal acts which elicited a response from a male. (The man approached the woman or talked to her within 15 seconds of the behavior.) The researchers fashioned a catalog of these "I'm-interested-in-meeting-you" signals. Here are some of the most frequent:

- Smiling
- Room-encompassing glance
- Solitary dance — keeping time with the music
- Darting glances
- Hair flip
- Leaning towards the man while seated
- Fixed gaze
- Head toss

Some less frequent signals were skirt hiking, primping, and knee touching. The researchers made the point that while you may see a lot of such behavior in a singles bar, you rarely see them in a library. In other words, these signals are flirtation-specific. Do they work? Moore reported that the women who signaled often were most frequently approached by men.[6]

Smiles are a key nonverbal signal in communicating both availability and continued interest. Interestingly, studies reveal that women smile much more than men do. Researchers have also found that smiles that are reciprocated tend to persist consistently longer than those which are not. An unreciprocated smile is likely to vanish as quickly as a prop under a magician's handkerchief. An unreturned smile functions like a red traffic light; the signal is "Forget it!"

Couples that have established a relationship sometimes use nonverbal signals when they are among other people to make their relationship clear. The late Erving Goffman, an acute observer of social interactions, referred to such behaviors as tie signs.[7] In her article in the *Psychological Bulletin*, DePaulo provides a nice illustration of tie signs in the behavior of a couple at a party: "Members of a couple who are attending a party, for example, might hold hands and gaze at each other; and if, during the course of the event, they drift apart from each other, they might periodically check back. All of these behaviors announce the 'withness' of the twosome ... to others in the gathering."[8]

Space and touch are important nonverbal signals in a romantic relationship. Try interposing yourself into a couple's space and you will probably see them close ranks. Watch the male in the couple. Does he keep his eyes on his partner and orient his body towards her? Notice how the woman smiles at her partner from time to time, touches him on the shoulder, or squeezes his hand. Reductions in space, changes in posture, touches, and looks, become tie signs when the unity of a couple is challenged. Space also offers a clue about the congeniality of a relationship. Try watching different couples sitting in a room. You will see some couples in which the man and woman sit very close together. You are likely to see the couple laughing, smiling, talking, and touching. You will see other couples in which the man and woman sit at an appreciable distance from one another. Here you are less likely to see smiles and laughter. The physical distance the partners maintain from each other is often a rough measure of the emotional closeness of the relationship.

Touching is an important signal that can have many meanings. In a well-defined relationship, touching conveys affection, reassurance, and a sense of togetherness. A touch on the shoulder to a romantic partner who feels blue can be comforting, for it conveys the message that he or she is not alone. Touching strangers is a different matter entirely, and in an era in which our consciousness has been raised about sexual harassment, one always has to be aware of what might be unwelcome.

How do I meet that special person?

For many people, this can be a very difficult problem. The chances of meeting someone that interests you depend in part on the number of eligible people that are in the area in which you live, and on how energetic you are in seeking them out. If there is nobody around, you could be out of luck, and if you wait patiently for something to happen, it could take a long time. In any event, there is a certain amount of blind luck involved, the two of you happening to be at the same place at the same time.

There are both traditional ways of meeting people and newer ways that reflect the technology and less restrictive sexual attitudes of our times. Some of the tried-and-true traditional ways are getting friends to introduce you to people, going to parties, and meeting people at school or work; joining clubs, organizations, churches and synagogues is also a traditional way of meeting people. The newer approaches include advertising your availability in personals columns, using a commercial dating service (these are organizations which provide introductions for a fee and employ such techniques as computer matching, videotapes, and voice recordings), and going to singles bars. Traditional approaches are still very much with us, and there is much to be said for them, for at least you are dealing with something of a known quantity. An introduction from a friend, for example, signifies that someone you know has some positive regard for the person. The potential downside to introductions from friends is that if things do not work out well, relationships between the three of you can become awkward.

Alan, a junior member of a large law firm, had become good friends with one of his associates, a married woman named Grace. At a dinner party at her home, Grace introduced Alan to her younger sister Kitty. Alan and Kitty hit it off well, and began a whirlwind romance which lasted for four months. Then, Kitty's ardor cooled. She told Alan that she was going to start dating other men. Alan was now deeply in love with Kitty, and was very upset. They continued to date for a while until, in an emotional scene, they finally called it quits. During this uncoupling process, the social and professional relationship between Alan and Grace became strained, as Grace found herself connected to both parting lovers. After the break-up, "Kitty" eventually became an unspoken word in the office, and "Alan" in the family.

Singles clubs and other groups organized by churches and synagogues are a good traditional way of offering people a way to meet. Your choices are obviously narrowed by restricting potential partners to a particular religion. However, that can be an advantage if similarity in religious affiliation is important to you. Clubs and professional organizations also offer excellent ways of meeting new people. If you are interested in politics, try the Young Democrats or Young Republicans. If you like the outdoors, look for a hiking club. Your local recreation department may have a wide variety of activities in which you can meet people. Don't overlook your community college; you may not only find a very interesting course to take, but may also meet new friends as well.

If traditional approaches have not proved productive, you might try some of the newer alternatives. Have you ever considered advertising? If America doesn't run on gasoline, coffee, or martinis, it probably runs on advertising. It has been said that you can sell anything from a new car to a presidential candidate if you advertise correctly. The thought occurred to someone that if advertising works for almost everything else, why not try it for people in search of romantic relationships. If you turn to the advertising pages of some upscale magazines like *The Washingtonian*, you will see several pages of notices which bring new meaning to the song "Hey, Look Me Over." As you peruse the ads, you will see that each notice comes with a box number address, so the advertiser has an opportunity to examine any replies without revealing his or her own address or phone number. If the person who responds to the ad is also able to work out a method to protect his or her privacy, such as "If you want to get together, leave your reply in the third volume of Gibbons' *Decline and Fall of the Roman Empire* on the top shelf of the second aisle in the local library on Thursday night," we could have intrigue as complicated as a spy swap during the Cold War.

In addition to the box number, which protects the advertiser's privacy, another feature of these personal notices is abbreviations to save space. SWF, for example, indicates a single white female. MWM stands for a married white male. Now, you might stop at this point and ask why a married man is advertising for a romantic partner. In the magazine pages I looked through, one married man was searching for a married couple for group activities. Presumably, the objective was group sex or wife-swapping. Another married man said he was looking for a discreet, intimate daytime relationship. A married woman stated she was all alone one weekend of the month, and was looking for a handsome man. She didn't specify further.

The advertiser's age usually follows the abbreviation, and then the "pitch" comes. If you're trying to stimulate some interest, you have to make it sound good, and I'm not sure truth-in-advertising laws apply here. A sampling of personal descriptions from one magazine included "open, sensitive, attractive"; "sweet, stunning"; "long dark hair, great legs, sexy lingerie"; "I am quite pretty, petite, sexy, sophisticated"; and "really cute." The last description was from a man. Occasionally, the personal descriptions border on the outlandish, with claims of exceptional powers to please sexually. Some ads include comments about one's wealth, and even statements that the writer is a millionaire. The cliché "I want someone to love me for myself, not for my money" seems to have fallen by the wayside.

Following the personal descriptions, there is usually a litany of the advertiser's interests. Typical interests listed are tennis, skiing, hiking, outdoor cafés, movies, cooking, classical music, dining, dancing, biking and theater. The last part of the notices specifies what sort of person and or relationship the advertiser is looking for. The objectives range from "discreet safe fun" to "a meaningful relationship" to marriage.

I have had a number of patients who have told me that they placed advertisements in these personal columns. The results were mixed. Some of the respondents proved to be interesting. At least one turned out to be a pest. The worst outcome of a personal ad that I have heard of was a story that broke in the newspapers in the summer of 1992. A divorced man placed an ad in a magazine, describing himself as warm, romantic and witty, and said he was looking for a woman with an open heart. When a woman responded, they began to date, and in a few months, she moved in with him. Several weeks later, he accidentally discovered that she was a fugitive from justice, wanted for stealing thousands of dollars. The revelation was devastating. Despite the fact that he was in love with her, he turned her in and testified at her trial. She was convicted and served a jail term. After she was released, she shot and killed him.

The story brings to mind the classic detective film, *The Maltese Falcon*. Do you remember the scene toward the end of the film where Sam Spade, played by Humphrey Bogart, confronts his beautiful client and romantic interest, played by Mary Astor, and accuses her of murder, then turns her in? While the chilling newspaper story is a rarity, it is certainly true that advertising in a magazine provides next to no screening of candidates. Commercial organizations which bring people together do offer some screening which may make the "let's-get-together" process less adventurous. However, you will need a larger checkbook if you pursue this route to romance.

Recognizing the difficulties many American singles have in finding suitable partners, entrepreneurs have tried to meet this need by turning the once discreet business of match-making into a corporate venture. Thornton Wilder, who many years ago authored the Broadway play *The Matchmaker*, which in its musical version became the fabulous success *Hello Dolly!*, would be amazed at what technology and mass marketing have done to an old idea. National chains using direct mail, the Yellow Pages, and magazine advertisements target singles offering introductions—at a cost—to interested applicants. While looking through the advertising columns of magazines, I have noticed ads that people have placed trying to sell at a discount blocks of unused introductions purchased from one of these organizations. One ad offered 24 introductions at a price of $2,100. That's $87.50 per introduction—and that's on sale. I was curious about the organization, and telephoned one of the local chapters. A young lady answered the telephone, then turned me over to a colleague who inquired appropriately "whom are you hunting for?"

If you are willing to spend $1.39 per minute, there are 900 numbers listed in magazines for calling potential dates. At this price, one hopes one's potential date is not a slow talker. Whoever thought up this scheme is certainly not in the poor house. There are other organizations listed in magazines which sound less crassly commercial, and at least to me more appealing. For example, one group states that it offers a way for unattached music lovers to meet. Another organization targets computer users, providing online introductions. The ad states that there is no fee for the first three introductions.

My boss asked me out. Is this my big moment or just trouble?

We cannot really consider this question without first looking at the issue of sexual harassment, because today's focus on sexual harassment is changing the ground rules for male-female relationships in the workplace. Sexual harassment in the workplace has been with us for years, but remained subliminal as an issue until television brought it to the surface. And it did so with a flourish. It happened during the confirmation hearings for Supreme Court Justice Clarence Thomas when one of Thomas' former aides, Anita Hill, accused him of sexual harassment when she worked for him.

Television has had its share of moments of high drama in broadcasting Congressional hearings. There were the Army-McCarthy hearings which led to the political demise of the demagogic senator from Wisconsin, the Watergate hearings, which led to the resignation of President Richard Nixon, and the Iran-Contra hearings, which revealed secret activities within the United States government attempting to circumvent prohibitions on foreign military assistance. While all of these hearings were of major political importance, and dealt with issues fundamental to the workings of our democracy, probably none of them approached the Clarence Thomas-Anita Hill confrontation for its frank portrayal of intimate human relationships. The focus of the hearings was not so much on politics as it was on sexual behavior and whether improper pressure had been exerted by a supervisor towards a subordinate in the workplace.

Traditionally, a certain amount of male-female interplay with sexual overtones has been considered within bounds — or at least tolerated on the job. Men and women flirt, touch each other circumspectly, compliment and kid each other, and at times tell off-color jokes. It is not uncommon for people to date coworkers. Nor are sexual affairs rare events. All of these behaviors continue after the Thomas-Hill confrontation. The difference is that if such behavior is pressed on an employee who finds it unwelcome, the perpetrator may find himself or herself in hot water, for sexual harassment in the workplace is a violation of the law.

In a paper, *Facts About Sexual Harassment*, the U.S. Equal Employment Opportunity Commission (E.E.O.C.) states that sexual harassment is "a form of sex discrimination that violates Title VII of the Civil Rights Act of 1964." The paper offers the following description of sexual harassment:

> Unwelcome sexual advances, requests for sexual favors, and other verbal or physical conduct of a sexual nature constitute sexual harassment when submission to or rejection of this conduct explicitly or implicitly affects an individual's employment, unreasonably interferes with an individual's work performance or creates an intimidating, hostile or offensive work environment.[9]

In considering sexual harassment in workplace relationships, it is important to note that the person who may be accused of harassment does not have to be the complaining employee's supervisor. It can be any coworker. Moreover, "The victim does not have to be the person harassed but could be anyone affected by the offensive conduct."[10] If unwelcome sexual attention creates an offensive work environment, it is sexual harassment.

While sexual harassment in the workplace is clearly most often perpetrated by men against women, the reverse is not unheard of. For example, an article in the *Washington Post* related how a woman deputy sheriff was placed on administrative leave after several instances of allegedly touching or attempting to touch the groin areas of her male colleagues. The men did not bring complaints against her. Someone else noticed her behavior. The law on sexual harassment places constraints on a person in a supervisory role when he or she asks someone down in the chain of command for a date. If the boss presses the invitation, and the employee remains unreceptive, the behavior could lead to charges of sexual harassment. The boss's behavior obviously puts the subordinate in a very awkward position as well. The office can become an uncomfortable place for him or her to work.

Even if the subordinate welcomes the idea of dating the boss, there are potential downsides. While things may work out beautifully, culminating in wedding bells and all the rest, what if it ends badly? Where does that leave the subordinate employee? Caroline, who has been a secretary in a small public relations firm for some years, is a case in point. Caroline dated her boss for about a year, and was physically intimate with him for most of that time. When they broke up, she still remained his secretary. Every day she saw him at the office, knowing he was now seeing other women. While this was very uncomfortable for her emotionally, times were hard and she needed the job. Finding another job that was as good would take time.

Another problem that may arise is office gossip. Keeping a developing relationship to ourselves, away from the eyes and ears of coworkers, may be difficult: it is very easy for romantically involved people to give themselves away in the way that they look at each other, and speak to one another. Being seen together outside the office may be inevitable. And when it becomes known that "she is dating the boss," it casts something of a cloud over whatever happens to her in the office. Take work assignments. What happens if someone else is given harder or more boring work to do than the "boss's girlfriend"? It may be difficult to persuade others that she is not profiting from the relationship. People deal with appearances as much as with reality.

Mixing business and romantic interests has other drawbacks. Having a romantic interest in a coworker can lead to biased perceptions of his or her ability on the job. If you are thinking about someone romantically, your views of his or her professional competence may be skewed. Susan Fiske and her colleagues at the University of Massachusetts provided a demonstration of this effect in an interesting study.[11] The researchers set up an experimental task in which young men supervised a female subordinate. Half of the men who participated in the study were led to believe that they would date the woman subsequently, and half were not told this. Now the woman who took the role of the subordinate was really part of the research team. Sometimes she performed competently in the task, sometimes incompetently. When the task was completed, the men were asked to evaluate her performance. The results showed that men who did not expect to date the woman were able to distinguish competent from incompetent performance. In contrast, the men who expected to date the woman did not make this distinction. Are blinders engendered by romantic interest restricted to men? Fiske reports the answer is no. The researchers repeated the study, but this time women supervised men; they found the same results.

Is that a sexual signal she is sending or is it something else?

He was a distinguished scientist who taught at a prestigious university. He was tall and bearded and had a twinkle in his eyes. She taught at a smaller school. She was dark-haired, petite, and attractive, and she was one of the few women going to the three-day symposium held at the quiet Midwestern college during the summer break. They met briefly at the airport, talked for a few minutes, then shared the limousine ride with other scientists to the campus. When the first day's proceedings of the conference were completed, he walked over to her and said, "It's a bit stuffy in the room. They have a lovely campus here. Would you like to take a walk?"

She was flattered by the invitation and thought it would be interesting to talk with him. So they set out for a walk across the campus and talked a lot about their respective research projects. It was all very pleasant. Then suddenly he put his arm around her and tried to kiss her. She backed away. He continued to press his advances and asked whether she would like to sleep with him. It was all unexpected and a bit overwhelming, and she avoided him during the rest of the conference.

Why had he acted this way? Did he suppose that by accepting his invitation for a walk and being friendly that she was interested in a sexual encounter? Or if we generalize, do men have a tendency to interpret friendly behavior by a woman in ways she did not intend?

In addressing this question, consider the following experiment. A young man and a young woman, both college students, are escorted to a small room where there are a table and chairs. They are told by the researcher to spend about ten minutes getting acquainted. The researcher leaves, and as instructed, the man and woman begin conversing. What they don't know at the time is that they are being observed through a one-way mirror by a group of other college students and that everything they say is being overheard through a sound system. When the conversation is over, the student observers are asked to make judgments about how the two people conversing were trying to behave. To make these judgments, the observers are given rating scales listing specific behaviors such as friendly, considerate, flirtatious, interesting, seductive, warm, intelligent, sincere, attractive, and promiscuous. The observers rate each of the conversationalists on these behaviors on a seven-point scale from (1) not at all to (7) very.

The observers in the experiment included both men and women. The interesting finding is that male observers saw more intended flirtatiousness, seductiveness, and promiscuity in both the conversationalists than did the female observers. The female observers were more likely to evaluate the intended behavior as friendly than were the male observers. The researchers repeated the experiment with a variation. This time they used a videotape rather than spontaneous, unrehearsed interactions. In the videotape, drama students portrayed a male assistant store manager explaining the store's policies and procedures to a recently hired female employee — a rather routine unglamorous business situation. Once again male observers saw more sexy behavior in the intended behaviors than did female observers. In this experiment, however, the strongest perception of sexy behavior was given to the female employee.

The researchers then ran a third variation of the experiment, using a videotape of a male professor and a female student. The script was designed to emphasize friendly, outgoing behavior and to avoid anything that might be construed as sexy or flirtatious. The results? The same. Male observers perceived more promiscuity, flirtatiousness, and seductiveness than did female observers, and women saw more friendliness than the men. And the strongest judgments of sexual intentions occurred when male observers considered the woman student.

These studies carried out at Kansas State University by Frank Saal and his colleagues following earlier studies at another university have a convincing consistency.[12] The conclusion is that men and women can look at the same male-female interaction and interpret it quite differently. Men see sexual implications in male-female interactions where women see friendliness. And for men, the woman's behavior, not the man's, is most likely to be judged as showing sexual intentions.

Do men see flirtatious behavior when it isn't necessarily intended, and react to women unduly as sexual objects? The answer from these experiments is yes. A woman who is friendly, outgoing and lively sends off signals to men that may be interpreted as flirtatious, seductive, and sexy. The results of these experiments could be taken as an argument for women who are uninterested in stirring up sexual interest in men to remain silent, fade into the woodwork, or wear veils. Failing this, women might well be forewarned that many men are likely to interpret sociable actions as having more sexual implications than the women had in mind. While it seems less than fair for women to have to keep such a possibility in mind when interacting with men, it is nonetheless a reality.

How can I ask him out without looking like I'm interested in a sexual encounter?

In the past, women seldom asked men out. If a girl had an interest in a guy, she might find many ways to communicate it, but she would usually stop short of asking him for a date. It was normally his prerogative to ask her. Fair or unfair, those were the rules of the game. The rules are no longer fixed in concrete. Women feel more free to ask men out. In doing so, however, there is a downside: their actions could be misinterpreted. We have already noted how many men look at a woman's behavior and see sexual intentions under the most innocent and mundane circumstances. If a woman takes the initiative and asks a man out, how much more probable is it that the man will assume that she has sex on her mind? And if he acts on this assumption and makes premature sexual advances, the prospects of getting the relationship off to a good start seem dim. How can a woman ask a man out and at the same time communicate the message that she wants to know him better and vice versa, that this is not an invitation for a casual sexual encounter?

Charlene Muehlenhard and Teresa Scardino carried out a study which suggests that a woman has a better chance of accomplishing this feat if she emphasizes her non-sexual qualities and interests in their conversation.[13] In the experiment, a large number of undergraduate male students watched videotapes of a female student initiating a conversation with a male student in a biology class. The students were portrayed by student actors. In one version, the female student portrayed herself as intelligent and both interested in and knowledgeable about the biology course they were taking. In another version, the same student actress portrayed herself as dumb and baffled by the course. In both cases, the tapes concluded with the woman saying "I don't know if you're interested—maybe you're dating someone else or something—but there's a good movie at the campus theater. If you're not busy, would you like to go with me?"

The male students who observed the tapes were asked to make ratings about the woman. Men who viewed the intelligent woman version rated her as less sexually active than men who viewed the unintelligent woman version. You might react by saying "Well, that sounds good, but would the men really want to date the more intelligent woman? Wouldn't they be intimidated by her, and prefer to date the other woman?" Not so, according to Muehlenhard and Scardino's data. The intelligent woman was rated as more likeable, tactful, interesting, flexible and agreeable than the unintelligent woman, and the men expressed more interest in dating her than the unintelligent woman. The experiment casts some doubt on the motion often passed off as worldly wisdom that a woman shouldn't appear very smart if she's going to attract and keep boyfriends. Quite the contrary seems true. Intelligent behavior seems more likely to stimulate interest in males than unintelligent behavior. And if one can generalize from this experiment, the more a woman projects herself as a multifaceted individual with significant non-sexual interests, the less likely her asking a man out will be interpreted as a sexual invitation.

If a woman is interested in a man and is unwilling to ask him out directly, are there other ways of taking the initiative? There are a number of ways including the old-fashioned method of having a friend put in a good word for you. Can you picture your friend talking with the object of your affections, saying something like "Joan and I were talking about you. She said a lot of nice things about you. I think she's interested in you." Not your style, you say. All right, how about dropping our own hints? An obvious one might be some pretext for giving him your phone number. If it comes down to hinting, however, you can't be too subtle, or the guy in question might never get the message. In her research, Muehlenhard showed videotapes of conversations between a man and a woman to a group of students. In the conversations, the woman threw out a variety of hints that she was interested in going out with the man. An example would be that she didn't have any plans for the weekend. Male students watching the tape didn't recognize the statement as a hint for a date. All things considered, the odds are that you're better off asking him out directly rather than beating around the bush.

What are some ways to make a positive impression in the first few dates?

Shakespeare used the phrase, "disguise fair nature,"[14] and I suppose most of us do that to an extent when we meet new people and would like to make a good impression. You can't expect to hide your blemishes, personality and character, forever, from the eyes and ears of your romantic partner, but the theory many of us operate on is that you will never attract that romantic partner in the first place if you allow too many of these blemishes to surface too soon.

The first rule that many people follow in their early dates with a new romantic interest is extra attention to grooming. I have pointed to the importance of physical attractiveness in interesting a romantic partner, and the message has not been lost. An interesting study carried out in restaurants and bars in the community around the University of Texas in Austin illustrates this point very well. Observers posted themselves in the restrooms of these restaurants and noted the amount of time men and women spend preening (straightening their clothes, fixing their hair, and spending time before the mirror). When the persons observed left the restrooms, they were accosted by another member of the research team. In a brief interview, the researchers asked how long he or she had been going with the person waiting in the restaurant. The researchers found that people in newer relationships spent more time in grooming than those in longer relationships.[15]

If rule one for new dates is good grooming, rule two is probably good listening. The idea is to convey the impression that your date's life story, activities and ideas interest you. If they don't, you are probably making a mistake dating him or her anyway. And if they do, there's no point in making a total secret of it. When he or she speaks, listen, pay attention and register the information in your memory banks. If he or she mentions a name or a place, remember it and use it later on in a subsequent conversation. Doing this will show that you are really paying attention and that you value what your date is saying. Do you know anyone who doesn't react favorably to someone who listens well and shows interest?

Asking questions is an obvious way of showing interest. The trick to asking questions is to use them to stimulate the flow of conversation and to not come over like a cross-examining district attorney. General questions such as "What happened then?" or "How did she feel?" or "What did you do?" are likely to elicit an interesting narrative. Questions that are personal or pointed, or that back your date up against a wall ("Why didn't you?") are likely to raise defenses and chill the relationship.

A patient who was in the early stages of a relationship once asked me when it would be strategic to discuss the skeletons in his closet. This might seem like an unusual question until you think about it, for almost everyone has a skeleton or two buried somewhere. Whether it's that you flunked out of grammar school, you did a five year stint in Sing-Sing, your mother is a political extremist, or your father made his money doing insider trading on Wall Street, there's likely to be something you may not feel comfortable about revealing. Should you be up-front with these things or hold off for a while? My own inclination would be to hold off for a while. To use a baseball cliché, you have to get to first base before you get to second.

6. *Rape*

What is the legal definition of rape?

Consider two incidents that are similar to events that happen every day. Incident one: It is night. The area is not well-lit and seems deserted except for a young woman, Megan, who is walking from a girlfriend's apartment building to her car which is parked in a large half-empty lot behind the building. As she opens her car door, she is suddenly accosted by a man who forces her into the car. Holding a knife against her, he instructs her to drive to a nearby wooded area where he forces her to have sexual intercourse.

Incident two: Denise and Gary, students at the state university, have been dating for two months. They now routinely see each other on Saturday night. Sometimes they go out to dinner or to a movie. Sometimes they study together or listen to music in Gary's apartment. On two occasions, they have had sexual intercourse. On this particular Saturday night, they are sitting on the couch in Gary's living room, Denise feels down-in-the-dumps. She did poorly on an economics test, had a row with her roommate during dinner and has a splitting headache. The last thing she wants is sex, but Gary has expectations and seems insistent. She says no several times and pushes him away when he makes advances. But, Gary keeps coming on. He doesn't pin her arms down or restrain her physically, but he just won't stop, until he finally has sex with her.

Think about the two incidents. Was Megan raped? According to almost any definition of the word, the answer is yes. The definition of rape, "carnal knowledge of a female forcibly and against her will,"[1] is an accurate description of what took place. The meaning of carnal knowledge in the traditional definition is restricted to penile penetration of the vagina. This traditional view of rape is the one that has been used by the Federal Bureau of Investigation in compiling rape statistics in its Uniform Crime Reports.

Was Denise raped? The answer is more equivocal, and one can see the ambiguities that surround the issue of date rape. There was clearly carnal knowledge, and the act clearly took place against Denise's will. There was certainly inordinate persuasion and coercion. But whether force was used is the question. When asked, Denise might first say that she wasn't raped. But upon reflection, she might conclude that she was. And while this conclusion might very well be correct, it could be difficult to prove if she wanted to press it. And Denise has no intention of doing so.

The traditional way of looking at rape is giving way to broader definitions that are becoming part of state laws in the United States. In her 1990 testimony before the Senate Judiciary Committee, researcher Mary Koss discussed these reform statutes. In these laws, rape is defined more broadly than before. An example she cited was "nonconcensual sexual penetration of an adolescent or adult obtained by physical force, by threat of bodily harm, or when the victim is incapable of giving consent by virtue of mental illness, mental retardation, or intoxication."[2] Koss goes on to state, "Reform statutes define *sexual penetration* as 'sexual intercourse, cunnilingus, fellation, anal intercourse, or any other intrusion, however slight, of any part of a person's body, but emission of semen is not required.'"[3]

So in many jurisdictions, rape now includes oral and anal sex as well as vaginal penetration. And intoxication has been added to outright force as a basis for making the charge. When we ask "What is date rape?" the answer is simply that rape is rape whether it is committed by a stranger or by an acquaintance. If the act is carried out by physical force, through the use of alcohol, or by any of the other conditions spelled out in the statutes, it is rape no matter who does it.

How prevalent is date rape?

It is difficult to estimate the number or rapes that occur yearly in the United States, because many of the incidents are unreported. Researchers believe that only a fraction of the sexual assaults committed—some say about half while others say as few as ten percent—are reported to police or victim assistance services. Very often the victim does not reveal the incident to anyone.

In the spring of 1992, the Department of Justice released preliminary data from a national crime survey carried out on a large number of American households. The department estimated that for the reporting period in 1991, there had been over 200,000 episodes of attempted or completed rape in the United States.[4] A few days later, a report released by the National Victim Center indicated that 683,000 women were raped in 1990.[5] With such divergent figures, one can't be precise about how many rapes occur during the span of a year; one can only state that the number is large, probably in the hundreds of thousands. Most rapes in the United States are carried out by persons who are acquainted with the victim, not by strangers. Research suggests that more than eight out of ten rapes are "acquaintance rapes."[6] And a large number of these are date rapes. In some instances, the man involved might be a causal date, perhaps a person the woman met at a party or a singles bar. In other instances, the perpetrator might be someone she has been seeing on a more regular basis.

To gauge the extent of date rape in this country, researchers have given out questionnaires to college students asking whether they have ever had sexual experiences in which they were coerced. A series of studies suggests that at least 12 percent of the college women surveyed experienced an attempt by a date to force them to have sexual intercourse.[7] In many instances, the woman was able to stop the man by pleading, screaming, or fighting back. In one study, about half the women surveyed reported that they had successfully avoided an acquaintance rape.

Coercive sexual behavior stopping short of intercourse occurs frequently. Judging from research, men often press sexual advances on dates who have made it clear that they are unreceptive and unwilling. In a study of college men, 60 percent reported they touched a woman's breast against her wishes, and 37 percent reported they touched her genital areas without consent. When their dates protested, the men often ignored the protests.[8] While the data are clear that most men do not physically force sexual intercourse on an unwilling date, many men feel verbal persuasion is within the rules. The various "lines" that have been employed as persuasive arguments run the gamut from "everybody does it" to "it will show you really love me." In addition, a small minority of men have admitted in studies that they have deliberately tried to get their dates intoxicated as a means of lowering their resistance to having sex. In doing so, they may be unaware that this is considered rape in many states. Twenty percent of women surveyed in the same study reported that on at least one occasion, a man had tried to get them high on alcohol or drugs as a means of getting them to have sexual intercourse.

When we ponder what kinds of men use coercive methods to obtain sex, the answers we get from research are that they are sexually promiscuous, have relatively little sense of responsibility, have hostile attitudes toward women, and countenance the use of force. When we ask what kind of woman becomes the victim of date rape, the most general answer is any woman. Women who are raped by dates are not really distinguishable from other women; they simply went out with the wrong guy and found themselves in circumstances that left them vulnerable to rape. While almost any woman is a potential rape victim, the women who seem most vulnerable to date rape are those who have experienced sexual abuse during childhood, go out with a lot of different men, and drink freely during dates. In considering the role of alcohol in rape, Mary Koss and Thomas Dinero commented:

> The role of alcohol as a risk variable deserves more research. It is possible that alcohol could yield physiological effects to impair the decoding of assault cues or to interfere with organized resistance behaviors. ... However, it is also possible that alcohol use in this sexualized context functions as a cue that sexually aggressive men see as willingness to have sex and that they use to rationalize away the victim's verbal assertions of nonconsent.[9]

In considering the circumstances that may promote date rape, researchers Charlene Muehlenhard and Melaney Linton suggest that the likelihood of date rape increases if a man believes he is being "led on" by his date and that she is interested in having sex, if the couple park in a car for sexual contact, and if the couple go to his apartment rather than hers.[10] The researchers also suggest that if a woman makes it very clear about the limitations she places on sexual behavior, she has a better chance of preventing this type of behavior from happening.

What are the psychological consequences of rape?

For many women, rape is a traumatic experience. Like other traumatic experiences such as combat and exposure to natural disasters, rape may have both short-term and long-term psychological effects. The term "post-traumatic stress syndrome" which is used to describe the long-term reactions of soldiers exposed to the stresses of combat applies to many rape victims as well. Generally, one would expect date rape to be less traumatizing than sexual assault by a stranger, because the act is less likely to be seen as life-threatening. The use of a lethal weapon is unusual in date rape. The weapons of a date rapist are more likely to be alcohol, verbal persuasion, and physical strength. Still, the breaking of trust and the use of coercion can be extremely upsetting.

When the experience of date rape is traumatic, we might expect reactions similar to those observed in studies of rape committed by strangers. These studies have reported that rape generates fear and avoidance behaviors which are usually most pronounced during the first one to three months following the incident, then tend to subside.[11] While many of the anxieties experienced by rape victims are clearly related to the rape itself, such as concern about personal safety, some rape victims also experience generalized anxiety reactions. In addition, many women report confusion and disruptions in the smooth flow of their usual routines in the days and weeks following the rape. Some women also experience symptoms of depression such as sleep disturbances, eating disturbances, fatigue, guilt, and feelings of worthlessness. These feelings may be exacerbated if the woman blames herself for the incident.

The unsettling effects of rape often extend into interpersonal relationships. Many rape victims find it more difficult to relate to other people; they may feel uncomfortable being around their friends, and are more easily hurt and offended by their friends. At the same time, they may feel lonely. Rape victims tend to be more careful about where they go and what they do. They may become more compulsive about locking the doors of their houses and cars, and more careful about the way they scrutinize people. Some women decrease their social activities, preferring the security of home. Interest in sex is often sharply diminished.

In the months following the rape, most women gradually put their lives back together, although lingering feelings of anxiety are not uncommon. One of the post-traumatic stress symptoms that may occur is "flashbacks." Flashbacks are instances where the victim vividly remembers the attack. While these flashbacks may happen in a variety of situations, Ann Burgess and Lynda Holmstrom reported in a study of the effects of rape on subsequent sexual experiences that these flashbacks often occurred during sex.

> Flashbacks ranged from thoughts of the rape and the way that it happened to feelings that the present partner was the rapist. ("I close my eyes and freak out with a substitution ... then have to explain to my partner.") Victims reacted to general behavior ("I always get a chill or freeze up when someone whispers in the dark like the rapist did whispering to me to shut up.") and to the sexual behaviors of partners ("My boyfriend was more forceful than I preferred and I started scratching at his chest like he was the guy").[12]

A woman's pleasure in having sex may be one of the long-term casualties of rape. Just beginning to have sexual relations again may be difficult for many women. If a partner pushes for sex too quickly, it may exacerbate the problem. One of the rape victims in Burgess and Holmstrom's study noted: "I was afraid to have any sexual contact. I really didn't want any. It was two nights before I could even think of it. Even when we did have sex on the third night, every time I closed my eyes, the scene of the attack went through my mind."[13] Another victim had a partner who was far more patient and sensitive. She reported, "In the first couple of weeks, it was good enough just to be close ... didn't have to do anything physical. He was patient. ... After that initial feeling of aversion died away, it was me who wanted it."[14]

When women who have been raped resume having sex, they may not enjoy it as much as they did formerly. Some women in the Burgess and Holmstrom study were no longer able to experience orgasm. One woman reported that is was "hard to have an orgasm for quite a while. Felt uptight and uncomfortable. It was on my mind how uncomfortable I was and I couldn't concentrate or relax."[15] Other women continued to have mixed if not negative feedback about sex:

> Q: Are you able to enjoy sex anymore now?
> A: It depends how I related to the man. If I'm in a position to enjoy it—a 50-50 thing—then I'm OK. But if I'm feeling that I'm only doing this for him and not for my own enjoyment, then I feel like the incident again … then sex is bad.[16]

Burgess and Holmstrom's study underscores the need for male partners of rape victims to be both patient and gentle in regard to sex. They should recognize that their partners may enjoy being held close and hugged, but it may take time for them to feel comfortable about having sex again.

Do some women pressure men into having sex on dates when they really do not want to?

The idea that women may pressure men into having sex when they don't want to goes back a long way. Do you recall the Biblical story of Joseph and Potiphar's wife? Potiphar's wife was attracted to Joseph, who was then a servant in her husband's household. She repeatedly urged Joseph to sleep with her, and when he steadfastly refused, she turned on him, publicly accusing him of trying to seduce her. A modern day version of the story was noted by researcher Charlene Muehlenhard, who related how one of her research subjects had received an "ultimatum" from his boss's wife.[17]

Research suggests that it is not uncommon for men to feel pushed, pulled, or lured into having sex when they don't really want to. According to the survey carried out by Muehlenhard and Stephen Cook at Texas A&M University, 63 percent of the male students questioned reported that they had engaged in sexual intercourse on occasions when they didn't really want to.[18] The reasons given usually did not involve coercion. Rather, the men reported that they believed they needed sexual experience, were intoxicated, and most often were enticed by their date into having sex. Fifty-seven percent of the men reported that they had unwanted sex because their dates enticed them into it. The scenario sounds something like another Biblical tale, Samson and Delilah. The seductive acts reported included teasing, flirting, touching, and the removal of her clothes or his clothes.

A small percentage of the men (13 percent) reported that women had verbally coerced them into having sex. Seven percent of the men reported that women had used physical coercion to get them to have sex. This physical coercion was for the most part non-violent (the woman might hold on to the man or block the doorway). However, there were a few instances reported which could be construed as a situation of females sexually assaulting males.

Muehlenhard has reported some anecdotal evidence, stories related by women which support the view that these acts of sexual coercion alleged by men are not pure invention. In interviews carried out in adult singles groups, women reported using "physical force and psychological pressure to obtain sex."

7. *Relationships*

What is important to you in a relationship?

Interested in exploring your own needs in a romantic relationship? Try answering the following questions. For each question check one of the following alternatives: "not important," "fairly important," "very important," "extremely important."

How important is it to you that your partner —

	Not Important	*Fairly Important*	*Very Important*	*Extremely Important*
1. Shows physical affection to you — like touching you on the shoulder or kissing you	( )	( )	( )	( )
2. Listens attentively when you have something to say	( )	( )	( )	( )
3. Does not flirt with others	( )	( )	( )	( )
4. Is dependable and reliable	( )	( )	( )	( )
5. Is a person you can really trust	( )	( )	( )	( )
6. Is well thought of by your family	( )	( )	( )	( )
7. Is well thought of by your friends	( )	( )	( )	( )
8. Acts in a way that makes you comfortable when the two of you are with other people	( )	( )	( )	( )
9. Feels free to disclose personal things to you	( )	( )	( )	( )
10. Excites you sexually	( )	( )	( )	( )
11. Is physically attractive	( )	( )	( )	( )

	Not Important	*Fairly Important*	*Very Important*	*Extremely Important*
12. Is sympathetic and supportive when you have problems	( )	( )	( )	( )
13. Is well educated	( )	( )	( )	( )
14. Has a good job	( )	( )	( )	( )
15. Is an interesting conversationalist	( )	( )	( )	( )
16. Likes to go places and do things	( )	( )	( )	( )
17. Is comfortable to be around	( )	( )	( )	( )
18. Genuinely likes you as a person	( )	( )	( )	( )
19. Is someone you can really respect	( )	( )	( )	( )
20. Shows in words or actions that he or she loves you	( )	( )	( )	( )
21. Is interested in your day-to-day concerns	( )	( )	( )	( )
22. Is a good lover	( )	( )	( )	( )
23. Doesn't try to control your behavior	( )	( )	( )	( )
24. Doesn't blow up at you	( )	( )	( )	( )
25. Gives you space to do your own things	( )	( )	( )	( )
26. Accepts you the way you are	( )	( )	( )	( )
27. Is a fun-loving person	( )	( )	( )	( )
28. Is a person who is an achiever	( )	( )	( )	( )
29. Is outgoing and sociable	( )	( )	( )	( )
30. Is a person you can look up to	( )	( )	( )	( )
31. Plans and makes decisions for the two of you	( )	( )	( )	( )
32. Isn't overly dependent on you	( )	( )	( )	( )
33. Tries to look his or her best	( )	( )	( )	( )
34. Will let you get close to him or her	( )	( )	( )	( )
35. Is caring	( )	( )	( )	( )
36. Is exciting to be with	( )	( )	( )	( )
37. Makes you feel you're appreciated	( )	( )	( )	( )

	Not Important	*Fairly Important*	*Very Important*	*Extremely Important*
38. Doesn't "put you down"	( )	( )	( )	( )
39. Has a positive attitude toward life	( )	( )	( )	( )
40. Makes you feel you're "in love"	( )	( )	( )	( )

Now go back and take a second look at the items which you checked "very important" or "extremely important." If these are qualities that are important to you in a romantic relationship, doesn't it make sense to keep them in mind when you search for that special person? There may be other qualities, too, that are important to you — things I may not have included. Go ahead and add them to the list.

What kind of baggage are you bringing into the relationship?

My definition of baggage includes (1) events that took place in your past, (2) your current life situation and (3) your aspirations for the future — any and all of these circumstances which might impact the way you relate to your romantic partner. Now this definition covers a lot of territory, but if you think about it, you can see how items in all three categories could affect a relationship. As an example of the intrusiveness of one's past, consider a broken romance. Dave had fallen deeply in love with Yvonne. Dave had never been in love before, and the relationship swiftly became the centerpiece of his life. When he was with Yvonne, he felt a surge of excitement that he had never experienced before. However, Yvonne did not share these feelings, and when she broke the relationship, it was devastating for Dave. Over a year elapsed before Dave could bring himself to date another woman, and when he did, he compared everyone he met to Yvonne. Dave had difficulty accepting a woman for herself, for who she was, as a unique individual. Nor could he give of himself freely into the relationship. The lingering memory of Yvonne was always in the background, always an impediment.

When one thinks of current life circumstances that impact on a romantic relationship, one might bring up Ted. Ted has a demanding job in a major multinational corporation, which requires him to bring work home and to frequently travel to Europe and the Far East. One of the casualties of his heavy workload and travel schedule is his relationship with Jean. Increasingly lonely and frustrated, Jean has become more and more receptive to the idea of seeing other men.

Future plans can affect relationships too. Have you heard this one?—"We can't get married because I have four years of medical school ahead of me, then an internship and a residency." Or is it law school, dental school, or foreign travel? While all of these goals are quite reasonable for a young person trying to make his or her way in the world, they can turn one's interest to casual rather than enduring relationships. Perhaps the most obvious example of a situation which impacts on new relationships is where one is divorced and is the custodial parent of young children. As one begins to date again, one has to consider the feelings of the children and how they relate to the new romantic partner. What happens if the children become attached to him or her and it doesn't work out? What happens if they resent your attachment? And how does your new romantic interest react to the realities of your having children? Even being the non-custodial parent brings its share of complications when you date again or remarry. A study of second wives reported in *Psychology Today* found that the husband's first marriage had left the new wife with a number of unresolved, residual problems. Among these were financial difficulties (the result of the divorce settlement and child support), lingering negative emotions, and problems caused by the ex-spouse herself.[1]

Try drawing on your own observations and experiences, and devise a list of circumstances that might affect the way a person relates to a romantic partner. Here is a short list of my own to get you started.

1. Emotional scars from a past relationship
2. Still stuck on someone who is not attainable
3. Strong need for independence—a wish not to be tied down
4. Negative attitudes toward the opposite sex
5. Demanding standards for potential romantic partners
6. Family obligations which limit your freedom to date
7. Bogged down in school work
8. Working long hours on the job
9. Financial situation is very limiting
10. Medical problems or disabilities
11. Feeling depressed
12. Personality patterns which make it hard to sustain a relationship
13. A tendency towards womanizing (or "manizing" if there is such a word)
14. Belief that your parents might not approve of your choice of romantic partner
15. Long-term plans which make commitments difficult
16. Too easily hurt by conflicts with romantic partners to take risks

Do any of these ring true for yourself? Now go ahead and add some of your own thoughts.

What kind of baggage does he or she have?

If your partner enjoys introspection and finds it comfortable to discuss very personal things with you, then you might approach this question by asking him or her to look through the previous section and share his or her ideas with you. If you feel your partner would be uneasy doing this, then it would be a mistake to press him or her with this request. As I have said, many people are uncomfortable disclosing personal matters. Still, the question posed is an interesting and potentially important one to keep in mind as you develop your relationship with your partner. Chances are, in time he or she will begin to volunteer some of the inhibitions, constraints and problems that are part and parcel of his or her existence. As you get to know each other better, and the level of intimacy deepens, such disclosure is likely to increase. Few of us come without some sort of baggage; it comes with living. The important thing is to try to understand your partner's experiences and how they seem to affect his or her behavior and the relationship with you. Such understanding may allow you to adjust your own expectations and behavior in ways that allow you to live more comfortably and happily with your partner. In fairness, it's an adjustment he or she should make with you, too.

What effect do age differences have on romantic relationships?

On the average, women live longer than men. To equalize things so that there would be fewer widows, wouldn't it make more sense for women to marry younger men? From the standpoint of numbers it might, but it does not work that way in practice. In fact, it works just the opposite way. If there is an age difference in a relationship, it's much more likely to be one in which the man is older than the woman. While there are probably a number of reasons for this, the pattern probably stems in part from traditional social roles. Until recently, men were usually the principal wage earners in the family, and one doesn't get to be an adequate provider without training, experience, and opportunity for advancement. These things take time. For their part, women traditionally found themselves in the roles of homemakers and mothers. In such circumstances, the biological clock which limits the age for reproduction would favor earlier marriage for women.

In his cross-cultural study of 37 different areas of the world, David Buss found that most men surveyed preferred having a mate who was several (two to three) years younger than themselves. Buss found that this was true in every country he studied. The desire of men to have a younger mate seems universal.[2] Do women buy into this scheme? The answer is yes, perhaps even more so than men. Buss reported that in every society studied, women preferred mates who were older than they were. The age difference preferred by women was if anything, slightly larger than the age difference men preferred.[3] In supplementing his inquiries, Buss analyzed data from the *Demographic Yearbook* and the *Demographic Fact Book.* He found that in actual practice, men tend to marry women who are about three years younger than they are, which is in line with the preferences expressed by both sexes in his cross-cultural survey.

Judging from Buss's data, men in Western and Northern Europe, the United States, Canada and Australia seem more comfortable marrying women close to their own ages than men in Africa, Asia, the Middle East and Latin America. The largest age difference reported by men was in Zambia (over seven years). The largest age difference reported by women was in Iran (over five years).

When we inquire about what effect age differences have on a romantic relationship, we have to begin with the premise that some age difference is the norm. Most people feel comfortable with the idea of a man's marrying a woman who is somewhat younger. Notwithstanding this preference, research suggests that when the ages of the partners are closer together, the chances of a successful marriage are higher than when the ages of the partners begin to diverge.[4]

A textbook case of a failing marriage was that between Pam and George. An attractive woman in her late thirties, Pam was divorced with a teenage son. George was much older than Pam. He was a widower and a well-off, retired stockbroker who lives in a large home in the suburbs. When George asked Pam to marry him, she agreed more out of a need for security than from any sense of romance. The marriage was a disaster for both of them. Pam soon became uncomfortable living the quiet, sedentary existence that George had fashioned for himself. She began to spend more and more time away from home, having a "good time" with her friends, leaving George to fend for himself. George soon became increasingly resentful and developed suspicions that she was having an affair. The atmosphere in the home became a deep chill, punctuated by occasional explosions. George and Pam developed patterns of antagonism and avoidance. In time, they slept in separate bedrooms and hardly spoke to each other. Finally, Pam packed her bags, left a note on the table telling her husband that it was over, and moved away.

The problems encountered by an older man and a younger wife is a theme that has captured the attention of novelists, playwrights, and filmmakers. Bring in a handsome younger man and you have the makings of a seething drama. John M. Cain's novel, the *Postman Always Rings Twice* and Eugene O'Neill's play *Desire Under the Elms* are both high-voltage treatments of this subject. Both stories have been made into films. One can envision a number of reasons for the marital instabilities that sometimes come with large age differences between the spouses. As was true in the marriage of Pam and George, large age differences are often reflected in differences in vitality, vigor, interests and attitudes. Older people may be more settled in their habits and more conservative in their outlooks. Moreover, older and younger partners are likely to have experienced a different set of realities as they grew up. The culture which shaped their tastes, attitudes and values may differ in many ways. If there is a truism in sociology, it is that we live in a time of rapid change.

Consider popular culture; today's popular singing group, the one at the top of the charts, may be a "golden oldies" in five or ten years. There was a story reported in the newspaper of a school teacher who was at a loss to improve conduct in some of the students. There were just too many smart alecks and troublemakers. He solved the problem by requiring the students sent to detention hall to listen to Frank Sinatra records for the hour. For these rock-conditioned youngsters, the experience of listening to yesteryear's romantic ballads was beyond endurance, and detention hall soon became an empty room.

The icons of popular culture rise and disappear. The gadgets and technology we use in our everyday lives are rapidly evolving. Standards in society shift. Even the language changes. Listen to the slang of a youngster and see if you fully understand the meaning of every phrase. Large differences in the ages of romantic partners mean that each grew up in somewhat different worlds; this fact makes it harder for the partners to have shared outlooks and understandings. It seems to me that the chances of a couple with large age differences minimizing these problems probably are better when they share interests which have an enduring quality. Common interests in a profession, religion, nature, gardening, sports, or the classical arts are less subject to the winds of rapid cultural change. Romantic partners of almost any age could equally enjoy a walk in the woods or listening to Mozart. If you both like such things, age is almost irrelevant.

While most men prefer to marry a younger woman, and most women want to marry a man older than themselves, there are reversals to this pattern. In a 1984 *Psychology Today* poll of 400 readers, 13 percent of those responding thought the woman should be older than the man.[5] Interestingly, wives are older than husbands in about 14 percent of the marriages in this country. In reporting on the survey data in *Psychology Today*, Elizabeth Stark suggested that the tendency of older women to marry younger men might be increasing. She reasoned that women are becoming less dependent on men for financial support and that as women mature their sex drive tends to get stronger, while that of men diminishes.

Hollywood has taken up the theme of love affairs between older women and younger men. In the 1950s and 1960s, it wasn't unusual to see aging film stars such as Cary Grant, Gary Cooper, or Fred Astaire romance much younger women. Since then, there have been a number of films depicting affairs between a younger man and an older woman. These films have ranged from a first sexual encounter such as *Summer of '42* to the development of a permanent relationship in *Forty Carats.*

What happens when people who come from widely different backgrounds fall in love?

Years ago, when I lived in Berkeley, California, I lived next door to a married couple. The backgrounds of the man and wife were radically different. She was tall, blonde, and very much the picture of Californian beauty. He was short, dark skinned, a scientist, and an expatriate from Burma. I wondered what storybook romance had brought them together. I also wondered how well things would go for them in the future.

The world of celebrities has provided us with notable examples of people coming from widely different backgrounds who married and had a difficult time of it. Rita Hayworth, the red-haired sex goddess of Hollywood's brightest days, first married theatrical genius Orson Welles and then Ali Khan, millionaire playboy from India. Both marriages failed. Another sex goddess of the silver screen, Marilyn Monroe, had equally unsuccessful marriages when she first tied the knot with baseball legend Joe DiMaggio and later with playwright Arthur Miller. More recently, the British royal family has provided tabloid readers with a steady fare of gossip about the marital troubles of princes and princesses of the realms, and their spouses who had been elevated into royalty.

For a marked contrast, think of Thornton Wilder's classic play *Our Town*; it was not hard for a boy to meet a girl in Wilder's fictional Grover's Corners. Boy and girl lived next door to one another. The community they lived in was homogenous. Everyone knew one another, went to the same schools, and attended the same churches. People understood what was expected of them: they shared a common outlook and accepted a way of life that seemed ordained for them. The marital commitment was fully understood. Divorce in a community like Grover's Corners would have been a rare event.

Social historian Edward Shorter points out in his book *The Making of the Modern Family* that the tendency of people with similar backgrounds to marry is a pattern with strong historical roots. He uses the somewhat forbidding term "class endogamy" to describe the fact that people tend to marry someone in the same social class. Shorter points out that one is not likely to marry someone one hasn't met and that the channels for meeting people are influenced by class.[6] The tradition of like marrying like is particularly strong in Western Europe. Shorter states that in Belgium, for example, farm families are three times more likely to marry among themselves than you would expect by chance.

If like marries like, does this increase the chances of marital success? Sociologists have found that similarity of education and religion seems to increase the odds of a successful marriage.[7] Dating someone with a similar background may seem less intriguing than dating that fascinating stranger who does things so differently, but it does offer more predictability. The adjustments required are easier to make. We all have expectations about how to live our daily lives — what we have learned to be comfortable with. When a man and a woman begin a relationship, there are adjustments to be made involving personality differences and gender differences. If you add to these marked cultural differences, you add appreciably to the problems. Can it be done? Certainly, but it probably won't be easy.

Is it important that we like the same things?

I've known the Jensens — Rob and Mary Ann — for many years. They've had a happy, solid relationship. One thing you can say about the Jensens is that they spend a lot of time together. They own a camper in which they take long trips; they are both devotees of folk music — he plays a banjo, she a guitar, and they are both involved in environmental causes, from protecting wildlife to cleaning up the air and water. I've always thought that one of the reasons for their successful marriage is that they both like the same things and do them together.

Research has shown that happy couples spend more of their elective time together than unhappy couples.[8] While sharing common interests is not a guarantee for a successful relationship, it usually helps. When romantic partners enjoy the same activities, they are both likely to experience pleasure when they do things together. Consider a contrasting situation in which many people find themselves at one time or another. One of the partners in a relationship is an enthusiast for a particular activity (e.g., watching a football game on television, playing bridge, camping, going shopping, dancing), while the other party has a lukewarm interest in the activity at best. If the person who is the enthusiast asks his or her partner to participate in the activity, what does the partner do? To go along occasionally may be okay, but to make a habit of it may create problems. Boredom, suffering in silence, or even a psychosomatic headache are possible outcomes. How much simpler it would be if they both liked camping, bridge, shopping or whatever.

Intuitively, the idea of liking the same things makes sense, and there is research to support the idea as well. To cite an example, Catherine Surra and Molly Longstreth studied dating couples at a large Midwestern University. The researchers asked both partners in the relationship to rate their preferences for various activities (e.g., sports, partying, sex) on a scale ranging from "dislike very much" to "like very much." The subjects were asked not to think about how much they liked doing the activity with their partner—just how much they liked the activity, period. The researchers found that for the women in the study, having similar interests with their partners was clearly related to their satisfaction with the relationships.[9] While the findings for the men were less clear, they still pointed to the importance of similar interests and shared activities. Enjoying the same things and doing them together are likely to increase satisfaction with the relationship.

Do you and your partner see eye-to-eye on values?

Here is a quiz about values—your beliefs about what is important in life and what is not. Try answering the questions below, then ask your partner to answer them. Compare your answers. What beliefs do you share? Where do your beliefs diverge?

Quiz on Values

In the list below, you will find brief descriptions of behaviors, things you may or may not do in your daily life. Some of these behaviors may be very important to you, acts that you place a high value upon. Other behaviors may seem less important to you. What I would like you to do is to read through the list of items, asking yourself how important the behavior is to you in your daily life. For each item, please check one of the following alternatives, "extremely important," "very important," "fairly important," or "not important."

	Extremely Important	*Very Important*	*Fairly Important*	*Not Important*
1. Keeping in touch with friends	( )	( )	( )	( )
2. Being supportive to friends	( )	( )	( )	( )

	Extremely Important	*Very Important*	*Fairly Important*	*Not Important*
3. Regular attendance at a church, synagogue, or other place of worship	( )	( )	( )	( )
4. Prayer	( )	( )	( )	( )
5. Getting additional formal education	( )	( )	( )	( )
6. Reading interesting books	( )	( )	( )	( )
7. Making a high income	( )	( )	( )	( )
8. Wearing fashionable clothes	( )	( )	( )	( )
9. Driving an expensive car	( )	( )	( )	( )
10. Having pets	( )	( )	( )	( )
11. Enjoying the outdoors	( )	( )	( )	( )
12. Not breaking the law	( )	( )	( )	( )
13. Being patriotic	( )	( )	( )	( )
14. Sticking up for my country	( )	( )	( )	( )
15. Observing the traditional holidays	( )	( )	( )	( )
16. Saving money	( )	( )	( )	( )
17. Thinking about long-range goals	( )	( )	( )	( )
18. Being prudent and careful in the things I do	( )	( )	( )	( )
19. Being willing to sacrifice today for better things tomorrow	( )	( )	( )	( )
20. Being on time	( )	( )	( )	( )
21. Being courteous and polite	( )	( )	( )	( )
22. Not hurting other people in the things I do	( )	( )	( )	( )
23. Not being prejudiced	( )	( )	( )	( )
24. Being fair in the way I treat others	( )	( )	( )	( )
25. Getting regular exercise	( )	( )	( )	( )
26. Exercising care in what I eat	( )	( )	( )	( )
27. Keeping myself in good physical shape	( )	( )	( )	( )
28. Going out for entertainment	( )	( )	( )	( )
29. Having fun	( )	( )	( )	( )
30. Busting loose and letting myself go	( )	( )	( )	( )

	Extremely Important	*Very Important*	*Fairly Important*	*Not Important*
31. Giving to charity	( )	( )	( )	( )
32. Volunteering time to community organizations	( )	( )	( )	( )
33. Sharing what I have with others	( )	( )	( )	( )
34. Having time for reflection and thinking about things	( )	( )	( )	( )
35. Enjoying the arts and cultural activities	( )	( )	( )	( )
36. Having a satisfying career	( )	( )	( )	( )
37. Doing whatever I do well	( )	( )	( )	( )
38. Working hard at my job or at school	( )	( )	( )	( )
39. Being personally responsible for my own actions	( )	( )	( )	( )
40. Looking after the needs of my family	( )	( )	( )	( )
41. Keeping my home neat and clean	( )	( )	( )	( )
42. Not turning a blind eye to wrong doing	( )	( )	( )	( )
43. Standing up for what I believe	( )	( )	( )	( )
44. Treating sex as very special	( )	( )	( )	( )
45. Having sex with only someone I love	( )	( )	( )	( )
46. Making sure I receive my fair share of things	( )	( )	( )	( )
47. Going after my goals aggressively	( )	( )	( )	( )

Does having similar or complementary personality needs best predict the success of a couple's relationship?

Nancy is described by her friends as a person who is very "supportive and giving," while her husband Eddie cheerfully admits that he constantly looks for help and emotional support. Nancy has a need to give; Eddie has a need to receive. It sounds like a match designed by a computer. The same might be said about Steve and Barbara. Steve is very assertive, exudes confidence, and is a born leader. Barbara is quiet, seldom shows initiative, and seems very comfortable following the lead of others. In each of these couples, the personalities of the man and woman seem to mesh together, like two pieces of an interlocking jigsaw puzzle. The partners appear to complement one another, filling important needs, one for the other.

Now imagine a contrasting situation. Think about a man and a woman who both have strong needs to be surrounded by lots of friends. Neither is happy without a constant buzz of people. Or picture a man and a woman who both have needs to express themselves in an artistic medium, like painting or music. The personality needs of these couples are similar, rather than complementary. One person does not fill a compelling need for the other person. However, there do seem to be greater possibilities for these couples to share mutually satisfying activities. One could imagine the first couple throwing a party, and the second couple taking their easels and canvases into the countryside for an afternoon of painting. Which of these pairings is likely to work out best — the couples with complementary personality needs, or the couples with similar personality needs? In an article which reviews research on this question, K. Daniel O'Leary and David Smith give the nod to the couples with similar needs.[10]

Here is an example of a study which points out the advantage of similar personality needs over complementary personality needs. Researchers P.M. Bentler and Michael Newcomb of U.C.L.A. located their subjects, newly married couples, using the records of a marriage license bureau. The researchers administered a wide-ranging personality inventory to the newlyweds, then put the data into file cabinets and waited. After four years had elapsed, they contacted as many couples as they could locate to find out how things had gone. As one might expect, things did not go well for all of the couples; some of them had divorced. The researchers then turned to their original data, and asked if the couples that stayed together were more alike in their personalities than the couples that had divorced. The answer was clearly yes. In discussing their findings, the authors observed: "Similarity between marital partners, based on personality traits measured at the beginning of a marriage, was substantially higher for couples who remained together after 4 years than couples who decided to end their marriage within that period of time.[11]

The results of the study do not mean that for some couples, complementary personality needs might not work out well. What this study and others suggest is that the odds favor couples who tend to be similar in their personality needs.

What ingredients in a relationship promote stability?

In approaching this question, I would like to first bring a theoretical perspective to the problem, and then offer some specific suggestions for keeping a relationship intact. Behavioral scientists have offered various theories about why romantic partners stay together and why they break up. I have found the views of Caryl Rusbult of the University of North Carolina particularly interesting, and will draw on her ideas as a way of beginning this discussion. In some of her earlier writings, Rusbult suggested that a combination of three factors makes a difference in whether a couple stayed together. These three factors were (1) how satisfied a person was with the relationship; (2) the quality of the "alternatives" that he or she saw available, and (3) the kind of investment he or she had made in the relationship. The more satisfied the person was, the less promising the alternatives appeared; and the more time and energy one had devoted to the relationship, the more likely the person would stay in it. Put simply, if you feel that you have something good, that you've worked at it and there's nothing better out there, you'll stay in the relationship.

While this analysis is straightforward, it does not probe very deeply into the dynamics of human relationships. Recently, Rusbult joined one of her students, Stephen Drigotas, in writing a paper which revisited the question of "staying or leaving."[12] In this version, which I find much more appealing than the earlier model, the authors view relationships as vehicles which provide satisfaction for an individual's needs. The needs might be for sex, security, companionship, intimacy, or a variety of others which come to mind. The authors theorize that the more dependent a person becomes on the relationship to satisfy these needs, the more he or she is likely to stay in the relationship. Staying put seems particularly likely if the person believes that there are no alternative partners available who could effectively satisfy these needs.

The theory suggests that the breakup of a relationship is likely to occur when a person recognizes that the romantic partner no longer satisfies his or her needs. Sometimes a judgment like this may be slow in coming. Drigotas and Rusbult present a hypothetical scenario of a slowly dissolving relationship.

> One day an individual may notice that he enjoys more laughs with his favorite colleague than with his partner, months later he may notice that making love has become routinized and unimaginative in comparison to what he imagines is available elsewhere, and months after that he may realize that his best friend expresses more spontaneous affection than his partner. That individual's feelings of dependence may gradually be eroded ... that by the time he makes the overt global judgment that the relationship has died, it may in fact have been devoid of meaning for some time.[13]

Individuals have different needs that are satisfied in a relationship. As long as some of a person's important needs are being satisfied in the relationship, there will be positive-attractive forces exerted from within the relationship to maintain its existence. There may also be external forces working to maintain the relationship, subtle and not so subtle pressures emanating from family and friends for the couple to stay together. In the case of married couples, the needs of children have to be considered as well as the economic burdens that would come with divorce. Divorced parents, especially the mother, often face severe economic problems.

While these forces act to hold a relationship together, there may be other forces both within and without the relationship pulling it apart. These forces may go beyond the failure of one person to meet the needs of the other person. These forces may be negative and destructive. Obvious examples would be physical and verbal abuse by one or both partners, a drum-beat of criticism from friends and relatives about one's partner, and hard economic times. Such forces can tear a relationship apart.

Looking at the relationship in these terms, whether a couple stays together or breaks up is the result of an interplay of forces — some pushing the couple apart (e.g., verbal and physical abuse), some pulling it together (e.g., satisfaction of important individual needs). When one's needs are no longer sufficiently satisfied in the relationship, the forces holding the partners together are weakened and are unable to counterbalance non-rewarding and aversive aspects of the relationship. The relationship, now in trouble, may unravel, particularly if the person who wants out believes it is possible to find a more satisfying partner.

Let's now move from this theoretical analysis of the stability of relationships to some suggestions for keeping a relationship intact.

1. **Choice.** Your choice of a romantic partner can make things easier or harder for you. When you become involved, exercise care. Listen to your head as well as your heart. If a person has a history of problem behaviors (e.g., abuse, promiscuity, irresponsibility), you are loading the dice against yourself. You load the dice in your favor when you choose someone you can trust and respect.
2. **Companionship.** Recall that friendships are often more stable than romantic relationships. A romantic relationship has a better chance to last if it incorporates the basics of a good friendship.
3. **Needs-satisfaction.** Discover what the important needs of your partner are and try to keep them in mind. When these needs are satisfied in the relationship, the chances are diminished that your partner will cast his or her eyes elsewhere.
4. **Communication.** This is an important, often crucial part of the relationship. When your partner wants to talk about something, listen! Sharing experiences and self-disclosure create bonds.
5. **Sexual relationship.** If it isn't satisfying, see what can be done to make it better. Mutual pleasures in a physical relationship increase intimacy and provide something special for both partners. Studies show that happy couples are more satisfied with their sexual relationship. In one study,

it was found that happy couples had sexual intercourse nearly twice as frequently as unhappy couples.

6. **Conflict.** Keep it within bounds. Constant bickering can shatter relationships.

7. **Investment.** A good relationship is as good as gold. Recognize that what you have is important and worth keeping. Doing things together and sharing help create this feeling of investment.

8. **Alternative partners.** If you have a good relationship, forget them.

I have kept this list short intentionally to keep it focused. As we move through this book, we will explore some of these ideas in more detail.

What works best in a relationship — male dominance, female dominance or none of the above?

Let's imagine three couples. Each couple has been married for about ten years. In our first couple, the Smiths, the husband is the boss. Mr. Smith is a very traditional head of the household, making all of the major decisions for the family, whether it's about major purchases, deciding where the family takes its vacation, or disciplining the children (Mrs. Smith's usual method of keeping the peace is to utter a thinly veiled warning to her children, "Wait 'til your father comes home!"). When there is a problem in the Smith household, he is the court of last resort. In our second couple, the Johnsons, the situation is reversed. Mr. Johnson has faded into the background. He spends most of his time at home, engulfed by his newspaper while Mrs. Johnson runs the home. It is Mrs. Johnson who organizes and supervises the children's activities and decides how she and her husband spend their spare time together. When there are unresolved difficulties, everyone defers to her. Mr. Johnson simply nods and acquiesces. In our third couple, the Fords, the usual process of decision-making is one of consultation. Mr. and Mrs. Ford talk through an issue and then come to a joint decision. They try to and usually do reach a consensus — a plan they can both accept.

Consider these three couples. Mr. Smith is clearly the dominant partner in the first couple; Mrs. Johnson is the dominant partner in the second, and in the third couple, neither partner is dominant. In the third couple, the relationship appears to be one of equals, and the term "egalitarian" is used to describe such a relationship. Take a moment and try to imagine yourself in each of these relationships. Now ask yourself, in which of these relationships would you feel most comfortable? In which of these relationships would you feel least comfortable? Let's see how your choices compare with the experience of other people. In a 1983 issue of the *Psychological Bulletin*, Bernadette

Gray-Little and Nancy Burks reviewed over 20 studies which related these three styles of husband-wife relationships to how satisfied the parties were with the marriage. Here are their conclusions.

> The most prevalent finding, which has appeared in the majority of studies ... is that marriages in which the wife is the dominant partner, whether in decision making or some other aspect of control, are more likely to be unhappy than any other type of marriage. Less conclusive, but nonetheless replicated in numerous studies, is the finding of highest levels of marital satisfaction among egalitarian couples.[14]

Among married couples, then, egalitarian relationships appear most satisfying; male-dominated relationships are intermediate, and female-dominated relationships are least satisfying. Why is this the case? Gray-Little and Burks offer a possible explanation.

> Women are brought up to expect a greater amount of leadership from their husbands than men expect from their wives. Some husbands do not take on a position of power equal to or greater than their wives, whether because of their own incapacity to take on such a role or because of their wife's unusually high ability to take on a leadership role. When this occurs, both spouses feel dissatisfied with the discrepancy between their leadership and their own internalized cultural norms.[15]

In their comments, the researchers seem to be suggesting that many women would like to find a relationship in which the men they choose would add strength, direction, and support to their lives. If it turns out that this is not the case, that instead of bringing strength, their partners lack direction, are unassertive, or are unable to handle responsibility, these women are likely to be disappointed and disillusioned. For their part, the men may feel a deep sense of inadequacy when they find they cannot meet both their wives' and their own expectations. If a frustrated woman pushes the man too hard to assume the leadership role, it may prove to be counterproductive. He may simply withdraw further from family responsibilities, creating the very situation she didn't want herself — where she is the dominant party, and he becomes a hapless bystander.

It has been said that nature abhors a vacuum. The idea probably holds in social relationships, as well. Usually, there has to be some leadership in a family, and the woman may step into this role by default. Our cultural expectations, however, make many men and women uneasy with female-dominated relationships, and in the marital situation such relationships seem less likely to be satisfying.

8. *Understanding Your Partner*

How would you evaluate your current romantic relationship?

In an earlier question I asked you about what was important to you in a relationship and particularly about the qualities you would like to have in a partner. Now, let's take a look at and evaluate the relationship that you have. For starters, imagine a rating scale with points ranging from zero to 100. Zero would be the pits, about as unsatisfactory a relationship as you can get. One hundred would be high in the clouds; you are living out a fantasy of happiness, and everything the poets and songwriters have written about, you've got—and more. If you say 100, you might do well to bottle the secret of your success and sell it.

For those who find themselves somewhere between zero and 100, let's break things down a bit and do some itemizing. Which aspects of your relationship are satisfactory and which are not? Below are "scales" for rating different facets of a romantic relationship. If you're game, try making the ratings for your own relationship. For each item, rate your relationship as "very satisfactory," "satisfactory," "unsatisfactory," or "very unsatisfactory."

	Very Satis-factory	*Satis-factory*	*Unsatis-factory*	*Very Unsatis-factory*
1. Amount of time he or she spends with you.	( )	( )	( )	( )
2. Quality of the time you spend together.	( )	( )	( )	( )
3. Willingness of your partner to listen to you.	( )	( )	( )	( )
4. Willingness of your partner to disclose personal things to you.	( )	( )	( )	( )

	Very Satis-factory	*Satis-factory*	*Unsatis-factory*	*Very Unsatis-factory*
5. Amount of affection your partner shows you.	( )	( )	( )	( )
6. Level of emotional support your partner gives you.	( )	( )	( )	( )
7. Your partner's willingness to help you when you need it.	( )	( )	( )	( )
8. The extent to which the two of you go places and do things together.	( )	( )	( )	( )
9. The way you and your partner resolve conflicts.	( )	( )	( )	( )
10. The dependability of your partner.	( )	( )	( )	( )
11. The extent to which your partner takes your wishes into account when the two of you make plans.	( )	( )	( )	( )
12. Your partner's reaction when you do nice things for him or her.	( )	( )	( )	( )
13. Your partner's responsiveness when you show affection to him or her.	( )	( )	( )	( )
14. The quality of your sexual relationship.	( )	( )	( )	( )
15. The extent to which your partner shows he or she cares for you by words or deeds.	( )	( )	( )	( )
16. The comfort level you experience when you are around your partner.	( )	( )	( )	( )
17. The respect you feel for your partner as an individual.	( )	( )	( )	( )
18. The respect your partner shows for you.	( )	( )	( )	( )
19. The level of trust you have in your partner.	( )	( )	( )	( )
20. The level of trust he or she has in you.	( )	( )	( )	( )
21. The degree to which you "like" your partner as a person.	( )	( )	( )	( )
22. The opinions your friends have of your partner.	( )	( )	( )	( )
23. The sense of well-being you experience just knowing that you have the relationship.	( )	( )	( )	( )

Here is a short supplementary quiz. Sometimes, a partner in a relationship may do things which are insensitive, even hurtful. How often does your partner act in the following ways?

	Very Often	*Fairly Often*	*Seldom*	*Never*
1. Excludes you from activities you want to share.	( )	( )	( )	( )
2. Encroaches on the time you want to use for other activities.	( )	( )	( )	( )
3. Is unreasonably jealous.	( )	( )	( )	( )
4. Is bossy or domineering.	( )	( )	( )	( )
5. Hurts you by the things he or she says.	( )	( )	( )	( )
6. Is physically abusive.	( )	( )	( )	( )
7. Flirts with other women or men.	( )	( )	( )	( )
8. Picks fights with you.	( )	( )	( )	( )
9. Cheats on you.	( )	( )	( )	( )

Now, go back and look at the first list. If almost all of the items are marked "very satisfactory," or "satisfactory," then all seems well. From your vantage point, the relationship is on a good course and it looks like smooth sailing. However, if there are many items marked "very unsatisfactory," or "unsatisfactory," then there are obvious signs of trouble. Ask yourself, how important to you are those items which you marked "unsatisfactory"? If they are important, your course looks particularly rocky. But before you decide to jump ship, ask yourself the following question: Are there sufficient compensations in the relationship, positive things that offer reason to stay and to work for change?

If you checked "very often" or "fairly often" to some of the items on the list of aversive behaviors, these are clear indications of problems. If you are being emotionally or physically abused in a relationship, it is certainly time to ask yourself some very basic questions: Why are you there and what's keeping you there?

How much do I love my partner?

Some traditional tests of love:

From the *Bible*: Jacob worked seven years for Laban to win the hand of Rachel, only to be tricked into taking her sister Leah. Then, he had to work another seven years to win Rachel. That's 14 years of labor.

From Greek mythology: Orpheus descended into Hades in an attempt to bring back his wife Eurydice from the underworld.

From the *Odyssey*: Penelope waited about 20 years for Odysseus to return from the Trojan War, never knowing whether he was alive or dead. While she waited, she was besieged and pressured by suitors.

From the days when knights were bold: To win the favor of the lady in tournaments, knights mounted on horseback would charge at each other, lances pointed forward, with the loser being hurled to the ground.

From opera: In Mozart's *Magic Flute*, Tamino had to undergo a series of tests (fire, water, silence) to win the hand of Pamina. In *Siegfried*, Siegfried had to pass through the magic fire to reach Brünnhilda. In *Turandot*, Calaf, the unknown prince, had to answer three riddles to win the hand of Turandot. If he failed to answer any of them, he forfeited his life.

From ancient history: Mark Antony gave up his family, his country, and ultimately his life to stay with Cleopatra.

From more recent history: Edward VIII gave up the throne of England to marry twice-divorced Wallis Simpson. When he addressed the British people by radio, he said he had found it impossible to carry the burdens and responsibilities of being King "without the help and support of the woman I love."

If the traditional tests are too exacting, try this ten-item quiz.

1. How do you feel when you have a quarrel with your partner?
( ) Extremely upset ( ) Very upset ( ) Moderately upset
( ) Slightly upset ( ) Not upset at all

2. How often do you think about your partner?
( ) It seems like all of the time ( ) Very often ( ) Fairly often
( ) Seldom

3. How would you feel if your partner left and you would not be seeing him or her again?
( ) Devastated ( ) Very upset ( ) Moderately upset
( ) Slightly upset

4. How strong is your love now, compared to the love you have felt before for others?
( ) Stronger now ( ) About the same ( ) Less strong

5. Would you willingly sacrifice your interests to advance your partner's interests?
( ) In most cases—yes ( ) In most cases—no
( ) I don't know

6. How much gratification do you feel when your partner achieves success in an undertaking?
( ) Tremendous amount ( ) A great deal ( ) A fair amount
( ) Little, if any

7. How resistant is your love to the charms and enticements of other attractive people?
( ) Very resistant ( ) Fairly resistant
( ) Not at all resistant — I could be easily swayed

8. If things began to go wrong in your relationship, how much of an effort would you make to try to work through the difficulties?
( ) Tremendous effort ( ) A great effort ( ) A reasonable effort ( ) Only a slight effort

9. If your partner asked for time before making a commitment, how much time would you give?
( ) As much time as he or she asked for ( ) A year or two, but no more ( ) Six months ( ) A few weeks ( ) None

10. On a thermometer scale of zero to one hundred, how would you gauge the intensity of your love?
HIGH 100 90 80 70 60 50 40 30 20 10 0 LOW

Take a look at your answers. If your responses were not near the top for most of the questions, you are no Tamino, Penelope, or Mark Antony.

How important is it to look at situations from your partner's perspective?

Your partner is a unique human being with his or her own set of values, needs, aspirations, concerns and fears. In taking our partner's perspective, you try as best you can to put yourself in your partner's shoes, to look at life as he or she is experiencing it. This can be a difficult task because it is not easy to really know another person, and it is often hard to divorce oneself from one's own perspectives when looking at an issue one's partner faces. Let's talk about some of the difficulties that may arise in getting to know your romantic partner. You may find, for example, that your partner is not a disclosing sort of person; he or she may not always share important concerns with you, and may wish to keep some things private. Or you may find that your partner is not that straightforward a communicator. Some people have difficulty stating what they really want. Perhaps they think it's unseemly to voice their own desires. They may even go so far as to say they don't want something when they do want it.

During his first years of marriage, Warren had this problem with his wife, Jan. "I don't know what it was," he said. "Maybe it was the way she was raised. Her mother's the same way. She did exactly the same thing. Jan would never tell me what she wanted. She would say 'No, don't get that for me,' when that's what she really wanted! She's changed now. She tells me what she wants. It makes it a lot easier." Not everyone says what he or she means, or worse, means what he or she says.

Sometimes the reasons romantic partners have for not leveling with each other are well intended. In their daily interactions, they find it wise to tread lightly when touching the sensitivities of the other, recognizing that there can be a heavy cost in always being candid and frank. When your partner withholds information from you or is less than candid, it obviously makes it harder to read what is on his or her mind.

Compounding the difficulty is the likelihood that our partners like most people are not fully appreciative of or even aware of all the issues that may be troubling them. If we subscribe at all to psychoanalytic theories of the unconscious, we have to entertain the possibility that people have hidden conflicts that influence their behavior. Even when our partners are open with us, we may find it difficult to make the mental switch to look at the world from our partners' points of view. Our natural tendency would be to look at a problem from our own perspectives — from what our own experiences have taught us. To try to understand how things appear to another person is an act many people find strange if not altogether alien. It is usually easier to toss off advice based on our own experiences than to patiently listen and try to understand what the other person is experiencing. Imagine, for example, the following fictional conversation. Notice how the woman misses the opportunity of being empathetic with her partner.

He: I had a bad day at the office. I feel rotten.

She: I had a bad day, too. *(Fails to respond to his situation. Brings up her own problem instead.)*

He: The boss chewed me out for something that wasn't my fault.

She: You should have told him that. *(Doesn't make any effort to find out what happened.)*

He: I couldn't. I think he made the mistake.

She: I know what I would have done. *(Again, changes focus to herself.)*

He: I couldn't tell him. He's not the type to admit making mistakes. And, I didn't want to appear defensive, either. I just had to take it. I felt sick.

She: You should always stand up for your rights. *(Doesn't pick up on his feelings. Instead, moralizes.)*

He: *(Shakes head.)*

She: *(Pauses.)* You'll never believe the bill I got from the insurance company today. *(Changes the subject.)*

If, as in this illustration, it is difficult for some people to enter into an empathetic relationship to a partner in need, how much more difficult it becomes to try to understand the other person's point of view when we ourselves are involved in the problem — when his or her interest conflicts with our own. When we are having disagreements and disputes with our partners, it becomes very difficult to turn away from our own agenda and ask what are they thinking and feeling. For these and other reasons, many people pay insufficient attention to the concerns and needs of their romantic partners. In a study of married couples, researchers Neil Jacobson and Danny Moore found that one spouse had only a vague idea of what the other spouse was doing. The researchers presented both husband and wife with a checklist of activities such as "spouse complimented me," and "we watched television together," and asked whether the spouse had done this in the preceding 24 hours. The spouses only agreed about half the time.[1]

With this evidence of inattention, if not indifference, to our partner's behavior, just how important is it that we try to take the perspective of our romantic partners? I would argue that it can be very important. The reasons are twofold. First, communicating to your partner that you are paying attention and trying to understand his or her needs, concerns and feelings helps build and deepen the relationship. Studies clearly show that for many women, the ability to talk with their partners and feel they are listening and understanding is a paramount need in a relationship. Second, as you become more aware of the needs and concerns of your partner, you are in a better position to help him or her successfully cope with the problems that he or she is facing. Whether the problems deal with the job, school, family or friends, you can often be of assistance as well as be supportive. Moreover, if the problems concern your own relationship, you should be in a better position to successfully work through the difficulties. Accurate information about what he or she is thinking and feeling can help you prevent conflicts and more easily resolve them when they occur.

To nail down the point, consider some findings from research. In a study carried out by Stephen Franzoi and his colleagues on student couples at Indiana University, it was reported that perspective-taking, especially by women, influenced the satisfaction both parties had with the relationship. In interpreting these findings, the authors suggested that "Perspective taking may enhance relationship satisfaction largely by eliminating some of the friction inherent in all social intercourse."[2] Similar results were reported by Edgar Long and David Andrews in a study of couples that had been married for many years. The authors concluded that "Married individuals who could adopt the point of view of others were more likely to have spouses who were well adjusted in their marriage."[3] The wives' feelings that their husbands were able to take their perspectives had particularly strong influence on how satisfied they were with the marriage.

How well do you understand your romantic partner?

Let's begin with how well you think you understand him or her. Edgar Long of Central Michigan University developed a scale to measure our beliefs about this. Try responding to some of Long's items using a scale from zero to four (zero does not describe you very well; four describes you very well).

> "I am good at understanding my partner's problems."
> "I very often seem to know how my partner feels."
> "I sometimes try to understand my partner better by imagining how things look from his/her perspective."
> "Even if my partner has difficulty in saying something, I usually understand what he/she means."[4]

If you responded to these statements with threes and fours, you probably view yourself as a person who both tries to and successfully understands your romantic partner. So far so good.

Would you like to try a little experiment to see how well your impressions of your partner coincide with those your partner has about himself or herself? Here are 35 items which can describe a person. For each item, please respond in the following way. If you think the statement is a very accurate description of your partner, check "very accurate." If you think the statement is a fairly accurate description of your partner, check "fairly accurate." If you think the statement is not at all accurate, check "not at all accurate." If you have no idea, check "not sure."

My partner…	*Very Accurate*	*Fairly Accurate*	*Not at All Accurate*	*Not Sure*
1. likes outdoor activities such as walking, jogging or bike riding.	( )	( )	( )	( )
2. loves to travel to distant places.	( )	( )	( )	( )
3. is an avid sports fan.	( )	( )	( )	( )
4. is extroverted — loves to be with people.	( )	( )	( )	( )
5. is interested in current events.	( )	( )	( )	( )

My partner…	*Very Accurate*	*Fairly Accurate*	*Not at All Accurate*	*Not Sure*
6. spends a lot of time reading books.	( )	( )	( )	( )
7. is fond of animals.	( )	( )	( )	( )
8. enjoys fixing and repairing things around the house.	( )	( )	( )	( )
9. enjoys cooking.	( )	( )	( )	( )
10. spends a lot of time listening to music.				
11. particularly enjoys spending time with children.	( )	( )	( )	( )
12. is more of an evening person than a morning person.	( )	( )	( )	( )
13. is funny and often makes people laugh.	( )	( )	( )	( )
14. is an avid television watcher.	( )	( )	( )	( )
15. has lots of up and down moods.	( )	( )	( )	( )
16. is very affectionate.	( )	( )	( )	( )
17. has a strong interest in sex.	( )	( )	( )	( )
18. is a workaholic.	( )	( )	( )	( )
19. is very religious.	( )	( )	( )	( )
20. often does things impulsively.	( )	( )	( )	( )
21. has conservative political views.	( )	( )	( )	( )
22. is more of a homebody than a person who enjoys going out on the town.	( )	( )	( )	( )
23. has an active fantasy life.	( )	( )	( )	( )
24. is neat and tidy.	( )	( )	( )	( )
25. likes to take risks.	( )	( )	( )	( )
26. is very controlled—should let himself or herself go more often.	( )	( )	( )	( )
27. is very focused and goal directed.	( )	( )	( )	( )
28. is a quiet sort of person.	( )	( )	( )	( )
29. seldom gets angry.	( )	( )	( )	( )
30. is a romantic.	( )	( )	( )	( )

Look back at your answers. Did you check a lot of "not sures"? If you did, perhaps you don't know your partner as well as you should. The next step in this exercise is only for people who feel secure in their relationship, for the procedure could stir up controversy. If either you or your partner feels uncomfortable about this exercise, don't do it. In the event you wish to go ahead, here are the rules. Ask your partner to answer the following questions without seeing your answers. Then you can compare how well your perceptions of your partner coincide with your partner's perception of himself or herself.

Instructions for your partner: Here are 30 items which can describe a person. For each item, please respond in the following way. If you think the statement is a very accurate description of you, check "very accurate." If you think the statement is a fairly accurate description of you, check "fairly accurate." If you think the statement is not at all accurate, check "not at all accurate." If you have no idea, check "not sure."

I...	*Very Accurate*	*Fairly Accurate*	*Not at All Accurate*	*Not Sure*
1. like outdoor activities such as walking, jogging, or bikeriding.	( )	( )	( )	( )
2. love to travel to distant places.	( )	( )	( )	( )
3. am an avid sports fan.	( )	( )	( )	( )
4. am extroverted — love to be with people.	( )	( )	( )	( )
5. am interested in current events.	( )	( )	( )	( )
6. spend a lot of time reading books.	( )	( )	( )	( )
7. am fond of animals.	( )	( )	( )	( )
8. enjoy fixing and repairing things around the house.	( )	( )	( )	( )
9. enjoy cooking.	( )	( )	( )	( )
10. spend a lot of time listening to music.	( )	( )	( )	( )
11. particularly enjoy spending time with children.	( )	( )	( )	( )
12. am more of an evening person than a morning person.	( )	( )	( )	( )
13. am funny and often make people laugh.	( )	( )	( )	( )
14. am an avid television watcher.	( )	( )	( )	( )
15. have lots of up and down moods.	( )	( )	( )	( )
16. am very affectionate.	( )	( )	( )	( )
17. have a strong interest in sex.	( )	( )	( )	( )
18. am a workaholic.	( )	( )	( )	( )
19. am very religious.	( )	( )	( )	( )
20. often do things impulsively.	( )	( )	( )	( )

I...	*Very Accurate*	*Fairly Accurate*	*Not at All Accurate*	*Not Sure*
21. have conservative political views.	( )	( )	( )	( )
22. am more of a homebody than a person who enjoys going out on the town.	( )	( )	( )	( )
23. have an active fantasy life.	( )	( )	( )	( )
24. am neat and tidy.	( )	( )	( )	( )
25. like to take risks.	( )	( )	( )	( )
26. am very controlled — should let myself go more often.	( )	( )	( )	( )
27. am very focused and goal directed.	( )	( )	( )	( )
28. am a quiet sort of person.	( )	( )	( )	( )
29. seldom get angry.	( )	( )	( )	( )
30. am a romantic.	( )	( )	( )	( )

How many of the questions did the two of you answer exactly the same way? On how many questions were your answers far apart — one person checked very accurate, the other not at all accurate? If there were a lot of the former and few of the latter, you seem to have a good reading of your partner. If you disagreed about most of the items, and you still have a good relationship, then ignorance must be bliss.

How well does my partner understand me?

If you were both comfortable with the procedure in the preceding question, now it's time to reverse roles. This time ask your partner to respond to the first set of 30 items while you respond to the second set. After you both have finished, compare your responses.

When things are not going well for me, is my partner the kind of person I can turn to for emotional support?

When Andrea discovered a small lump in her left breast, she consulted her physician, Dr. Harding. After Dr. Harding examined her, she told Andrea that she was concerned about the possibility of malignancy, and scheduled her for a biopsy. Andrea was extremely upset when she left her physician's office. Only a few months earlier her best friend, June, had undergone a radical mastectomy, and the thought of cancer was terrifying. Andrea felt an urgent need to talk to someone about what she was feeling, to vent the emotions that were welling up within her. She thought immediately of her boyfriend Mike, but then shook her head. Mike would become so uncomfortable, it would make her feel even more upset.

She remembered that she had tried to talk to Mike before about personal problems that were bothering her, and that she had found Mike barely able to listen to her. When she tried to tell him about the difficulties she was having with her mother, he would fidget, try to change the subject, or become irritable. The same thing happened when Andrea became upset by a problem at work; she felt she had not been considered for a supervisory promotion when she should have been. The more she expressed her feelings of anger and disappointment to Mike, the more uncomfortable he became. It was as if he wanted to open the door and run away.

When it comes to listening to the problems of other people, most of us have a kind of comfort zone. For some people, this zone of acceptance is very wide and encompassing. Such people usually listen patiently and sympathetically, so friends turn to them when in need. You may even find them volunteering for service on "hotlines." Take Warren, for example. He's a minister at a small church not far from a community college campus. One night, a student dropped into the church. He was feeling desperate, suicidal. He wasn't a member of Warren's church, not even of the same faith. Yet Warren spent hours talking with him, gave him his home telephone number, and kept in contact with him until the crisis was resolved. Warren is a giving type of person who is comfortable dealing with the raw emotions of people experiencing stress.

Mike, of course, is very different, and he's not unusual. There are many people like Mike, whose tolerance for listening to the problems and concerns of others is very limited; they avoid such situations like the plague. Andrea has learned that if she has a problem, the last person to turn to is Mike. You will find individual differences in comfort zones even among people working in the helping professions—social workers, nurses, psychologists and physicians. Some physicians will make a point of listening carefully to the concerns and anxieties of their patients, trying to find out what is happening in their lives that may have contributed to or complicated the problems that the patients are experiencing. Other physicians may be far from comfortable in this role, preferring the more traditional facets of patient care, such as physical diagnosis and prescribing medications.

In choosing a romantic partner for the long haul, there are questions of dependability and stability to think about. No one can read the future, and it is nice to know that the person you have cast your lot with is going to be there when times are tough. It is also a comforting thought that your partner will listen to you when things happen that are distressing and you really need to talk. You can find someone else to fill this role, but it's nice when you don't have to.

Do I want to make a commitment? Can I make a commitment?

Let's consider the question of whether or not you can make a commitment first, because it is more fundamental. Take a few moments and look back at your personal history. Would you characterize yourself as a person who has been indecisive — someone who has experienced a great deal of difficulty in making up his or her mind? Consider a few "for instances." When you chose a college, did you wrestle for months between possibilities? When you make a major purchase like that of an automobile, do you agonize about the decision? How confident did you feel when you made your career choice? Did you waver back and forth? When you make big decisions, do you make lists of positives and negatives, then put the list away for a while and then can't find it again?

While prudence is a virtue, indecisiveness can lead to no decision which then becomes a decision. It can leave you in a vague state of dissatisfaction. Indecisiveness is a first cousin to procrastination. Both states are inhibitory; you don't do something because — if you are inventive enough, you can make up a long list of "becauses." However, if you analyze these reasons for inaction, it often leads to a trail of underlying anxiety. Some of this anxiety has to do with the consequences of sticking your neck out. Taking action means taking risks. You may experience unpleasant results.

As is true for making any decision, there are downsides to making intimate, romantic commitments. Obviously you will lose some of your freedom. When you commit yourself to someone, that attractive stranger you encounter at the bar must remain an attractive stranger, not become an intriguing possibility for a new romance. Your time is much less your own. There are expectations for sharing your time with someone else; maybe in amounts that make you uncomfortable. Your space may no longer be your own. You may be sharing an apartment or house. Your closets are full of someone else's clothes, your bookshelves with someone else's books, your bathroom with someone else's cosmetics. And where did all those wet towels come from? If you're used to your own space, it may be a bit overwhelming.

And you may have to give of yourself more than you are accustomed to doing. Your partner may want to share the experiences of the day with you at a time you would rather be reading the paper or watching your favorite television program. He or she may want to lean on you for support when things have gone bad, and your shoulders may not be very strong for this. Your partner may want you to "open up," and you may not be comfortable doing this. And perhaps most worrisome, you expose yourself to the chances of being hurt when things go wrong between the two of you. If you've been badly burned before in a love affair, this can be an overriding concern. You give up your freedom when you make a commitment. You become linked to someone else. It is a big decision with lots of consequences, some unforeseen.

The upside of the equation can make all of these problems and risks seem insignificant, if he or she is the right person for you. So we turn to the first part of the question. Do you want to make a commitment? Think about him or her. Picture in your mind what it would be like living with him or her. What would it be like going to bed at night together and waking together in the morning? What would it be like sharing meals or having quiet conversations together in the evening? What would it be like sharing coffee and a Sunday morning paper? Picture in your mind what it would be like seeing him or her more than anyone else. If the thoughts fill you with delight, it sounds as if you're ready. If they don't, think twice.

Does my partner want to make a commitment? Can my partner make a commitment?

It's not easy to get into the mind of your partner so that you can answer these questions with precision, but if you've been seeing each other for a while, you have probably amassed some pretty good clues. Consider, for example, what your partner may have said to you about making a deeper commitment. Has he or she ever broached the subject? Can you recall the conversation — the words, the tone? And if you broached the subject, how did he or she respond? Was there enthusiasm? Or was there a sense of hesitation, reluctance, or evasiveness? If your partner has never brought up the possibility of making a commitment, has he or she even hinted at it? If not, why not?

There can be a negative twist to conversations about commitments. Some people bring up the subject and come right out and tell you that they're not interested in making a commitment. Madeleine, for example, tells of a man she met who on their second date said "I haven't gotten over my divorce. I'm not ready for a serious relationship. I want you to understand that." Should we award her date a point for candor or assume some devious motivation to push the relationship into narrow parameters?

If your partner hasn't talked about the possibility of a commitment, has he said anything that tells you that you are special or could be special in his life? Words provide clues. So do deeds. Consider the obvious things. Does your partner remember you on Valentine's Day and your birthday? When you are with his or her friends, does your partner make it clear to them in words and nonverbal signals that the two of you are a couple, that you have an ongoing relationship? Do his or her friends treat the two of you as a couple? And how about his or her family? Have you met them? And if so, in what terms do your partner's parents see you? Do they act as it you are only a casual friend of their son or daughter, or do they see you as a serious interest? And most importantly, is he or she still dating other people? If you've been seeing each other for some time, shouldn't this stop? As you think about such questions, you may be able to assess your partner's readiness to make the commitment to an exclusive relationship. You may also want to consider your partner's potential to stay in such a relationship. What do you know of his or her past history or romantic relationships? If there is a pattern of sleeping around or a succession of unsuccessful, unstable relationships, you may be becoming involved with someone who has difficulties entering into committed relationships and staying with them.

While most of us reach a point where we are comfortable with the idea of making a commitment, there are some people who find it very difficult. Let's hope you are not unlucky enough to fall in love with such a person. Did you ever see the musical play or motion picture version of *Guys and Dolls*, based on Damon Runyon's wonderful collection of stories about New York City horse players, gamblers, mobsters, and their women? One of the characters in the play, Nathan Detroit, was not only "the proprietor of the longest running floating craps game in New York," but also may have had the longest running engagement as well. His long-suffering fiancée, Adelaide, who has waited seemingly forever to tie the knot, finally laments in song how she has developed a psychosomatic illness waiting for something that never seems to happen.

9. *Conflict Resolution*

What is communication like between distressed partners?

One thinks of distressed couples as those in which the partners are not getting along well, have repeated conflicts, and express a great deal of dissatisfaction with the relationship. If you're around such couples any length of time, you can usually spot them, for things often get acrimonious. Researchers have studied the behavior of such couples in experimental situations: the partners are asked to "role play" common problem situations such as managing household responsibilities or planning leisure time activities. While the spouses are talking, their conversation is recorded. Researchers have also observed the spontaneous, ongoing behavior of such couples in their homes. The results of these studies are clear and consistent. When compared with couples who are not distressed, communication between distressed partners is extremely negative.

Researchers have found that members of happy couples who served as their control subjects were much more likely to listen to each other and respect each other's ideas. Criticisms of one another tend to be muted and restrained. The conversations of distressed couples, in contrast, are often destructive. In discussing their research on distressed couples, Paul Koren and his colleagues remarked:

> Distressed couples were more likely than nondistressed couples to rely on criticism in attempting to influence each other's position. Thus, instead of describing issues of disagreement in neutral terms, they tended to attach elements of blame or accusation so that the other spouse was made to appear at fault.[1]

For some couples about to terminate their relationship, communications may deteriorate into dreadful arguments. Do you remember the lovely Jerome Kern song "All the Things You Are"? For these couples, the title may as well be "All the Things You've Done to Me." Both parties have a long list of grievances which they may vent in sometimes hellacious disputes. It's not very pleasant to listen to, but if you are ever tempted to pursue marriage counseling as a vocation, you will find such arguments sometimes come with the territory.

The negative tone observed in the conversation of distressed couples extends to the interpretations the partners make about each other's behavior and motivations. It's not only what they say to each other, it's also what they think about each other. Members of distressed couples are less likely to give their partners credit for the positive things they say and do and they are more likely to put the worst light on the negative things they do. For example, when their partners exercise poor judgment, make mistakes, or forget to do something they promised, they are more likely to believe their partners acted intentionally ("He did it deliberately!"), rather than to assume it was an inadvertence. They are more likely to see the act as part of a pattern ("That's what she always does. It's the same thing all the time!") than as an isolated, transitory event. Members of distressed couples are more likely to describe their partner's motivation for the act as selfish or self-centered ("He only thinks of himself"). They are likely to view the act as evidence of lack of love, respect, and regard for themselves ("She doesn't love me. She doesn't even like me."), and they are more likely to blame their partners.

In contrast, among couples who have a basically healthy relationship, the partners are likely to give each other the benefit of a doubt. When something goes wrong, it may be seen as an accident, or written off as "just one of those things." The underlying feelings of love and respect are not seriously affected. Partners in good relationships are more likely to keep a sense of perspective when something goes badly, and are less likely to overreact.

How is it possible to be so angry with someone you love?

It was in the middle of a group therapy session. All eyes were focused on Roy, a short blonde-haired man of twenty-five. You could see the anger in his face. His hands were clenched into tight fists. As he spoke, his voice got louder and louder. He soon worked himself into a rage. And whom was he speaking about? Whom was he complaining about and abusing so vociferously? It wasn't his boss or a coworker in the engineering firm in which he worked; it was not an unfair teacher in the university where he was doing his graduate work. No. It was the girl with whom he was intimately involved; the girl he loved passionately; the most important person in his life.

In trying to explain this seeming paradox of feeling so much anger about someone one loves, we have to first have some appreciation of the causes of anger. While the causes of angry feelings are not always observable, one can see from everyday experience that anger often arises from feelings of frustration, from feelings that one had been denied something that one wants or desires. Sometimes you can see this very clearly with young children. When some children can't do what they want or get what they want, they may erupt with outbursts of anger. Adults are supposed to be mature enough not to engage in fits of anger when frustrated. However, broken plates, slammed doors, shouts, screams, insults, and accusations are all too common evidences that many adults react to frustration with angry outbursts. And even when one's anger is controlled, not showing itself outwardly in aggressive behavior, you can often recognize it in that hours-long sulk, curt tone of voice and unsmiling facial expression.

Many of the frustrations that give rise to anger occur in interactions with other people. In our research using diaries to monitor daily activities, Roland Tanck and I asked college students to note the days on which they felt angry and to explain what happened that made them feel that way. While some of the reasons given for angry feelings were pressures from school work such as too much studying to do, most often the reasons given were interpersonal problems, difficulties with friends, roommates, acquaintances and romantic partners. A young woman, for example, reported that she felt angry on three consecutive days. When asked what happened to make her feel this way, her responses for the three days were "With boyfriend about our relationship," "My boyfriend is trying to control my life," and "I had to deal with my boyfriend's moodiness." Two days later, she reported that she felt angry again, stating she had to confront her boyfriend about his lying to her.[2]

Many of the frustrations in a dating relationship involve disappointments (one's expectations are not fulfilled), feelings of unfairness and lack of equity, and feelings of rejection. Occasional difficulties and disappointments in a dating relationship are almost inevitable. In a marital relationship where the parties are involved in daily interaction, frustrations of one sort or another are not only inevitable, they may occur frequently. Feelings of disappointment, unfairness, lack of appreciation and perceived insensitivity may occur at times in the best of relationships and are chronic in distressed relationships. When frustrations occur in romantic relationships, transitory feelings of anger are likely to arise. Such feelings coexist with more stable feelings of respect, friendship, and love. Psychologists refer to the coexistence of both positive and negative feelings towards the same person as ambivalence.

A transitory feeling of anger in an otherwise secure relationship is something like a solitary cloud in an otherwise clear sky. Like the passing cloud that might block out the sun for a moment, a transitory feeling of anger passes away and is of little consequence. The problem arises when these feelings of anger become frequent and negative feelings deepen. Like a darkening sky the love in the relationship becomes harder and harder to find.

As we could see with Roy, it is possible to develop strong, sometimes wrenching ambivalences. On one side of the psychological balance scale, one finds feelings of love, sometimes stemming from memories of happier days when the relationship looked bright and promising. On the other side of the scale, one finds waves of anger coalescing into lingering resentments. Sometimes these resentments become catalogued into what I like to call a "mental file cabinet." The frustrated, disappointed and disillusioned lover gradually assembles a list of grievances ready to be called from his or her memory banks, much as one might access data from a computer. When that big explosion happens — when he and she raise their voices and begin to scream at each other — those grievances may be recited with the force of a declaration of war. Anger has temporarily, and in some instances permanently, triumphed over love.

How do I handle my angry feelings?

This is a question that is likely to elicit many different opinions. I doubt that there is a consensus among psychologists as to what is the best approach for dealing with angry feelings, and the analysis that I will offer may be at odds with what other therapists have written. With this caveat, I would offer the general rule that the expression of anger towards another person is more likely to be harmful than helpful. In coming to this conclusion, I was particularly impressed by a study carried out by Roy Baumeister and his colleagues at Case Western Reserve University.[3] These investigators asked people about what happened after another person had expressed anger towards them, what were the consequences of this behavior. A substantial number of the people responded that the incident had damaged the relationship between the person expressing the anger and themselves. Moreover, the damage in many cases was long-lasting. Over one-third of the people questioned were still angry about the incident at the time of the interview. Relatively few of the respondents — only four percent — saw any positive effects stemming from the incident.

From time to time, one hears the opinion that a person should not hold back angry feelings; rather, he or she should express them. The theory seems to be that in the ensuing discussion (or confrontation), ventilation of grievances will clear the air. Both parties will experience a catharsis, feel better and will come closer together. This is a fight, kiss and make-up scenario. This "fighting-is-healthy" idea may indeed work for some romantic partners. It might work particularly well when both partners are used to fighting and both get over their angry feelings quickly after expressing them and neither holds grudges. But the Baumeister study suggests that such relationships are far from typical. Most people feel hurt when they are targets of anger. The effects of an argument are more likely to be destructive than constructive, and the effects may linger.

A good example is Cary, a quiet-spoken man in his late twenties. Still getting over the emotional reactions to his recent divorce, Cary shook his head when he talked about his ex-wife Jenny. "She'd come home after visiting her friends or going to the store and suddenly, without warning, she'd blow up at me. Half of the time I wasn't even sure what the problem was. It was something I did or didn't do, I guess. She'd really let me have it. Then, later, Jenny would settle down and be as nice as she could be. I never knew what to expect. It was too much. I don't like fights. After a while, I just couldn't take it."

Jenny could not control her angry feelings. When anger built up, she usually exploded. Her marriage could not sustain these frequent outbursts. If frequent explosions are likely to prove destructive, what about the other extreme of always holding anger in and never expressing it? This is unlikely to be a healthy alternative. Living with unexpressed angry feelings can be very uncomfortable. Can you imagine what it would be like if you're really steaming about something and can't ventilate these feelings? Some people have come to see me that seem to be almost consumed by a sea of rage. It has been theorized, and there is evidence to support this view, that such persons are more prone to develop physical symptoms (psychosomatic illnesses). At best, feeling angry much of the time is a very unpleasant way to live.

Another unconstructive way that some people have for dealing with angry feelings is to displace these feelings onto other objects. One does not strike back at the person or persons who provoked one's anger; rather, one lashes out at another target. People may do this without fully realizing what they are doing. Displacement of anger may be symbolic such as pounding one's fist on a table, or worse, swatting one's pet or shouting at one's child. Most of us have probably been the victims of anger provoked not by our own actions but generated from another source.

One of the more self-destructive ways of dealing with anger resulting from romantic difficulties is to redirect this anger inwardly, towards oneself. Freud viewed this form of displacement as an unconscious process that occurs when one cannot admit or even recognize having hostile feelings towards one's beloved.[4] Anger is turned outside-in. One becomes self-accusatory and gets very down on oneself, and the result can be depression. I'm not sure this scenario happens quite the way Freud theorizes, but being angry with oneself is often part of the clinical picture in people who are depressed. So where does that leave us? Behaving in an angry way with your romantic partner is likely to be counter productive, almost certainly so if one makes a habit of it. Living with chronic unexpressed angry feelings is very uncomfortable, and may be physically harmful. If displacing anger onto other targets or onto oneself will only generate other problems, what then do we do?

The approach I would offer is not easy to do. For some people it may be very difficult. And it is certainly not a panacea. Still, it may prove helpful. What I would suggest is to put aside your anger as much as you can, and to direct your efforts towards solving the problems that have led you to feel disappointed, unappreciated, treated unfairly or rejected. And even if it is not possible to fully resolve these problems, you may find ways to measurably improve your situation, so that you feel less frustrated and angry. A sense that things are getting better may allow the tender feelings in your relationship to reassert themselves and turn the relationship back towards what you had hoped it would be.

In implementing this approach to dealing with anger, it is important to accurately identify the sources of the problems and to use reasonable and effective ways of dealing with them. I shall have more to say about problem-solving approaches in the next section. Still, you may find that you will need some help in pursuing these ideas, for being caught up in an angry conflict can diminish both one's objectivity and coping abilities.

What are some strategies for resolving conflicts?

Some conflicts in a relationship are almost inevitable. Conflicts may be minor, like a dispute over which television program to watch, or major, like excessive drinking and infidelity. For some couples, conflicts occur infrequently; for others conflict seems incessant; peace and quiet seem like uncertain truces in an ongoing battle. As conflict between partners over desires and lifestyles cannot be avoided altogether, it becomes a matter of importance how these conflicts are resolved. Are there ways of resolving conflicts which do not damage the relationship? Or better yet, are there ways that act to strengthen the relationship?

In approaching this question, I would like to discuss three types of responses to conflict — aggression, disengagement, and problem-solving. In our previous discussions about angry feelings, I voiced the belief that expressing anger towards one's romantic partner is usually counterproductive. The same thing may be said about other forms of aggression, either verbal (e.g., intimidation, threats, scorn) or physical. Although aggressive behavior may resolve a conflict in your favor, it is likely to be a hollow victory, for the aggressive behavior is more likely to exacerbate the problems between the two people than solve them. Aggressive responses to conflict are not always overt and clear-cut; sometimes aggressive behavior can be subtle, even passive. Are you familiar with the term passive-aggression? It sounds like an oxymoron, a contradiction within the word itself. Still, passive-aggression can be very real.

When the Rowans have a conflict, you can see elements of both active and passive aggression. Their latest problem has to do with his mother's plans to visit. Mrs. Rowan does not get along with her mother-in-law. She finds her interfering and intrusive. When Mrs. Rowan voiced her unhappiness at her mother-in-law's impending visit, Mr. Rowan blew up at his wife for her attitude. Mrs. Rowan retaliated by not speaking to him for two days.

In working with couples in the Veterans' Affairs Mental Health Clinic in San Diego, Gary Birchler and his colleagues developed a questionnaire which assesses both active and passive responses to conflict.[5] For active aggression, the questionnaire items include such behaviors as hitting, biting, scratching, yelling, screaming, swearing, and nagging. The items for the passive-aggressive pattern include such behaviors as sulking, the silent treatment, leaving the scene, and refusing to discuss the matter. Interestingly, the researchers reported that young couples are more likely to respond to conflict with active aggressive responses than older couples.

While the second type of response, disengagement, may not resolve conflicts in a completely satisfactory manner, the effects of disengagement are likely to be less destructive than aggression. Disengagement, which means pulling away from, may take various forms. One form is a preventative strategy, staying away from possible areas of conflict. In their interactions, one or both partners learn that there are "red zones" in the relationship, areas into which one treads at the risk of provoking a fight. By avoiding these zones, one avoids trouble. Many people have touchy areas, subjects that elicit angry or defensive reactions. John, for example, is very touchy about his first marriage. Martha will bristle if you bring up the subject of her weight. Political issues like gun control will get Fred all steamed up. Their partners have learned not to touch these hot buttons as a way of preventing conflict from erupting.

When a fight has taken place, another form of disengagement is a "cooling off period." This is a truce — tacit or explicit — a time to allow angry feelings to subside and to give the partners a chance to think things over. In a basically sound relationship, it should become apparent to both parties that the conflict is not that important measured against what the relationship offers. A cooling off period may enable the parties to deal with the problem in a more conciliatory manner.

Disengagement may also take the form of the partners' giving each other space. The partners may explicitly or implicitly yield to each other some personal physical space, a piece of private turf where one can spread one's things out the way one wants to, a place to which one can retreat for solitude. It can also mean affording to one another the freedom to do things alone. While disengagement as a strategy to deal with conflicts has much to recommend it, there are clear limitations. Disengagement avoids problems rather than solves them. And if there is too much disengagement, you may have little left of the relationship. The strategy of disengagement requires a delicate balance. It may serve a couple well up to a point, but if carried too far, may loosen the bonds of the relationship.

In my judgment, the third type of strategy for resolving conflicts, problem-solving, offers the greatest potential for building and strengthening relationships. Of the three strategies, it is probably the hardest to carry out. Interpersonal conflicts often generate strong emotions, raise defenses, and foster aggressive responses. Almost by definition, problem-solving is a rational approach. And it's hard to be rational when one is caught up in a swell of emotions. Let's sketch some of the features of a problem-solving approach. Many psychologists look at problem-solving as a series of steps. While this is a convenient way to describe problem-solving, one must recognize that in practice, some of the steps may blend together or disappear entirely, particularly when one experiences an overall creative flash, "I've got it!" With this qualification, here is a representative list of steps in problem solving.

1. Accurate assessment of what the problems are.
2. Listing of possible alternative solutions to the problem.
3. Examining and evaluating these alternatives.
4. Selecting what appears to be the most promising alternative or alternatives and putting them into the form of a plan.
5. Trying out the plan and evaluating how it works.
6. Modifying or changing the plan if it does not prove satisfactory.

Problem-solving by romantic partners can be a delicate process, and sensitivities to each other's needs is of paramount importance if the process is to work well. Here are a few potential pitfalls to watch out for. He and she may not assess the problem the same way. Suppose she says, "He does not spend enough time talking with me," and he says, "She just chatters and doesn't say anything." If the couple cannot define the problem in the same terms, they may never get to first base in solving it. In the illustration just cited, the couple might begin by jointly recognizing, "We have a problem in communicating. It's souring our relationship. What can we do about it?" Defining the problem this way offers an opportunity for movement.

Another hazard looms when the time comes for proposing solutions, for putting ideas on the table. If one partner dismisses the other partner's ideas out of hand, if immediate reactions are negative, or worse, derisive, it can put a chill on the entire process. Both partners have to communicate an attitude of open-mindedness and a willingness to consider the other party's suggestions if the process is going to have any chance of working. The crux of the process comes when the suggestions offered are discussed and evaluated, and most importantly, when a plan is drawn up which incorporates the best of the ideas. A really satisfactory plan should be one in which both parties feel they will benefit from it. If either party feels like a loser in these "negotiations," the relationship is only likely to suffer. This is not a competition where one tries to win. This is a relationship to be fostered.

What are some options when he wants to watch the football game and she wants to go visiting?

If you ask a group of men and a group of women what activities they enjoy, you are likely to find differences in their responses. We have previously mentioned a study carried out by Catherine Surra and Molly Longstreth in which they presented a list of activities (e.g., partying, sports, games, sex) to dating couples and asked the man and woman separately to indicate how much they liked or disliked the activities on a nine point scale.[6] It will not come as a great surprise that the men liked sex, sports and games more than the women, or that the women's preference was for companionship and relationship-maintenance activities, entertainment and cultural activities. The study suggests that for many couples, romantic partners will differ in important ways in the things they like to do. As these differences can create conflicts, we will want to keep in mind some of the strategies for conflict resolution discussed in the previous section.

I have seen cases in my clinical practice where conflicts about activities were avoided, at least temporarily by virtue of marked personality differences in the partners. Roger and Betty particularly come to mind. Roger was a dominant sort of person. Tall, dark-haired, well built, he had a commanding presence and a take-charge manner. His wife Betty was quiet, respectful, and unassuming. The personalities of the two seemed to complement one another, and during the first years of their marriage, Roger made the decisions about what to do and when, and Betty acquiesced. There was no outward sign of trouble. As the years went by, however, the marriage went downhill. While Roger did the things he wanted to do, developing his skills and pursuing his interests, Betty lagged behind. She simply languished. Living in Roger's shadow, her potential for growth and self-actualization was never realized. Her deference to Roger created a gulf between the two of them. Roger lost interest in her and she became depressed.

One can't, of course, generalize from a story like Roger and Betty's and conclude that one person's dominance will inevitably lead to serious problems, but this pattern of male-female interaction hardly seems like a good bet in today's world which more and more emphasizes equality between the sexes. In an egalitarian relationship, a premium would have to be placed on fairness. The question becomes what strategies can achieve both the perception and reality of fairness.

When there are conflicts about what to do and when, the two obvious strategies that come to mind are alternating choices and doing things separately. Neither strategy is perfectly satisfying, but, as has been often stated, this is an imperfect world. The strategy of alternating choices is simplicity itself: First doing something together that she likes, then doing something that he likes. What could be more fair? What could be more equitable? And for partners with widely divergent interests, what could be more boring 50 percent of the time? The strategy of alternating choices probably works best if it is applied with some sensitivity to the likes and dislikes of one's partner. The strategy is not a license to subject one's partner to an afternoon or evening of some activity he or she detests. There is merit to taking turns selecting a television program or choosing a movie. But even here the possibilities of a frustrating evening are evident if he has his heart set on watching a quiet love story and she wants to watch an action-packed thriller filled with violence and mayhem.

Doing things separately, a form of disengagement, can be a useful strategy for many couples in coping with this type of conflict. I say this recognizing the importance that shared activities have in deepening a relationship and promoting both satisfaction and stability. However, for many couples, too much togetherness can turn a good thing into a bad thing. I would offer a case for balance: do the things you both enjoy together; do the things you like and he or she doesn't like separately. Try to find a balance between separateness and togetherness that offers the best opportunities for both individual growth and relationship growth. This would be a balance that allows the activities and pastimes that you have developed over years of maturing — that have made you unique individuals — to continue, while at the same time affords the two of you the time together to enjoy the pleasure of your relationship. In this scheme of things, the pressures of too much togetherness are relaxed. A dash of separateness acts as a safety valve dissipating the build-up of interpersonal tension. Transitory absence may well make the heart grow fonder. And the greatest boon of all might be that you will have new things to tell each other.

How does alcohol affect relationships?

A small amount of alcohol often makes a person feel relaxed. Part of the effect is from the drink itself, part from expectations the drinker has that he or she will feel relaxed because of the alcohol. As the quantity of alcohol consumed substantially increases, the effects go well beyond relaxation. Take Jack, for example. After several drinks, his judgment and motor coordination, as well as his ability to listen, think, reason and communicate deteriorate. Three drinks turn him into a caricature of his sober self. He rambles on repetitively, paying little attention to what other people say. Sometimes, he becomes nasty and aggressive. So far he has not physically abused his wife, Sarah; nonetheless, Sarah is having a very difficult time coping with her husband's drinking. And the same can be said for many men and women whose romantic partners abuse alcohol.

The extent to which one is drinking may not be readily apparent to others. Alcohol abusers are sometimes able to cover up what they are doing for some time. The bottle of gin may be hidden in a safe place. It may look like straight orange juice she has on the kitchen table, but it's really laced with vodka. And a lot of drinking takes place away from home. Sooner or later, however, the problem becomes inescapable, and alcohol-induced behavior begins to undermine a relationship. Feelings of confusion, anger, and resentment are engendered. The hopes of the non-alcoholic partner are dashed repeatedly and resignation often sets in. In discussing the clinical literature on the effects of alcoholism on family relations, researcher Theodore Jacob talked about "alcohol's deleterious impact on family life in which conflict and dissension are the norm," and "the great disturbance and disruption that is often brought on during states of heavy drinking and intoxication."[7]

You can see the antagonistic behavior of couples where alcohol is a problem even in brief samples of time. With his colleague Gloria Krahn, Jacob observed the interaction of couples in which the husband was an alcoholic and compared them with non-alcoholic couples. These observational sessions lasted only about ten minutes, yet the researchers found important differences in the way these couples interacted. Where the spouse was an alcoholic, there was "less conviviality and good-natured communication than [among] the social control couples, as reflected in clearly different rates of smiling, laughing, humor, and talk."[8] When it came to negative interactions (e.g., criticisms, putdowns), the alcoholic spouse's interactions were more negative, and this was especially true with the husband was drinking.

One interesting theory that has been advanced about the hostile and destructive acts of the heavy drinker is that alcohol provides a cover or excuse for his or her behavior. Drinking provides a way of not taking full responsibility for one's actions. During periods of intoxication, a person may be very hostile, and afterwards offer the explanation, "I'm not really responsible — I didn't know what I was doing. It was the alcohol." The "sober periods" in the lives of couples in which one person is an alcoholic are not necessarily periods of love and peace. Interviews carried out with the wives of alcoholics suggest that wives may use this time to complain how the husbands made them suffer during drunken episodes.[9] Such recrimination may only have the effect of increasing the alcoholic's discomfort which he or she may relieve by returning to drinking.

Based on some of his preliminary findings, Jacob has offered the interesting theory that episodic drinking may lead to more conflict between spouses than constant drinking. Constant drinking, particularly in the home, may become an accepted feature of daily existence that the spouse gets used to and learns to live with, while drinking bouts out of the blue may lead to a state of unpredictability and increased tension. By the time alcoholics enter treatment for the problem, they usually recognize the destructive effects of their behavior on their spouses and families. In a study I carried out with J. F. Nugent on alcoholic patients at a Veterans' Administration Hospital, 76 percent of the patients we surveyed acknowledged that their drinking had "strained their relationship with members of their own families."[10] Interestingly, divorce is more frequent for husbands of alcoholic wives than for wives of alcoholic husbands. For economic and social reasons, wives are more likely to stay in an alcohol damaged marriage.

When a relationship is dissolved it often leads to loneliness for alcoholics. In his autobiographical book, *Conspiracy of Silence*, Leo Hennigan talks about how this loneliness manifests itself in "telephonitis."

> Another definite symptom of alcoholism, related to our profound feeling of loneliness, is the use of the telephone. We often call people from our distant past. It can of course be somewhat indiscreet, to say nothing of being dangerous to one's health, to call old girlfriends of 10 to 15 years ago. When loneliness was profound, I called Information and asked the telephone number of the Smithsonian Institution at 3:00 A.M., just to hear a human voice.[11]

How widespread is physical abuse in relationships?

Violence of men against the women in their lives is widespread in the United States. In October 1992 the majority staff of the Senate Judiciary Committee released a report entitled "Violence Against Women: A Week in the Life of America." In speaking of domestic violence, the report states that "More than *1.13 million women* are victims of *reported* domestic violence every year — by some estimates, as many as 3 million more domestic violence crimes go unreported each year." The report further states that "Almost one fifth of all aggravated assaults (20 percent) reported to the police are aggravated assaults in the home." And yet one more statistic to drive home the point: "Some experts estimate that a woman has between a 1 in 5 and a 1 in 3 chance of being physically assaulted by a partner or ex-partner during her lifetime.[12]

The committee report went beyond simply compiling statistics. The report also presented accounts collected from emergency rooms, police stations, and domestic violence and rape crisis centers which describe what this violence was like. As you can see from some excerpts below, many of these violent acts go far beyond pushing and shoving: they are cases of beating and battering.

> 12:45 A.M.—Rural California—A woman with five children (11 months old to 11 years old) is physically abused by her husband. He punches her in the head with his fist. She sustains bruises. She escapes and runs to a friend's house for the night. She reports that she is afraid to call the sheriff because her husband threatens to take their 11-month-old baby.
>
> Early morning—Rural Texas—A 33-year-old woman enters a local shelter after 15 years of abuse by her husband. She reports that he has tried to choke her and pulled a knife on her. She is seeking a protective order.
>
> 3:30 P.M.—A large city in Kansas—A 22-year-old woman comes into a domestic violence shelter because she wants to leave her 27-year-old live-in boyfriend who locks her and her two children in the bathroom. She escapes through the bathroom window fearing further violence.
>
> 4:23 P.M.—A city in West Virginia—A call from the hospital comes into a local hotline. A woman has been brought into the emergency room because her husband has severely beaten her in a drunken rage.
>
> Early evening—A town in Michigan—A 44-year-old woman is beaten by her husband when he returns home from work. She reports that he has choked her and beaten her with his fists and various household objects. Their two young children are present.
>
> 11:00 P.M.—A small city in Connecticut—A 30-year-old woman is attacked by her husband of five years. He uses his closed fist to assault her, knocking out her front tooth and causing a black eye. Their three children are present during the attack. She obtains a restraining order.[13]

The perpetrators of violence against women include husbands, ex-husbands, and boyfriends. Researchers at Yale University published a study in *Women's Health Data Book* which suggests that among a woman's intimates, separated or divorced spouses are the ones most likely to commit violence against her.[14] Boyfriends are next, while current husbands trail. The implication is that violence is more likely to be associated with unstable, conflicted and transitory relationships.

The results of a study carried out in a facility for battered women in Detroit, Michigan, suggest that violence against women falls into different patterns. The authors of the study, Douglas Snyder and Lisa Fruchtman, describe five types of wife-battering situations that they encountered in exploring the histories of these women.[15]

Type I women

> are distinguished by the relative stability of their relationship with the assailant, who nearly always is the current husband. Abuse of women in this group is relatively infrequent and rarely involves concurrent abuse of the children. Sexual assault is virtually nonexistent, and sexual relations are rarely used to cement the relationship following a violent exchange. Type I women are most likely to rationalize their abuse by attributing the assailant's response to alcohol or external pressures.

Type II women are "characterized by a highly unstable, explosive relationship with their assailant. Recurrent separations are common. ... Abuse frequently results in injury. Abuse often involves a sexual component both during the assault and in response to it."

Type III women are described as "victims of the most chronic and most severe forms of physical violence. These women live in fear, under constant threat of further assault; they are least likely to retaliate with violence of their own toward their partner." Their children are often included in the violence as well. The histories of these women show that they have experienced little abuse in the past. When they leave their partner, they seldom return.

Type IV women are those who are not abused as much as their children are. They seek refuge for their children as much as for themselves.

Type V women have experienced a history of violence throughout their lives. They reported "extensive parental neglect and actual physical abuse as a child on a monthly basis. Physical violence pervades their interpersonal relationships. ... Type V women have grown to expect violence and accept it as part of their lives."

We should note that violence between romantic partners is not confined to male towards female. Acts of violence of women towards men, sometimes in self-defense, sometimes in retaliation and sometimes self-initiated, are hardly rare. As a point of reference, the Senate Judiciary Committee's report estimated that there is six times as much male violence towards females as vice versa. (I assume that they are speaking for the most part about acts of major violence.) With the estimated number of acts of violence against women in the four million range annually, simple arithmetic shows that the number of violent acts committed annually by women against men is in the hundreds of thousands. Interestingly, when we move away from the level of severe battering to the level of grabbing, shoving and slapping, research suggests that women are more likely to commit acts against their partners than vice versa. About four out of ten women surveyed in some recent studies reported that they have attacked their spouses in such ways during the past year.[16]

Physical attacks by romantic partners upon each other do not always begin with marriage; such behavior often surfaces during dating and courtship. In a study of college students, it was found that 30 percent of those questioned had either attacked their date or had been attacked. K. Daniel O'Leary and his colleagues at the State University of New York at Stony Brook followed couples over a period of time, as they moved from engagement through the first 30 months of marriage. Here is what they reported. "According to self-reports, 31% of the men and 44% of the women indicated that they had engaged in aggression against their partners in the year prior to marriage."[17] (Aggression was defined as "throwing something at partner," "pushing, grabbing, or shoving," "slapping," "kicking, biting, or hitting with a fist," "hitting or trying to hit with something," "beating up" and "threatening with a knife or gun.") Most of the acts reported were in the first four categories; there were practically no instances of threatening with a knife or gun.

So many people begin marriage knowing full well that their partners may get testy and physical. What effect does the reality of marriage have on these explosive tendencies? Does aggressive behavior increase or decrease? O'Leary and his colleagues reported that after 30 months, the percentage of men who attacked their partners dropped from 31 percent to 25 percent, and the percentage of women attackers dropped from 44 percent to 32 percent. It may be that the slogan "make love, not war" was finally taking hold, or maybe it was just battle fatigue. Research suggests that most forms of violence decrease substantially with age.

Why do women stay in a relationship when they are battered?

In the report released by the Senate Judiciary Committee on violence against women, there were accounts of women who had been married for many years being badly beaten by their husbands. In one case, for example, a 45-year-old woman was assaulted in a bar by her husband of 20 years. Suffering a black eye and many bruises, she had to be taken to the hospital. Her husband was arrested for drunken and disorderly conduct.[18]

In many marriages, wife battering is not an isolated event, but a repetitive pattern. The obvious question that arises is why women stay in such relationships? Lenore Walker has interviewed hundreds of battered women.

In an essay published in the *American Psychologist*, she offered an analysis which sheds light on this question. Walker describes the battering relationship as a three phase cycle of violence.[19] The first phase is one of "tension building." The phase itself conjures up an image of conflict, irritability and rising tempers. In this phase, the woman can still exert some control over her partner's violent outbursts. By one means or another (e.g., making concessions), she can prevent or minimize an attack. In phase two, the domestic situation deteriorates. These preventative strategies no longer work. Conflict leads to explosions and battering. Phase two is a time of high risks of serious physical harm. The woman may end up in the emergency room of a hospital. The police often become involved. The third phase is a period of remission. Violence temporarily ceases and there is often a period of "loving contrition"; one can almost hear the man's words, "I'm sorry ... I don't know what got into me. I swear to you it will never happen again."

It is easy to see how many women who find themselves in this third phase of a relationship can arrive at the conclusion "Maybe it will be okay. Maybe things will be all right from here on." In their decision-making process, it is this hope added to the memories of better days in the relationship plus the fear of change which tips the scale in favor of staying. Walker's analysis suggests that many women who stay in battering relationships are entertaining unrealistic hopes, and that their perceptions of their partners are skewed, off the mark. They have discounted vital realities in favor of more palliative memories. One thinks of the ostrich with its head in the sand. Walker writes:

> Battered women often describe the batterers as having a Dr. Jekyll/Mr. Hyde personality. A battered woman believes that if she somehow could find the right way to help this man, with whom she has a strong love bond, then the mean part of him would disappear. ... A battered woman may hope to elicit the man's "good side," which is frequently the only side she observed during a relatively short but emotionally intense courtship phase. Obviously, this does not happen; instead, the "good side" shrinks as the abusive behavior increases in frequency and severity.[20]

In her essay, Walker makes another point which further illuminates why some women stay in such destructive relationships. Walker believes that many of the women develop a sense of helplessness in the situation. They become fearful of doing anything that might irritate their partners. Some women lapse into what would appear to an outside observer to be a kind of paralysis. Even the idea of escape arouses anxiety. They ask themselves such questions as "What would I do?" or worse, "What might he do?"

One should stress that fears of retaliation can be quite legitimate. In many cases, they are anything but fanciful. I have already mentioned data that suggest that ex-spouses and estranged partners are the men most likely to engage in violent acts. A dramatic example of a violent reaction to a wife's ill-timed attempt to escape from her husband was included in the Judiciary Committee's report on violence against women:

> 6:00 P.M.— A city in Washington state—A 34-year-old woman with two children (ages nine and six) reports that her husband of 15 years has slapped her, threatened to kill her, and accused her of losing some important documents from his work. He returns home to find her packing. He drags her across the kitchen by her hair as the children try to stop him. He draws a gun on all three when one of the children tries to call 911. Eventually, the woman and her children escape to the police station.[21]

The lingering fear that some women have of retaliation is expressed in another story from the Committee's report:

> 12:45 P.M.—A city in the Southwest—A woman enters a shelter after fleeing from a northern state. She reports that her husband has beaten her repeatedly and has threatened to find her and kill her. She hopes he will not look for her and her two children in her new home.[22]

Many women who find themselves in this position, fearful of the retribution of a former boyfriend or estranged husband, seek relief from the courts in the form of a restraining order that forbids the offending party from having contact with her. While these restraining orders are often effective, they obviously cannot stop someone who is reckless and is indifferent to the consequences of his actions.

What have we learned about men who batter women?

L. Kevin Hamberger and James Hastings of the Medical College of Wisconsin, have been interested in this question for some time and have written a review of research findings. Here is a summary of some of the most important points they make in their article.[23]

1. While batterers are found in all socioeconomic classes, battering by men is more often reported in the lower socioeconomic classes.
2. Batterers often have a previous history of getting into trouble, being unable to conform to established rules. For example, they have higher rates of early disciplinary discharge from the military for violent behavior, alcoholism, and desertion.
3. Many men who batter women have drinking problems. One survey reported that about half of the batterers studied had alcohol problems.
4. Batterers are often violent with other people—not just their spouses.

Their targets may include children, parents, and people who are not members of their families.

5. On psychological tests, batterers tend to score high on a number of areas indicating emotional difficulties. Batterers tend to be more alienated, moody, emotionally changeable, and passive-aggressive. They may have lower self-esteem and higher power needs.
6. Batterers are more likely than non-violent men to have witnessed parental violence in the homes in which they grew up.
7. Batterers are more likely than non-violent men to have been abused themselves, as children.

In discussing the findings from research, Hamberger and Hastings stress that wife batterers are a heterogeneous group. There is no single personality pattern that describes men that batter women. While one may look for certain tendencies such as a history of experiencing child abuse or current heavy drinking, one won't find these tendencies in all batterers.

With the recognition that there is no single personality pattern which describes all wife batterers, researchers have tried to utilize psychological tests and interviews to classify wife batterers into different types. Writing in the *American Journal of Orthopsychiatry*, David Saunders developed a typology which I find particularly useful.[24] He described three types of wife-batterers. The first type was "family-only" aggressors. Normally, these men are not angry or jealous, and feel satisfied in the relationship. Their violent outbursts are frequently associated with drinking.

The second type of abuser was labeled "generally violent," meaning such men are apt to be violent both with the family and with other people. These men frequently have a history of being severely abused when they were children. Like the first group of men, their violent acts are often associated with drinking and many have arrest records for drunk-driving and violence.

The third classification of wife batterer was called "emotionally volatile." These men are apt to be dissatisfied with the relationship, and psychologically abusive to their spouses. At the same time, they are often fearful of losing their partners; they are jealous, depressed, angry, and sometimes suicidal. Interestingly, they often have rigid sex-role attitudes. These men are less likely to be severely violent, and more likely to seek counseling for their problems. Men who fall in this category appear to have severe problems in sustaining intimate relationships.

Is there help for spouse abusers?

Many women and men do not want to give up on their abusive partners. The sometimes desperate question they ask is can anything be done short of terminating the relationship to end the violence? In her essay on spousal abuse, Lenore Walker took a very pessimistic view of the likelihood that a man who batters his wife will permanently stop what he is doing. However, the findings from research do offer hope for some couples. Many men cease the violence against their wives for extended periods. Statistical data suggest that about one-third of wife batterers alter their violent behavior without outside assistance. For one reason or another, perhaps a threat from the spouse to leave, perhaps a personal recognition that such behavior is unacceptable, they stop. In a study carried out by the Family Research Laboratory of the University of New Hampshire, men who had committed violent acts against their wives were followed for the next two years. Forty percent of the men ceased or interrupted such violence for the two-year follow-up period.

Even these data, however, suggest that it is a chancy business for a woman to remain in such a relationship. The author of the research report, Etiony Aldarondo, strikes a cautionary note:

> The finding that over half of the men recorded as violent in the first year of this study were involved in either persistent or inconsistent patterns of wife assault is indicative that violence tends to become scripted in many relationships. Although the relatively high rates of the cessation of wife assault bring hope for change in the lives of couples where men are violent towards their female partners, these data show that men who use physical violence against their female partners are more likely to continue using violence in the future.[25]

So while many spouse abusers stop such behavior without outside intervention, many men continue. What can be done, if anything, to change their behavior? One way to end wife battering which sometimes works is to call the police. When police become involved in cases of domestic violence, they may try a number of approaches including conflict mediation and temporarily separating the spouses. But according to studies reviewed by the University of Virginia's Barry Rosenfeld, what seems to work best is plain and simple arrest. Arrest sends a message like little else. In one study, 19 percent of those who were arrested committed subsequent assaults, compared to 28 percent of those temporarily separated and 37 percent given police mediation.[26]

Arrest can be traumatic and may have a deterrent effect on future spouse violence. But even arrest is not foolproof. What else can one do? The answer may be one of the treatment programs that have been established for spouse abusers. Some of these programs involve group therapy. Some focus on reeducation, teaching such skills as more effective communication, conflict resolution, and problem-solving. How effective are spouse abuse treatment programs in stopping violence? Rosenfeld carried out a survey of the research literature and found 25 studies presenting data on the number of men who abstained from violence after participation in a treatment program. The average rate of recidivism for spouse abusers was close to 30 percent. While this figure indicates that spouse abuse programs are not effective for all participants, most men who complete these programs will benefit from them.

The problem for wives is getting their husbands into a treatment program and having them stay there until they complete the program. Dropout rates for spouse abuse programs are often high. One estimate based on a national survey of these programs was that the dropout rate was of the order of 40 percent.[27] The men who drop out are more likely to be younger, to have more prior police contacts for alcohol and drug-related offenses, and to evidence more problems on psychological tests. If a man is unwilling to enter a spouse-abuse program or if treatment fails, the ray of hope that violence will end may not be extinguished, but it certainly is dimmed. A woman stays in such a relationship at considerable risk. A statistic cited in Rosenfeld's article makes the point in stark terms. In a study of women seeking treatment in a New Haven emergency room with an injury or other complaint, nearly 20 percent of the injuries were found to have resulted from spouse abuse.[28]

What causes jealousy?

Have you ever heard stories about men who sit in cars in the evening unobtrusively watching their girlfriends' home to see if other men are visiting them? These things do happen and are a pretty extreme form of an emotion we call jealousy. Jealousy may be thought of as an emotional response to a real or imagined loss in an important relationship. It's easy to understand a strong response, even an intense reaction, to the thought of losing one's loved one. When you think of the emotional investment you make in a romantic relationship, all of the shared experiences and personal intimacies, to imagine that these will fall by the wayside and that someone else will now experience such pleasures with your loved one has to be a very upsetting idea.

The threatened loss of one's loved one to another hits home in very deep ways. Among these losses that weigh on one's mind are the loss of an exclusive sexual relationship, the loss of a partnership that has provided meaning and stability in one's life, and the loss of face in the eyes of one's peers. The idea that one's beloved has fallen for someone else can be a fundamental jolt to one's accustomed patterns of living as well as a jolt to one's ego and self-esteem. When a person feels threatened by the possible loss of his or her romantic partner to someone else, there is often a reaction of increased vigilance to confirm or deny these suspicions. A wife who suspects her husband of infidelity may begin to closely question him about his whereabouts: "Where have you been?" "Whom did you see?" "What took you so long to get home?"

A jealous person may watch his partner's response to the attentions of others. Did she smile too much at that men in the bar? Did she touch him? Jealous people may feel distrustful, anxious, and angry. Jealous behavior may be wide-ranging: quarreling, withholding, withdrawing, and taking revenge. Jealous thoughts and behavior have given rise to songs, ballads, movies and plays including Shakespeare's tragedy of *Othello*. In *Othello*, the emotion of jealousy was given its ultimate metaphor: "O, beware, my lord, of jealousy!; It is a green-ey'd monster which doth mock the meat it feeds on."[29]

While jealousy rarely plays itself out in the deadly fashion of Shakespeare's *Othello*, it certainly is a commonly experienced emotion. A study carried out by Yale researchers Peter Salovey and Judith Rodin suggests that jealousy is easily aroused. The authors conducted a survey of *Psychology Today* readers in which almost 25,000 people responded. As part of the survey, the researchers posed hypothetical situations to the readers and asked them to react. One situation described a couple attending a party. During the party, one partner does things like conversing a long time with a stranger, dancing with the person, or putting his or her arm around the person. The *Psychology Today* readers said that all of these actions would arouse jealousy in them. When the researchers went one step further, and asked how the readers would act if their partner left the party with the attractive stranger, hundreds of respondents commented spontaneously on the margin of the questionnaire with such remarks as "I'd kill him."[30]

The researchers reported some interesting findings about how marital status relates to jealous behaviors. Married and widowed individuals seemed less jealous than unmarrieds living together, and separated or divorced individuals. Separated and divorced individuals were the ones most likely to call their lovers unexpectedly, to listen in on their lovers' phone conversations, and even rummage through their lovers' personal belongings. Perhaps the key to understanding these data is feelings of insecurity about one's relationship. When one is in the midst of a difficult romantic experience or does not have a reliable commitment, these circumstances heighten feelings of insecurity. You can imagine the questions dogging the individual: "Where do I stand?" "Does he really care?" "Is she just leading me on?" "Is there someone else?" It is not a long step from posing such questions to exercising vigilance to relieve these anxieties, to verify or refute one's suspicions.

The connection between feelings of jealousy and feelings of insecurity is broadened in Salovey and Rodin's study. The researchers found that people who were quite jealous had a low opinion of themselves and saw a larger discrepancy between what they were and what they wanted to be.[31] Other studies support the idea that jealous persons tend to be self-depreciating, dissatisfied, and anxious. How does one cope with jealous feelings? Salovey and Rodin suggest that the best approach is prevention: If couples are very clear about the kinds of behavior that are acceptable and unacceptable in their relationship, there will be fewer situations that arise which can create reason for jealousy.

Lately the person I really care for has been depressed, and I would rather not be around him. What should I do?

Your problem may be something like Mark's. Mark has been married to Carol for over a year. For most of the time that Mark has known Carol, she has been an outgoing, cheerful person. In the last few weeks, however, she's seemed dispirited, at times, downcast. She told Mark that she hasn't been sleeping well. When the two of them went out to dinner, she ate very little. At times Carol seemed sluggish, almost listless. And she didn't enjoy the things they had always enjoyed doing together, such as visiting their friends and going to the movies on the weekend. The fun had gone out of the relationship. Being around Carol was becoming difficult, uncomfortable. Carol's conversation had a negative bent; almost everything looked dark to her. When she talked about her job, her family, or herself, there was a bleakness in her tone and a sense of hopelessness in her outlook. She looked sad, and she felt worse than she looked.

Worried and confused, Mark confided to his family, "I don't know what to do. I don't know what's wrong." Fortunately, Carol's problem was soon diagnosed and she began treatment. She was suffering from depression, an emotional illness that affects a great many people. I am not talking of a transitory case of the blues, but something more prolonged and much deeper. Young adults are at risk as much as anyone for depression. It is an unhappy, bleak experience for the person affected; it also poses difficulties for his or her friends and loved ones.

In my book *Understanding Depression*, I made a number of suggestions for those who are in a close relationship with a person who is depressed.[32] I would like to reiterate a few of these points here. First, depression often turns people off. Many people find it uncomfortable being around a person who is depressed. If you experience such a feeling, it is not unusual. While your basic impulse will be to help as much as you can, don't be surprised if you have avoidance feelings too; they often come with the territory.

Second, depression is usually treatable by either medication or by short-term psychotherapy. While the results of both treatments are usually good, there is a fairly high chance of recurrence somewhere down the road. If your romantic partner has depressive symptoms, educate yourself as much as you can about the problem. It will help you help him or her find appropriate therapy and will help you better understand and cope with the problem.

Third, depression is a stress-sensitive problem. If the person you care about is depressed or depressive-prone, do what you can to keep the level of stress in your life together from becoming excessive. Try to stop a stress-overload from developing when stress appears to be building up.

Fourth, do things together that both of you find pleasant. Exercising, such as walking in the park or bike-riding, can be a particularly good idea, for exercise has an anti-depressant effect. Finally, if you love your partner, be patient. Depressed people usually get a lot better.

When does love become an obsession?

Amy is an artist in her late twenties. She is still struggling for success in a difficult field. During the spring, Amy met David at a party at a friend's apartment. David is a young physician taking a residency in pediatrics at one of the city's major hospitals. Amy really liked David right from the start. On Sunday afternoons, they took walks together in the park or strolled through the city's art galleries. When David was free of hospital duties, they dined together in a charming French restaurant. They quickly became sexually intimate and sometimes spent the night together in Amy's small apartment. Sleeping in David's arms gave Amy a feeling of comfort and togetherness she had never experienced before. To Amy, the romance was a picture-perfect love story. She told her friends that David was the most wonderful man she had ever met. Then for reasons that Amy could not understand, David's interest in her began to wane. One night he seemed particularly withdrawn and said that he needed space.

As the weeks went by, he began to distance himself. Telephoning less and less often, he explained that he was very busy at the hospital. The more David pulled back, the more Amy thought about him. She wondered what he was doing. She wondered what had gone wrong. Was it something she had done? With increasing anxiety, she waited for his telephone calls. At night the problem became acute. She couldn't sleep. She would try to read or listen to music, but nothing seemed to work. Her thoughts kept drifting back to David. It was almost automatic. When David stopped telephoning altogether, Amy began to experience almost overwhelming impulses to call him. But she held back, thinking that he would respond coolly. Finally, she called, but just hung up when she heard his voice. Sometimes, she drove to the hospital, and waited in the parking lot, just hoping to see him. It was a vague, hopeless, almost desperate longing.

Have Amy's feelings for David become an obsession? A dictionary definition of "obsession" is a persistent idea or desire that can't be reasoned away. Looking at obsession this way, Amy is clearly obsessed with David. If love can be obsessive, does it follow that it's pathological in a psychiatric sense, that it could be considered an obsessive-compulsive disorder? Not necessarily. While there are important similarities, there are also important differences. Obsessions are defined in the American Psychiatric Association's *Diagnostic and Statistical Manual (DSM III)* as "recurrent, persistent ideas, thoughts, images, or impulses that are ego-dystonic, that is, they are not experienced as voluntarily produced, but rather as thoughts that invade consciousness and are experienced as senseless or repugnant."[33] In Amy's case, her thoughts of David were indeed persistent and involuntary, but her impulses were of desire and longing; they were not experienced as senseless or repugnant.

While Amy doesn't appear to have a classical psychiatric disorder, she is nonetheless badly hung up on David and very uncomfortable. She has an emotional problem that is interfering with her ability to function normally and could profit from counseling or therapy. When love becomes absorbing and all-consuming, it can be obsessive. We are talking about a person who is possessed by an overwhelming interest in and need for another person. Writing from a psychoanalytic perspective, Michael Sperling calls this situation "desperate love." Desperate love is characterized by a sense of merging with the lover, an idealizing of the lover, a reduced ability to perceive the person and the relationship accurately, a tendency to extol the qualities of the lover and the relationship, an insatiable need to give and receive affection, and feelings of urgency and anxiety when separating from the loved one. The boundaries between oneself and one's beloved can become indistinct. In an extreme case, desperate love may go far beyond one's legitimate need for closeness to a denial of the lover's right to a separate identity.

Sperling theorizes that desperate love is more likely to occur in a person who had really not developed a clear sense of self.[34] A person who does not know whom he or she is, who has not developed into a self-reliant, confident individual, might fall into a desperate love relationship as a way of filling the gaps in his or her own persona.

Are "codependent" relationships as unhealthy as they sound?

Codependent is a "psychiatric type" of label that is becoming part of popular speech. The term is not always used in a clear and precise way, and can mean different things to different people. In an article discussing codependency, Maurcio Gaborit and his colleagues at Saint Louis University relate how the term emerged from research on the wives of alcoholics. It was observed that these wives sometimes went to great lengths to cope with and control the behavior of their spouses; these efforts became a central, if not *the* central focus of their lives. In a way, meaning in their own lives became largely dependent on the actions of their spouses. The term codependency describes a disengagement from one's own goals and plans; instead one becomes heavily involved in the activities of someone else. One becomes focused on another person's aspirations and activities, rather than on one's own. Gaborit and his colleagues put it this way: "Simply stated, it can be conceptualized as an excessive preoccupation in the lives, feelings, and problems of others."[35]

According to studies carried out by the Saint Louis University researchers, codependent people tend to have some of the following characteristics. They express a strong need to take care of others and solve their problems. Codependent people derive their sense of well-being from these actions. They believe that the interests and concerns of these other people are more important than their own needs and concerns. Codependent people may have trouble standing up for themselves or taking risks in relationships. They also may have a negative self-image, needing approval from others to feel good about themselves.

You may see examples of codependent behavior in your own circle of friends. Perhaps it is a mother who talks only about her children, who thinks of nothing else and whose day is totally consumed by them. Perhaps it is a man or woman who is devoted to the care of a sick or disabled parent. Perhaps it is a father who is caught up in the problems of a child's drug addictions, or it may be the spouse of someone who has a highly successful career in politics or the arts. In codependency, one sees a loss of personal identity and an absorption in the activities and concerns of another.

One problem with the term codependency is that the boundaries of the term may not be clear. What do we mean by excessive preoccupation? Where does normal caring about someone end and an unhealthy preoccupation begin? The problem becomes especially murky when we consider the role women have traditionally held in our society. Until recent times, the traditional role for most women in American society was to be a homemaker and mother. In filling these roles, women often subordinate their own needs for achievement to the careers of their husbands and the needs of their children. To be loving, giving, supportive and self-sacrificing was not considered pathological; it was a cultural expectation and was often idealized. To look back at such behavior from a contemporary "revisionist" perspective and label what millions of women did in their daily lives as a form of codependency seems unfair to the women to say the least.

Clearly, we have moved into a different age where women are much more independent and career-minded. Self-sacrifice may be viewed as less normative and more unusual. Still, it remains far from clear when excessive preoccupation with the needs of others should be labeled codependency or simply a lifestyle choice. Codependency sounds like a way of dealing with personality inadequacies which might have an unhealthy basis. A lifestyle choice to be family-focused rather than career-oriented is a matter of individual preferences and values as well as the family's financial needs.

What happens when your partner begins to cling and becomes anxious about being dumped?

Have you ever known a person who was a "clinging vine"? Someone who was uncomfortable being alone, couldn't do things for himself or herself, was passive and indecisive, and sought help from others as the primary way of coping with even minor problems? Such people have exaggerated dependency tendencies and have been referred to in psychiatric language as "dependent personalities." You are more likely to find women with dependent personalities than men. This gender difference has its roots in child-rearing, where traditionally boys have been raised to be more independent than girls. Still, there is no shortage of dependent personalities of either sex. Two good illustrations are Jenny and Gerald who are in group therapy in a community mental health clinic.

Jenny is 40 years old. She lives with her boyfriend Dick, who is a freelance writer. To make a living, Dick spends his mornings religiously sitting in front of his word-processor writing articles for popular magazines and working on a book. While Dick writes, Jenny fidgets around the old rented house they live in. Every half hour or so she knocks on the door of the room where Dick is working, interrupting him about one thing or another. Dick tries to be patient, but the frequent interruptions do not help his concentration. Jenny is uncomfortable being alone, does not know what to do with herself, and is almost petrified at the idea of holding a job.

Gerald, a tall, blonde, 24-year-old X-ray technician, has gone from one girlfriend to another. The girlfriends, typically a few years older than Gerald, have a striking similarity. They all have nurturing personalities; they are givers who freely extend mothering to adults as well as to children. After a few dates, Gerald falls into the role of a little-boy-lost, and feeds on these maternal tendencies, using his girlfriends as mothers, lovers, therapists, and sometimes providers. When he has a problem, he calls them on the phone, and when the problem persists, he calls them again. He leans on his girlfriends until he wears them out.

Like many people with dependent personalities, Jenny and Gerald behave in ways that eventually turn off their romantic partners. Their clinging behavior smothers their partners, and their lack of self-reliance engenders a lack of respect. When the partners of dependent personalities begin to pull away, a fear of abandonment is generated in the dependent person. This fear may manifest itself in anxiety, more clinging, abasement, tears, and pleading. Responsibility for the dependent person's emotional well-being is placed on the shoulders of the stronger person who may feel emotionally blackmailed. The message conveyed is something like this: "If you leave me, I will be devastated."

In a study carried out by Nancy Collins and Stephen Read, there was clear evidence that men are particularly uncomfortable with women who appear anxious about being abandoned or unloved.[36] When men are in such relationships, they tend to be less satisfied, feel less positive toward their partners, feel more conflict in the relationship, and are less likely to consider marriage. The women who took part in Collins' and Read's study were less turned off by men who had a fear of abandonment but still were less willing to entertain the prospect of marriage. Fear of abandonment has some of the same properties as self-fulfilling prophecies. Fear of abandonment turns off partners, often bringing about the very situation the partner is afraid of—termination of the relationship.

10. *Sexual Activity*

What factors influence restraint in becoming sexually active?

Gail did not want to sleep with Todd until after months of dating and lots of thought. She waited until she was fully convinced it was what she wanted to do and she felt a strong sense of commitment from Todd. Sex began for Rita and Brian after what amounted to no decision at all; it was simply the end game of a passionate exchange one evening after dinner and drinks in Brian's apartment. As Rita put it, "We simply did not have good brakes." People differ markedly in the degree of restraint they exercise in becoming sexually active. When we try to account for these differences, a variety of explanations comes to mind. These explanations include differences among individuals in the strength of their sex drives, in their expectations for sexual experience stemming from the culture in which they live, in the sexual behavior of their peers, in their beliefs and values, in their perception of risk factors, and in their individual personalities. Depending on the way these forces play out, the decision to become sexually active may be a quick, almost casual act, like Rita and Brian's, or a carefully reasoned choice like Gail's.

Let's discuss some of these factors beginning with sex drive and culture. Individuals, of course, differ in the strength of their sex drives, and these differences reflect differences in biological makeup. Like all biologically based drives, the way in which the sex drive is expressed is strongly influenced by the society in which one lives. Sexual desire may be heightened by both internal stimuli (sensations within the body, thoughts, sexual fantasies) and external events (seeing an attractive person of the opposite sex, watching an erotic film). In the abstract world of psychological theory, other things being equal, heightened sexual desire leads to sexually-driven behavior in an attempt to find some way to satisfy the aroused need. However, in the real world, other things are generally not equal, and sexual desire is often left unsatisfied. As a textbook example of this, I recall a story related by evangelist Billy Graham during a television interview in which he described a colleague who was so concerned about controlling his mounting sexual desire that he locked himself in his hotel room and threw away the key.

When we think about external events or stimuli that activate or increase sexual desire, we have more than enough examples in contemporary American society. One only has to open up a magazine to see advertisements which attempt to sell products through the implied promise of making the buyer more sexually enticing. Sex is frequently on display on television in varying degrees of explicitness. Motion pictures often feature bedroom scenes, and the lyrics of pop music have at times been so sexually explicit that some alarmed citizens have urged the record companies to place labels on their products to warn parents about what their children might be listening to.

While society goes out of its way to stimulate sexual desire, it sends a mixture of often conflicting messages about sexual behavior. Parents, ministers, and teachers urge young people to be abstinent, pointing out the problems and risks involved in early and casual sexual behaviors, while movies, television, and peers often suggest the opposite. The cumulative impact of these cultural messages is that sex is okay and it's not okay. The result is often confusion.

The perception of what one's peers are doing makes a difference in whether one becomes sexually active, and this is especially true for teenagers. The belief that one's peers are having sexual relations provides both feelings of justification for and pressure toward becoming sexually active oneself. Early sexual behavior is also associated with drinking and experimentation with drugs. Attitudes and values make a difference. People who view sex as a casual act are more likely to be sexually active with multiple partners than people who believe that sex should be restricted to committed relationships. Attitudes based on religious convictions often exert a restraining influence on sexual behavior. Research has shown that women college students raised in religious households are less likely to enter sexual relationships.[1] Research also suggests that students with conservative orientations tend to have less permissive sexual attitudes and behavior than their more liberal counterparts.[2]

There are significant risk factors in becoming sexually active. Sexually transmitted diseases including AIDS make casual sex a risky and sometimes dangerous act. Unwanted pregnancy is an ever present possibility. People differ in how much attention they pay to these risks. While some people restrict sex to a committed relationship with a reliable partner, other people have sex with partners they hardly know at all. One's personality plays a part in the decision to become sexually active. In the 1970s, Marvin Zuckerman and his colleagues at the University of Delaware asked male and female undergraduates to complete some personality inventories and to indicate the extent of their previous sexual experiences. The personality inventories included a measure dealing with risk-taking (thrill and adventure seeking). As one might expect, students who scored high on this measure had more extensive sexual experience. The authors also reported some other findings which suggest that sexual expression is linked to different personality needs in males and females. "In males, sexuality seems more related to self-expressive needs, such as exhibitionism, play, impulsivity ... in females, sexuality seems to be more intimately involved with social needs, such as dominance, affiliation, and social recognition."[3]

So, we have a man and a woman who begin to see each other. Each has a unique combination of sex drive and attitudes towards sex. Each may or may not have serious restraints about sexual conduct. As they begin to interact, situational factors begin to exert an influence on the level of sexual play that may ensue. The atmosphere where they go on a date may heighten sexual desire; the clothes they wear or scents they use may stimulate sexual feelings; and drinking may lower inhibitions. These situational factors can have a powerful effect and may tip the balance in a new or short-term relationship. In a long-term relationship, the decision to have sex is usually an integral part of the type of commitment the partners make to each other.

How much truth is there to the idea that when a woman says "no" she really means "yes"?

A car is parked on a dimly lit road overlooking the river. It is a road often used by couples who want to be alone and undisturbed, and it has the reputation of being a Lovers' Lane. A man and a woman are together in the back seat of the car. Her clothes have been loosened and the buttons on her blouse are undone. She snuggles up against the man's body. They have been petting passionately for a long time. He makes a move toward having intercourse, and she grips his hand and says "no." They stop what they are doing for a moment, then they kiss and resume petting. In a while, he tries again to have intercourse with her. Again she stops him. Now they talk for a while. He tries to persuade her and is reassuring. When they being to make love again, she makes no further effort to stop him and they have sex.

Is this scene a male fantasy? Or is it an often repeated reality with only minor variations in staging and scenario? Do some women offer token resistance when they really want sex? Or as Charlene Muelenhard and Lisa Hollabaugh posed the question in a provocative study: "Do women sometimes say no when they mean yes?" In the beginning of their research report, Muelenhard and Hollabaugh framed the issue:

> There is a common belief that many women offer token resistance to sex: that they say no to sex even when they mean yes and that their protests are not to be taken seriously. This belief is based on the traditional sexual script in which women's role is to act resistant to sex and men's role is to persist in their sexual advances despite women's resistance.... A typical scenario in pornography, movies, and jokes portrays a woman who refuses a man's sexual advances and who subsequently becomes highly sexually aroused when he ignores her protests.[4]

The researchers then cite evidence which suggests that many men believe this sexual script. In their study, they set out to determine if this scenario has any basis in fact. The researchers gave out questionnaires to 610 undergraduate women students at Texas A&M University. One of the items in the questionnaire described the following situation:

> You were with a guy who wanted to engage in sexual intercourse and you wanted to also, but for some reason you indicated that you didn't want to, although *you had every intention to and were willing to engage in sexual intercourse.* In other words, you indicated "no" and you meant "yes."[5]

The women were asked to recall the number of times they had been in such a situation. Two hundred and forty of the 610 women reported that they had indeed experienced this situation on at least one occasion. That's about 40 percent. So a large number of young women have been with men and said "no" when they meant "yes." The statistics on "how often" this had occurred are revealing. For the majority of the women, saying "no" but meaning "yes" was not a one-time event. Forty-five percent of those who reported doing this at all did so two to five times, 11 percent six to ten times and about ten percent more than ten times. These data indicate that there are some women — clearly a minority — who often, perhaps routinely, say "no" when they mean "yes."

The researchers asked the 240 women for their reasons for offering token resistance when they really wanted to have sex. The reason most often given was the fear of appearing promiscuous. The show of reluctance was intended to communicate the message that the woman was not an easy mark and that her eventual consent would not lead to a lack of respect. Other reasons cited were situational problems (e.g., her roommate might return soon), uncertainty about her partner's feelings, self-consciousness about her body, religious and moral scruples, game playing and a desire to be in control. Game playing included such ideas as wishing to get her partner more aroused by making him wait, wanting him to talk her into it, and wanting him to be more aggressive. Being in control meant that she would make the decision when it was going to happen.

The token resistance scenario may have some value for women who wish to convey an impression to their partners that they are not easy marks. However, the fact that many women act out this script presents ambiguities for men. They may mistakenly interpret a woman's refusal to have sex as a charade and push their dates aggressively when they should not. It certainly creates problems for the majority of women who mean "no" when they say "no." The expectation that a woman's refusal is not for real may well contribute to the high incidence of date rape.

What turns men on?

It's no secret that most men are easily turned on to sex. Before we discuss this non-secret, it may come as a bit more of a surprise that many a man's ardor can be fairly easily switched off. Picture this scene: A man and a woman are seated together on a living room couch. The lights are dim. Romantic music plays from a stereo in the corner of the room. She is half-reclined, resting in his arms looking up at him. He looks into her eyes, draws her close and kisses her. Then they kiss a second time. He feels aroused. When he eagerly seeks her lips a third time, she looks at him lovingly, opens her mouth and says, "Did I tell you about the crazy experience I had at work today?"

In their ground breaking book, *Sexual Behavior in the Human Female,* Alfred Kinsey and his associates pointed out that during the height of sexual passion, men may become insensitive to distractions.[6] Indeed, prostitutes confided to them that their confederates often robbed their customers during intercourse because the man would be unaware of what was happening around him. Still, long before a man reaches a point of insensitivity, mental distractions can interfere with, if not undermine, the arousal process. Witness this experiment carried out by James Geer and Robert Fuhr.

Young men at the State University of New York were recruited to take part in a study of responses to erotic materials. Tested individually, the men were first fitted with a device that measured penile swelling. Then the men listened to a tape recorded woman's voice vividly describing a highly erotic sexual encounter. While the men listened, they were asked to perform certain mental tasks using a series of numbers. The more complicated the mental tasks became, the less responsive the men were to the description of the erotic encounter.[7]

An acquaintance of mine who was struggling with a problem of premature ejaculation tried to control the pressure building to ejaculate during sexual intercourse by mentally reciting the multiplication tables. If you think "there must be a better way," you're right. While thumbing through the pages of a popular magazine, I came across an article which discussed the question of what turns a man on. The article contained quotes from a few men stating what turned them on. One of the things mentioned was seeing a woman in sexy clothes or lingerie. Now it is certainly true that what a woman wears or doesn't wear can be stimulating to many men. Some companies make a livelihood out of promoting sexy lingerie. Judging from research on male sexual fantasies, the idea of an attractive woman undressing is an image that many men find arousing. This idea, of course, was the basis for a whole industry, the striptease shows that once flourished in the downtown white light districts of big cities. In these burlesque houses, women moved about the stage, to the rhythms of a small orchestra in the pit, seductively shedding their clothes, little by little, while a roomful of men sat transfixed, hoping the performer might take off a little bit more than the law allowed.

Striptease joints gave way to X-rated movie houses in the 1960s and 1970s. In the beginning the novelty of seeing explicit sex on the screen drew a substantial audience (which was mostly male), but in time interest waned. In the area in which I live, public pressure closed most of the theaters and the X-rated video arcades that were nearby. Pornographic movies continue to sell in the home video market. There has been considerable interest in what effect such films have on men. The research I have read suggests that some exposure to pornographic films is usually sexually stimulating to men. Continued viewing, however, is more likely to be boring than stimulating. If the films contain scenes of aggressive sexual behavior towards women, they may stimulate such ideas in some viewers. While heterosexual men are aroused by viewing films of sex between men and women, they are likely to be turned off by viewing sex between gay males. In commenting on the findings of their experiments with pornographic films, David Mosher and Kevin O'Grady remarked, "It was the males watching the film of homosexual behavior who reported the highest levels of disgust, anger, shame, and guilt."[8]

Researchers have studied the reactions of men viewing sexy pictures of women and reading erotic literature. As is true for X-rated movies, such stimuli are sexually arousing to many men. To cite one study as an example, Joseph Campagna gave a sexual arousal checklist asking about transient sexual feelings and the need for sexual release to college males. Then, he gave them both erotic photographs clipped from magazines and erotic literature to look through. Campagna retested the subjects and found higher scores on the sexual arousal checklist.[9]

The fact that many men respond to erotic literature has led to a growth industry in magazines which feature erotica in varying degrees. *Playboy* magazine and *Penthouse* are among the biggest sellers. *Penthouse*'s 1992 circulation was well over a million. The 1993 edition of *Writer's Market* lists the titles of several magazines that appear to be blatantly erotic. One magazine, *Turn-on Letters*, publishes sexually explicit materials in the form of letters. *Buxom* reports a circulation of 81,000, while *Thigh High* reports 89,000. How is this for a magazine title—*Climax, Sex Crazed Couples Come Together*? The magazine's circulation was reported to be 83,000.[10] While these are hardly huge circulations, it is clear that there are plenty of men who buy and read erotically oriented magazines. Researchers Neil Malamuth and Robert McIlwraith were interested in the readers of *Playboy* and *Penthouse*. They wondered whether men who fantasized a lot about sex would be more frequent readers of these magazines. The researchers did find a relationship between reading *Penthouse* and sexual fantasizing, but not so for *Playboy*.[11]

The sense of vision is, of course, only one of the modes of sexual arousal. Manufacturers of perfumes and scents for women swear by their effectiveness in turning men on. A rationale advanced by one maker of perfumes is that the olfactory system is connected to the limbic system which governs sexual appetite. I'll leave the merits of that argument up to students of physiology. The claims of scent manufacturers can be interesting, to say the least. One ad for a cologne stated that its use was designed to enhance the pheromones naturally emitted from the body when one was attracted to someone of the opposite sex. The ad suggested that when the winds were right, your augmented personal scent could "ignite the fire."

How about a woman's voice? Do you find that some women's voices turn you on while others turn you off? How do you respond to a southern drawl? Do you react to British, French or other foreign accents? The legendary German born film star Marlene Dietrich has a voice that turned on a whole generation of movie-goers.

What turns women on?

In their book *Sexual Behavior in the Human Female*, Alfred Kinsey and his associates made the point that men are often surprised that women are not aroused by the same kinds of stimuli that arouse them. Kinsey related a story of a 16th century prince who used to serve wine to his ladies in a cup that was covered with illustrations of couples engaged in sex. The prince would ask the ladies whether the cup had stimulated them. The answers were usually negative.[12]

Most men are aroused by the sight of a nude woman. Among Kinsey's sample of several thousand women, only about 20 percent reported that they had a significant response to viewing a man's genitals.[13] Many men are excited by viewing photographs or drawings of nude women. Relatively few women are excited by drawings of nude men. The X-rated film houses have few women in the audiences. Kinsey observed that women are more likely to be sexually stimulated by reading romantic literature than by more explicit references to sex. He noted that five times as many women said they were responsive to romantic writings as were responsive to looking at photographs or drawings of nude males.[14]

The fact that there is a very large readership for romantic novels seems consistent with Kinsey's observation that a romantic story can be a turn-on for many women. An interesting experiment carried out by Denise Moreault and Diane Fulingstad demonstrates the power of romantic imagination to arouse women sexually. The researchers asked women to read some romantic fantasies that included no explicit sexual content, then to make up some of their own sexual fantasies. Afterwards, the women were asked about their own level of sexual arousal. Not only was their level of sexual arousal heightened as compared to a control group which read non-romantic materials, they also reported more genital and breast sensations.[15]

Does this mean that women are not responsive to explicit eroticism in literature? Not necessarily. While women are generally less aroused by visual depictions of sex than men, they may be receptive to explicit erotic literature if it conveys a sense of caring and tenderness. A study carried out by Donald Mosher and Irene Greenberg demonstrates this point. The researchers asked women students at Ohio State University to read one of two passages. The first group of women read a passage from a psychology text book. (How exciting can you get?) The second group read a passage from a novel, *Eternal Fire*, by Calder Willingham. Mosher and Greenberg summarize the passage from *Eternal Fire* as follows: "The passage describes the seduction of a virginal girl by a young man. Sexual petting and foreplay lead to mounting sexual arousal in the girl, and her conflicts about sexual intercourse give way until she actively encourages the young man to have sexual intercourse with her. The literary style is vivid and realistically descriptive." They go on further to say, "The sexual descriptions were accompanied by indications of apparent tenderness and concern."[16]

After reading one of the two passages, the women were asked to respond to a list of adjectives which described their mood. Included among the many adjectives listed were the words "titillated, passionate, excited, sensuous, aroused, tantalized, and hot." The women who read the erotic passage were more likely to check such adjectives indicating sexual arousal than the women who read the academic passage. The suggestion from such studies is that the response of women to erotic literature is influenced by the context and manner in which the erotic passages are presented. Simple depictions of sexuality in the absence of romantic feeling are likely to be a turnoff. Throw in love and tenderness, however, and a chance for a woman to exercise her romantic imagination, and a dash or two of eroticism may be much more acceptable.

In his romantic comedy, *Twelfth Night*, Shakespeare voiced the lines, "If music be the food of love, play on!"[17] Music certainly can put many men and women into a romantic mood. And this could be any genre of music — depending on what one likes — from classical, to romantic ballads, to country-western, to contemporary rock. As part of a study on sexual symbolism, researcher Michael Wallach wanted to put his female subjects into an aroused mood and elected to use classical music as his stimulus. He chose impressionist music. To select the best musical candidate, he asked a group of Radcliffe undergraduates to rate a number of musical selections in terms of how sexually aroused they felt while listening to the music. The winning composer was Debussy. The music was a selection from the *Petite Suite*.[18]

While many women may not be aroused by male nudity, they are hardly indifferent to the appearance men present. Let's talk a bit about some of the physical characteristics of a man that women find most attractive. April Fallon and Paul Rozin showed drawings of male bodies to female undergraduates at the University of Pennsylvania. The drawings ranged from very thin to very heavy. The thinnest figure was given a value of one; the heaviest was given a value of nine. The women were asked to select the drawing they found most attractive. The average rating for the women was about 3.7 — that is a bit on the thin side.[19] Interestingly, when men were asked about which drawing women would find most attractive, their guesses were somewhat heavier than what the women actually chose.

You've heard the phrase, "tall, dark and handsome"? Do women really find men taller than themselves attractive? Yes, according to a study reported in *Psychology Today*.[20] Shown photographs of a man and woman conversing together, undergraduate women students judged men more attractive when they were taller than the woman they stood next to. If a man is tall and slender, he should consider himself fortunate.

Do men and women experience similar patterns of arousal during sexual contact?

James Geer and Deborah Broussard carried out a study in which students were shown cards describing different sex acts, including kissing, various kinds of foreplay, and intercourse. The students were asked to examine the cards two at a time and to select the act which would come first in a "typical sexual encounter." From these data, the researchers were able to construct a clear cut sequence of acts beginning with kissing and ending with vaginal intercourse. This research showed that men and women shared a similar road map — a set of expectations — as to the order in which events will take place in a sexual encounter. Now, consider this question: Would the level of sexual arousal people experience intensify steadily as they proceed through this sequence of sexual behaviors? If you think that sexual arousal would intensify steadily as one moves from kissing to vaginal intercourse, you would probably be right for men, but not necessarily for women. Geer and Broussard asked their subjects to make judgments about how sexually arousing the behaviors described on each card would be. The men's responses revealed a steady increase in perceived sexual arousal as one moves through the sequence. Not so, the women. Acts near the end of the sequence were not seen as that much more arousing than acts near the beginning of the sequence. While men may experience an increasing surge of passion during sexual play, women may experience more of a steady state of arousal.

The authors of the study note that this gender difference could lead to unwitting conflicts between partners. "The difference in perceived arousal value sets the stage for miscommunication between the sexes. If, as is likely, individuals assume that acts they perceive as arousing are seen by their partners as equally arousing, the potential for confusion and conflict is high. What we have found is that such differences typify the sexes."[21] The implication from these data is that men should not assume that their partners are feeling what they are feeling at any given point during sexual play.

11. Drugs and AIDS

How do drugs affect sex?

There are some drugs which are said to act as aphrodisiacs; that is to say, they are supposed to increase sexual desire and performance. I would imagine that the term aphrodisiac comes from the Greek goddess Aphrodite who was the goddess of love and beauty. If Aphrodite was successful in turning men's mind to love and lovemaking, the drugs which are her namesake are much less so. According to *The Handbook of Non Prescription Drugs*, not only are these substances ineffective, some of them are dangerous.[1]

Perhaps the most widely talked about aphrodisiac is Spanish Fly. I can remember years ago listening to schoolyard conversation which extolled the power of Spanish Fly in arousing girls. I doubt that any of the boys who talked about Spanish Fly had ever seen it, much less used it, but it sounded very knowing and sophisticated to talk about such mysterious things. Spanish Fly is a preparation made from dried, ground up insects of a species of cantharis that is found in Spain among other places, hence , the name Spanish Fly. This unappetizing sounding preparation has been described as a dangerous blistering agent. While it may act as an irritant stimulus to the genitals, it does not increase sexual desire. According to *The Handbook of Non Prescription Drugs*, Spanish Fly is both ineffective as an aphrodisiac and is dangerous.

The Handbook of Non Prescription Drugs lists a number of other substances for which similar claims have been made. The list includes Ginseng Sarsaparilla, a root extract from smilax plants; Yohimbine, an alkaloid derived from the bark of a tree named *Coryanthe* Yohimbe; and Pega Palo which is an extract of a plant named *Rhynohosia pyramidalis*. Do any of these preparations work? Since controlled scientific evaluations of the effects of these substances are hard to come by, one has to be very skeptical about any claims made.

While the claims made for the aforementioned aphrodisiacs are questionable to say the least, there are drugs which do have relaxing and inhibition-lowering effects and as such have become associated with sex. One substance which comes quickly to mind is marijuana. Although illegal throughout the United States, marijuana remains a heavily used drug; in 1992, it was estimated that it was used by 78 percent of the people that used illegal drugs. Many marijuana users believe that the drug enhances their sexual pleasure. Users have reported that the drug enhances their feelings of emotional closeness during sex and the experience of orgasm. Marijuana users have also reported that the drug prolongs sexual excitement. These perceptions may stem from the fact that marijuana does have disinhibiting, relaxing, mild psychedelic and time-distorting effects, any of which could influence subjective sexual pleasure.[2]

Some years ago, when I was doing research on marijuana, I asked students about their reactions to the drug. The question asked was "Now, please tell us in your own words what it is like to smoke marijuana. How would you describe the feelings and sensations you experience?" In these illustrations from the student responses, you can see these various effects:

> "Very relaxed, everything very amusing, constantly smiling, very warm and floating, erotic."
>
> "Lightheadedness, perception is not totally accurate, giddiness."
>
> "Horny and less inhibited."[3]

It is well to point out that the drug may also have adverse affects such as anxious and depressive reactions.

Marijuana use seems to be associated with increased sexual desire. Roland Tanck and I asked university students to fill out diaries every night for a ten-day period in regard to what the students had experienced during the day. We compared the days in which students reported that they used marijuana with the days in which they did not. We found that reports of sexual desire were higher on days in which the students used marijuana.[4]

Let's consider the other side of the coin. Are there drugs which can reduce sexual desire or interfere with the ability to have sex? The answer is yes. There are some prescription drugs that may have an adverse effect on the sexual functioning of some people who use them. Here are two examples. Beta blockers are widely prescribed in the treatment of hypertension (high blood pressure). According to the *Physician's Desk Reference* (PDR), these drugs can cause impotence in some users.[5] Diazepam, a drug widely prescribed for the treatment of anxiety, is best known under the trade name Valium. One of the possible adverse effects of this drug is that it can cause changes in sexual drive. According to an article in *U.S. News and World Report* (Nov. 8, 1993, p. 78), most of the antidepressive medications now being used can reduce sex drive and delay orgasm.

How has AIDS affected patterns of sexual behavior?

Acquired Immunodeficiency syndrome, AIDS, is a disorder that results from being infected with a retrovirus called HIV-Type I. The virus is transmitted through sex, through exchange of blood or blood products and from mother to child during pregnancy, the perinatal period and through breast milk. A few weeks following infection, many persons will experience a two or three week bout of symptoms such as fever, night sweats, headaches and swollen lymph nodes. After the initial symptoms abate, infected persons will remain without symptoms of AIDS for a number of years. Then he or she will develop a full blown case of the disorder. What the virus does is severely damage the body's immune system, leaving the person vulnerable to multiple opportunistic infections. As things stand currently, most afflicted people will die in a matter of months to a few years.[6] At present, there is no known cure for AIDS, and vaccines to prevent the disease are still in the research stage. The only way to prevent infection current is to practice low risk behaviors. And for the vast majority of people who are not intravenous drug users, this means exercising prudence in sexual behavior for that is where the risk lies.

The chances of becoming infected with AIDS through sexual contact can be eliminated by abstinence. Alternatively, one can find a sexual partner who is not infected with the virus, and to remain safe, the partners must keep their sexual relationship exclusive. Failing this, the use of latex condoms can substantially reduce the likelihood of one's getting AIDS. A 1992 report of the House of Representatives Select Committee on Children, Youth and Families entitled *A Decade of Denial* stated, "The CDC [Center for Disease Control] and numerous researchers have found that correct and consistent use of latex condoms lubricated with the spermicide nonoxyol 9 prevents transmissions of STDs [sexually transmitted diseases] including HIV."[7]

With these preventive behaviors in mind, I will focus on three questions: (1) Are more Americans becoming abstinent? (2) Are more Americans forming exclusive sexual relationships? (3) Are more Americans using condoms during sexual intercourse? But to first cast some perspective on the scope of the problem, consider this statement from the report, *A Decade of Denial*: "By age 20, 68% of adolescent females and 86% of adolescent males are sexually active. Among sexually experienced teens ages 18–19, nearly 25% of females report having had six or more partners and nearly 20% of males report having had six to ten partners ... only 47% of females and 55% of males report use of condoms at first intercourse."[8]

In a word, very large numbers of young people are currently sexually active, having multiple partners and not using condoms. Is the situation changing at all? Studies carried out on college students in the late 1980s indicate that many students have changed their sexual behavior because of AIDS. In the studies I have seen, the numbers range from about a third to one-half of the students surveyed. So the situation does appear to be improving.

Let's look at the three types of specific preventive behaviors mentioned, starting with abstinence. Studies of college students suggest that from 3 to 10 percent of the students surveyed have abstained from sexual intercourse because of AIDS.[9] The figures are higher for those carefully choosing and remaining with one sexual partner. The questions asked of college students do not quite put it in these terms, but they do ask about becoming more selective in choosing a partner. In one of the studies, 18 percent of the students said they were being more selective because of AIDS.

Finally, consider the use of condoms. In a June 1991 report from the National Commission on Children, it was stated that among sexually active teens, the number using condoms had risen from about one-fifth in 1982 to about one-third in 1988.[10] The recent report, *A Decade of Denial*, suggests that the number of young people using condoms may approach 50 percent. So, in all three categories of preventive sexual behaviors, there has been a trend towards more widespread acceptance of the need to exercise prudence, a small increase in abstinence, and larger increases in partner selectivity and condom use. However, a very large number of people remain as sexually risky in their behavior as ever. It is as if AIDS was a disease someone else had to worry about.

With the AIDS epidemic, how can I be sure of my partner?

Unfortunately, for many persons, the answer is "you can't." Remember the old cliché, "I'd stake my life on it"? Well, you might just be doing that if you're not careful. Here are a few tough-minded rules you might want to consider to help you play it safe.

The first rule is to avoid having sexual relations with anyone who is using intravenous drugs or has shown any tendency to use them. Drug users can become infected with AIDS by sharing needles and then passing the HIV virus to others through sexual contact.

The second rule is that refraining from vaginal intercourse and substituting oral sex or anal intercourse is not helpful in preventing infection. AIDS can be transmitted during both acts.

Rule three is to stay away from anyone with a reputation for promiscuity. You'd have to have very good reason to believe that a person who has been sleeping around is going to stop sleeping around.

Rule four, don't necessarily believe what someone tells you about his or her past sexual behaviors. Questioning students in California, researchers Susan Cochran and Vickie Mays found that many of the men and women studied said they might distort details of their past sexual experience when talking with potential new partners.[11] Nearly a quarter of the men indicated that they would not reveal the fact of an ongoing sexual relationship, and about one man in five might say, if pressed, that he has had a blood test for the AIDS virus when in fact he hasn't—if it would help persuade a woman to have sex with him.

Rule five. Use a condom. Even without spermicide (which by the way should be included for safety, if.you have any doubts), using condoms substantially reduces your risk.

12. Sexual Fantasies

What are typical male sexual fantasies?

Here are two sexual fantasies. The first is from a normal 26-year-old man. The second is from a man arrested for sexual offenses. The difference in content between the two fantasies speaks volumes about what is typical for men and what is not.

"When I lie in bed I sometimes fantasize about a girl I had a blind date with last year. Her name is Lois. She had flown in from Seattle to visit a friend, Anne, for the weekend. Now Anne has been dating a guy I know from law school named Donnie. Well, Donnie arranged a double date, and the four of us first went to a movie and then to a cocktail lounge where we had drinks and listened to a blues singer. When we left, Donnie parked the car near his apartment. It was one of those old large cars with a roomy back seat. They were in the front and we were in the back. Lois and I had really hit it off well; we just liked each other, and when we were in the back seat, we went at it hot and heavy. We were all over each other. We both wanted to go further, but there was no place where we could really have privacy, so we just stopped things midway. In my fantasy, I imagine that instead of stopping I get the keys to Donnie's apartment and they drive off. Lois and I go to Donnie's place and we pick up where we left off in the car. We take each other's clothes off, make passionate love and spend the night together."

The second fantasy was taken from an article on treatment of sexual deviations, authored by Kelly Brownell and his colleagues. The subject "was a 22-year-old engaged male college student, seeking treatment following arrest for exhibitionism. He had a 10-year history of exposure incidents in which he publicly masturbated." His fantasies were violent and masochistic. He imagined "women kicking his groin, crushing his testicles, biting his penis and cutting out his abdominal organs with knives."[1]

The first fantasy was a reexperiencing and extension in imagination of a previous sexual experience. As we shall see from the research literature, reexperiencing past sexual encounters is a typical fantasy for most men. The second fantasy is off the wall. Although some men entertain kinky sexual fantasies, they are not the usual bill-of-fare. What do young men daydream about? Is it usually about sex? I doubt it. I previously mentioned a study Roland Tanck and I were doing in which we asked university students to write down their daydreams over a period of ten days. Sometimes, these daydreams were escapist; sometimes they were about becoming rich and famous or simply going home for a vacation. While the young men most often daydreamed about their girlfriends and the young women about their boyfriends, only a few students related anything explicitly sexual in their reports. Admittedly, if we had asked specifically for reports of sexual fantasies, we would have picked up more of this, but daydreams do not seem typically focused on sex. The exception to this generalization is when daydreams occur during masturbation. These fantasies are usually sexual, pure and simple.

Researcher Anthony Campagna found that 88 percent of his sample of college males reported masturbating on occasion. Most of these young men had sexual fantasies while masturbating. Campagna wanted to know what these fantasies were like. He drew up a list of 53 fantasies and asked the students how often they had such fantasies on a scale ranging from "never" to "every time." Campagna reported that sexual fantasy during masturbation was diverse. "Every daydream in the questionnaire was endorsed by some of the men in the sample and forty-six items were endorsed by at least 25 percent of the students."[2] Campagna reported that sexual fantasies tended to cluster into several types. The most prominent group of sexual fantasies included thoughts of women in erotic situations and memories of prior sexual experiences. Examples were, "I try to picture a woman I know and what she would look like naked"; "I imagine that I am watching a very sexy woman slowly undressing"; "I think about sexual experiences I have had in the past"; and "I imagine that I am having sex with my girlfriend."[3]

A second cluster of sexual fantasies, much less prominent than the first, was those with sexually aggressive and kinky sexual behaviors. A third group of fantasies, also not very prominent, was having passive or anonymous sexual experiences. An example was, "I imagine that I am having sex with a beautiful woman who does all the work while I just lie back and enjoy it." Finally, there was a group of fantasies that had a make-believe flavor to them, such as having sex with a famous movie actress.

Campagna's study indicates that the sexual fantasies of young men are typically straightforward. They think about a sexually enticing woman, or they imagine themselves making love to a woman, often someone they know. Some men may at times fantasize about participating in more unusual sexual situations, but this is apparently not the rule. Sexual fantasies, of course, are not restricted to masturbation. Many men have fantasies during intercourse or when they are not engaged in any physical sexual activity. Danielle Knafo and Yoram Jaffe studied sexual fantasizing among a group of American students at Tel-Aviv University in Israel. Knafo and Jaffe reported that 60 percent of the men studied indicated that they often fantasized during sexual intercourse, and 80 percent of them often had such fantasies when not engaging in sexual activity.[4] Among the most frequent fantasies reported were thoughts of an imaginary lover, having sex with an older, experienced lover, reliving a past sexual experience, and delighting many women. As was true in Campagna's study, fantasizing about kinky or bizarre sexual themes was infrequent.

What are typical female sexual fantasies?

Many women have sexual fantasies. It is a common experience, particularly for women who fantasize frequently about lots of other things. Sometimes these sexual fantasies occur where the woman is not physically involved in any kind of sexual activity. Sometimes these fantasies occur during masturbation. They may even occur during sex play with a lover and during intercourse itself. A 1974 study carried out by Barbara Hariton and Jerome Singer on a group of married women living in an upper-middle-class New York suburb revealed that 65 percent of these women reported erotic fantasies during sexual intercourse with their husbands, and 37 percent had such fantasies very often.

What did these women fantasize about when they were having intercourse? The most frequent idea was thoughts of an imaginary romantic lover. Other typical fantasies were reliving a previous sexual experience, pretending that they were doing something wicked or forbidden, being in a different place like the beach or the woods, and being overpowered.[5] The latter fantasy, which sounds similar in many respects to a rape fantasy, was reported by nearly half of the women. Other ideas which are also outside the bounds of normally acceptable behavior were reported by a surprisingly high percentage of these suburban women. These fantasies included imagining oneself delighting many men, observing oneself or others having sex, being made love to by more than one man at a time, and imagining oneself as a prostitute. During sexual intercourse, these women sometimes imagined themselves doing things they would never do in reality.

The Hariton and Singer study revealed that many women occasionally entertain erotic if not X-rated fantasies while engaging in sex with their husbands. How often are erotic fantasies entertained outside of sexual relations? In a 1991 study carried out in an Australian university, Ingrid Meuwissen and Ray Over asked a group of women students how often they had sexual fantasies while masturbating, while not engaging in sexual activity, and while participating in heterosexual sexual activity. They found that sexual fantasy occurred more often outside of sexual activity than during heterosexual activity and most often during masturbation. Some of the fantasies most often reported by these young women were lying in bed with a partner, having intercourse with herself on top, cuddling with a partner, having a partner stimulate her genitals manually, and having a partner stimulate her orally. Stimulating her partner was a less frequent activity, and activities such as group sex and fantasies of being overpowered were far down on the list.[6] When asked which fantasies were most arousing, the top rated fantasies were having intercourse with her on top, having sex in an unusual setting, and having a partner stimulate her genitals orally. The arousal value of being raped was very low.

Women's sexual fantasies that occur during intercourse may be a bit wilder and more likely to include the idea of being overpowered and forced to have sex than fantasies accompanying autoeroticism or sexual fantasies that are just passing thoughts. Researchers Danielle Knafo and Yoram Jaffe reported that the sexual fantasy of pretending to struggle and resist before becoming aroused and surrendering was more likely to occur during sexual intercourse than at other times.[7] In commenting on this finding, the researchers observed that this might reflect the needs of some women to escape responsibility and blame for sex. For women who have been brought up to feel guilty about sex, what better way to make the act permissible than to fantasize that what she is doing is the result of coercion.

If the researchers' speculations are right, that is one possible reason for sexual fantasizing. Other more straightforward reasons for sexual fantasy for both men and women are that fantasy serves as a substitute for gratifying sexual needs when a sexual partner is unavailable. This is the case when fantasy is accompanied by masturbation. Fantasy also serves to heighten sexual pleasures even when one is making love with a partner. Hariton and Singer found that some "women who reported that their husbands were ineffective lovers made use of fantasy to increase their enjoyment."[8] Additional evidence for this view of sexual fantasy comes from a 1980 study appearing in the *British Journal of Social and Clinical Psychology* which reported that 91 percent of the women questioned regularly used sexual fantasy to initiate or heighten sexual arousal.[9]

What if I dream of having sex?

Two women graduate students were strolling across the campus of the state university. As they neared the library, one of them, a tall woman with auburn colored hair, said to her companion, "You know I had a dream last night. I dreamed that I was having sex with Professor Hamilton." (Dr. Hamilton was a good looking young man who taught the English class the students were taking.) The second student smiled at her companion, looked knowingly and asked, "How was it?"

Have you ever had an explicit sexual dream — that you were making love or being made love to by someone you knew or perhaps someone you didn't know? If you have had such dreams, have you wondered what the implications were? While explicit sexual dreams are not all that unusual, they are not the typical fare of the many dreams we experience night after night. Looking through a collection of 1,000 dream reports, researchers Calvin Hall and Robert Van de Castle found that about 8 percent of the dreams contained some types of overt sexual behavior (e.g., kissing, petting, sexual intercourse). Dreams are much more likely to portray other types of behavior (e.g., aggressive acts) than sex.[10]

While explicit sexual dreams occur infrequently, most men and women will have such dreams at one time or another. In their book, *Sexual Behavior in the Human Female*, Alfred Kinsey and his colleagues reported that about two out of three women they studied had experienced at least one such dream. What were these dreams like? Sometimes the dreams went no further than petting; sometimes the dreams were of having sexual intercourse. Kinsey reported that over 30 percent of the women had dreamed of having intercourse on at least one occasion. Interestingly, for 20 percent of the women, sex in the dream proceeded to the point of orgasm.[11]

Sigmund Freud believed that sexual impulses were a driving force behind many if not most dreams, but you wouldn't necessarily find overt sexuality in the content of the dream. Freud believed that you would be much more likely to uncover these sexual ideas if you applied his technique of free association to the dream. In using this technique, the dreamer thinks about the various parts of the dream one at a time and reports whatever ideas come into his or her mind. This free association technique can be a very powerful tool that helps unravel the ideas that have given rise to the dream. Freud's experience was that the trail of ideas often led to sexuality. So, if one accepts Freud's view, the fact that you seldom have erotic dreams doesn't necessarily mean that there are not sexual energies working in your unconscious seeking expression in your dream.

Freud held the view that many of the commonplace objects that are part and parcel of our dreams function sometimes as symbols, representing sexual ideas. He believed that elongated objects (e.g., sticks, tree trunks, umbrellas) were often male sexual symbols and that vessels and containers (e.g., boxes, cases, chests) were often female symbols. Freud believed that sexual ideas in dreams were sometimes disguised in this manner.[12]

The evidence for Freud's theory of dream symbolism is sketchy at best. In some of my own research studies carried out at George Washington University with Roland Tanck and Farzaneh Houshi, we found some modest support for the hypothesis that the presence of such symbols in dreams was related to sexual deprivation. However, we found that the presence of Freudian symbols in dreams was more clearly related to anxiety than sexuality.[13] I remain skeptical of the theory.

What does it mean if you do have explicit sexual dreams? For many men such dreams occur with nocturnal emissions. An erotic dream experience occurs during the night; semen stained sheets are visible in the morning. The connection between dream imagery and physiological functioning is clear. The type of erotic dream seems analogous to the sexual fantasies that occur during masturbation. Beyond the obvious association between such erotic dreams and nocturnal emissions for men and some parallel phenomena for women (Kinsey reported that some women who reported sexual dreams also reported muscular spasms and vaginal secretions), I am not sure that there is a pat answer to the question of what these erotic dreams mean. It has been my experience that one is safest in making dream interpretations when one takes a close look at the individual dreamer, assessing his or her needs, circumstances and personal history before venturing any interpretation. It is also usually very helpful to ask the dreamer for any associations that the dream brings to mind.

In my book, *The Psychology of Dreams*, I presented the view, similar to Jung's, that many dreams tend to bring up unresolved issues in a person's life.[14] If you do have frequent erotic dreams, it would suggest that there are unresolved issues worth examining. You might want to take a close look at your sexual needs and your sex life. If you conclude that you're not happy with the way things are, consider making some adjustments to bring your sexual needs and your sexual experience into a more satisfying balance.

13. Relationships and Marriage

Some people feel they cannot get close to others. What can be done about it?

In our earlier discussions about attachment, we showed how this problem often has its roots in childhood experiences and particularly in parent-child relationships. Patterns of difficult relationships with peers are often noticeable in the early years of school. If a person is unable to feel close to others as an adult, there is often a long history behind the problem, and consequently it is not easy to remedy. There is unlikely to be any kind of quick fix. If a person with such problem is lucky, he or she may encounter someone who is open, kind and sensitive — someone who is non-threatening and accepting and can allow the gradual building of trust and the creation of bonds. On the assumption that such saints are few and far between, therapy may be the more realistic alternative. Therapy may not work for everyone, but for many people therapy can point out the probable causes of the problem and can help the person move toward ameliorating it.

Here is an example of a case in which psychotherapy was effective in dealing with difficulties relating to closeness. The case was presented by Leonard Horowitz and his colleagues in the *Journal of Consulting and Clinical Psychology*. Mrs. C. was described as a "prim, married, school teacher in her late 20's who came to treatment complaining of sexual frigidity, difficulty experiencing pleasurable feelings, and low self-esteem."[1] When she entered therapy, she had been married for over a year. "She felt that her sexual inadequacy created a major marital problem." Before she entered therapy she felt "beleaguered and upset. In situations that called for intimacy, she experienced intense ambivalence, which left her feeling confused and in turmoil."

As is so often the case, the problem appeared to stem from her early childhood. "Mrs. C.'s parents were described as controlled people, undemonstrative of any affection." Her mother was further described as "very controlling." The child sometimes responded to her mother with anger and once struck her in the stomach. She began to develop guilt feelings about her aggressiveness and assertiveness and experienced "recurrent nightmares of something happening to her mother." The therapist believed that Mrs. C.'s problem with intimacy and her sexual frigidity might be related to her continued difficulties in dealing with aggression. The therapist hypothesized that if Mrs. C. could "develop a better capacity to defend herself against other people," such as being able to disagree without feeling guilty, her fears of being close to people might diminish.

In the process of therapy, Mrs. C. became increasingly able to disagree with and oppose people. Subsequently, she seemed less vulnerable and was able to feel closer and more compassionate toward other people. As these changes occurred, her reactions to sexual relations with her husband changed. In one of the earlier hours of therapy it was noted, "Sometimes when she is trying to make herself have intercourse with Bill, she feels as though she wants to hurt him. She just doesn't understand it. She'll go from feeling very warm to feeling nothing toward him suddenly." Many sessions later, it was noted, "This weekend she and Bill had intercourse, and she was thinking how different it can be when she's thinking about him and feeling close to him and not all wrapped up in herself."

Therapy for Mrs. C. led to significant changes in her ability to accept intimacy. Her problem was deep-seated, and it took a lot of time to work through.

Obviously, not all problems of being comfortable with intimacy stem from difficulties with aggressiveness as was the case for Mrs. C. The causes of such problems are likely to be many and varied. As was true for Mrs. C., dealing with the problem through therapy is likely to take considerable time. It is a problem requiring patience and perseverance on the part of both romantic partners.

What can I do when I am in a committed relationship and become attracted to someone else?

The world is full of attractive people, and not to feel attracted to someone who is "out of bounds" at some time or other would be unusual. The problem arises when one contemplates acting on his or her feelings. Then a major conflict looms which can engender a heavy dose of guilt and the possibilities of destroying one's committed relationship. This can be a steep price to pay.

After seven years of marriage, Margo found herself in just such a dilemma. Margo was an unusually attractive woman with very dark, almost raven colored hair. Her marriage to Kevin, a successful architect, had been solid, though unspectacular. The marriage had never quite lived up to the romantic dreams that Margo had fashioned for it. The couple lived in a condominium in a well-to-do area of the city. They had a daughter, Carol, who was in the second grade. Kevin was kind, if not overly romantic, and he was receptive to any wishes that Margo had. Because of Kevin's financial success, Margo had the option of staying home or going to work. As she was not happy being a housewife, she looked for a job and found one in a small community theater in a suburb, an hour's drive south of the city.

The theater director, Norman, was good looking and exceptionally dynamic and over the years had attracted the interest of any number of young actresses. Margo became infatuated with Norman almost at first sight. In the weeks that followed her employment at the theater, she became almost obsessed by thoughts of him. Her fantasies began to run wild about being with him. On a summer afternoon, when things were slack at the theater, Norman asked Margo out to lunch. Margo found lunching with Norman a delight. They had an animated conversation, punctuated with wit, smiles and laughter. When Norman asked her to stop by his apartment so he could pick up some scripts he wanted to read, she readily assented. After they entered his apartment, they each had a drink. Then Norman began to make love to her. Margo was more than willing. She was living out her fantasies.

In the weeks that followed, Margo had sex several times with Norman. But it soon became apparent that for Norman the relationship would not go beyond an affair and perhaps a short one at that. Margo, however, was now caught up in a terrible conflict. While sleeping with Norman, she was living with Kevin and her daughter and trying to act as if things were the same and they were not. She was cheating on Kevin and was beginning to feel miserable about it. Recognizing that nothing would come of the relationship with Norman, she went to his office and told him it was over. She left her job at the theater abruptly.

Even after the brief affair ended, her guilt feelings lingered. She had trouble sleeping at night. She began to be afraid that somehow Kevin would find out that she had been unfaithful. At times, she came close to telling him herself, but was afraid he could not handle it. She finally decided never to tell him. Margo blamed herself for her behavior, yet sometimes she would take it out on Kevin with outbursts of anger, as if he was somehow at fault. She had tied herself up in knots and didn't know what to do. Many men and women have been caught up in conflicts like Margo's, but unlike Margo, they stopped short of having an affair. To fantasize is one thing; to act on one's fantasies is something else. To fantasize is retrievable, to cheat may not be.

There are several questions I would pose to any person in a committed relationship who feels attracted to someone else. First, how substantial is the committed relationship? If there is meaning and vitality in the relationship, it may make little sense to place it in jeopardy. If the relationship is essentially sound, you ought to ask yourself, "What am I doing?" Good relationships are hard enough to find. Is gratifying the desires of what may be a transitory infatuation worth putting everything else at risk?

Second, is your relationship in a period of vulnerability now? Are you becoming interested in other people because things have not gone well lately in your relationship and have left you feeling upset and dissatisfied? There are many situations which can injure a relationship and put it at risk. Separation for an extended period of time, physical illness, emotional problems, financial difficulties, family problems—all of these can impact on a relationship, making it less satisfying. If this is the case, the question becomes, "Are these difficulties transitory or do they appear more or less permanent?" If the problems in the relationship are clearly transitory, then isn't prudence reasonable counsel?

Third, how accurately are you perceiving your new romantic interest? "The grass is always greener on the other side of the fence" may be more than just a cliché. How long did it take you to discover all the quirks and foibles of your present partner? If you think that your new romantic interest would be without a series of comparable, though different, blemishes, think again. He or she may look terrific, but you will probably find less charm and more problems as you really get to know the person.

Are you staying with your partner because you want to or do you think you have no choice?

A very short play:

Two women, ages about 35, are seated in an otherwise empty restaurant. They are sipping coffee and talking softly.

Mary Ann: How long have you been seeing Mike?

Janet: It's about three years now.

Mary Ann: That long. I can't figure out why you stay with him. Why do you?

Janet: *(Shrugs)* I don't know. Habit, I guess. It sure isn't any fun being together. We never seem to talk to each other, and you know how important that is to me. We really don't do that much either. He never wants to go anywhere. He comes over. I cook dinner. We watch TV for a while. That's about it.

Mary Ann: Sounds a little grim. How's your love life?

Janet: *(Laughs)* We don't have much of one. I don't enjoy sex with him. Never have really.

Mary Ann: Do you have strong feelings for him?

Janet: Do you mean — do I love him?

Mary Ann: Yes — do you love him?

Janet: *(Shakes her head)* No. I don't love him. Sometimes, I'm not even sure I like him that much.

Mary Ann: *(Shakes her head)* Doesn't sound like much of a relationship. No love, no talk, no nothing. There's not much in it for you.

Janet: I guess not. *(Laughs)* I don't think there's much in it for him either.

Mary Ann: *(Smiles and nods)* I wonder why he stays in it.

Janet: The same reason I do, I guess.

Mary Ann: Habit?

Janet: *(Nods, then smiles)* Maybe there's another reason.

Mary Ann: What's that?

Janet: Before I met Mike, I was pretty lonely. Having no one to see on the weekends wasn't any fun. I don't want to go through that again. That's worse.

Mary Ann: Why don't you find someone else? Someone who's better for you.

Janet: *(Forced laughter)* If I thought I could find somebody, I'd do it in a minute. I don't think I can. I don't know anybody.

Mary Ann: That's why you stick with Mike?

Janet: Yeah, I'd feel rotten if I didn't have someone. And I don't know anyone else.

Many people stay in unsatisfying relationships because they don't see an alternative other than loneliness. If they believed that they could easily find someone new, they would break the relationship and look elsewhere — and they might do so with little distress. In a study of undergraduate dating couples, Jeffrey Simpson of Texas A&M University found that the perceived ease of finding another dating partner was one of the factors that predicted how much distress people experienced when breaking a romantic relationship. When a person believed that he or she could indeed find someone else, it was easier to dissolve the relationship.[2]

Janet seems convinced that there is no one else out there for her. Is this simply a perception on her part, or is it a reality? There is only one sure way of finding out and that is to take a look and test the waters.

What are memories like for past loves?

There is little more poignant in life than the breakup of a love affair. The emotional swells that rise from the occasion can be overwhelming. But when the distress subsides and time places a shield over one's feelings, it becomes easier to look back and remember. For many people, the memories are something like a novel — a story about oneself with a beginning, middle, and end. And the recollections are often bittersweet.

Researchers have tried to capture such memories. John Harvey of the University of Iowa and his colleagues asked men and women in their late twenties, thirties, and forties to think about their most emotionally significant relationship of the past and to describe their most vivid memories. Some of those questioned recalled the beginnings of the relationship. "I met him at a small party given by our apartment manager. It was like in the movies — our eyes kept meeting across the room as we sat in a circle and got to know each other. When the party was over, we both managed to saunter out the door at the same time."[3]

Some subjects recalled the endings of the relationship. "We were lying in bed at the end of the weekend. We were both aware that the end was upon us, but we had waited until the end of his visit to talk about things. I remember lying there stiff with the sun streaming in the window, telling him what I wanted from a marriage and how I doubted he was willing to fulfill that expectation. I lay there wanting him to say I was wrong, but knowing that he wouldn't. He just turned, looked at me sadly, and said, 'You're right.'" Interestingly, the memory most often recalled by both men and women was the first sexual encounter. For example, "The first time we slept together I was living alone in a little house in a tiny town in the middle of nowhere. We stayed in bed for fourteen hours — it was wonderful."

Harvey's subjects also recalled significant moments and special occasions. Some of these incidents were very positive like the "first time he told me how he loved me." Others were negative like "some birthday. Father absent, no note, no message. Returned late the next evening with makeup on his shirt." Perhaps the ultimate in bittersweet sentiments was the simple statement "August 15 — The date we intended to marry."

Even after the passage of years, this mix of tender, sad and angry feelings may return, sometimes spontaneously, sometimes triggered by special occasions such as holidays and anniversaries. Some of the people interviewed by Harvey's group reported continuing curiosity about the lives of their former partners, wondering what they were doing and with whom.

What is the difference between normal grieving and depression when one breaks a romantic relationship?

When Mel broke up with her, Viki took it really hard. She was still very much in love with him. They had gone to concerts, movies and restaurants together, were sexually intimate, and had been accepted by each other's family and friends, and for a while it looked like they might marry. And now it was all over. Where there had been someone who filled her thoughts and shared her life, now there was a void. She felt this emptiness. She was sad, listless and lonely. During the weeks that followed the breakup, Viki slept poorly. Sometimes it took hours just to fall asleep. While she lay in bed, her mind drifted from thought to thought, mostly about Mel. Memories of the moments she shared with him filtered through her consciousness. At times these thoughts seemed to come of their own volition, almost automatically. At other times, it was as if she was trying to re-create, to bring back, something that was gone. Sometimes while she lay in bed, thinking about Mel, a mixture of strong emotions overwhelmed her. She felt angry, disappointed and sad. Sometimes she just sobbed. Viki's appetite was poor. There were days when she missed meals and hardly noticed it. In the months following the breakup, she lost 10 pounds. At work she went through the motions, but her heart wasn't in it. She was grieving for a lost love. She was also suffering from depression.

Grief and depression are not always easy to distinguish from one another. Grief is an intense emotional experience of suffering and sadness, brought on by the loss of someone or something that is very important to the individual. Depression is a constellation of symptoms that includes sadness along with a plethora of other symptoms such as sleeping and eating disturbances, loss of energy, loss of interest in one's usual activities, a sense of hopelessness and sometimes suicidal thoughts. Many people who are depressed can point to a precipitating event, usually stressful, often involving a loss. The loss may be a job, status, or one's hopes, or as in Viki's case, the loss may be of a loved one. So grief and depression may, at times, appear very similar. They both involve deep sadness and they may both involve loss. Moreover, both emotions can persist over time. But depression is a problem with broad ramifications for one's ability to function, and for many people it has biological as well as psychological causes.

The sadness that follows the breakup of a relationship is a normal expected reaction. To grieve in such circumstances is normal; many psychological theorists view grieving as a healthy and even necessary step in the process of healing oneself and making it possible to reconnect with someone else. "Getting over it" is a process that most of us go through at one time or another. In Viki's case, however, we have gone beyond grief. We see grief and depression coexisting. The normal expected reaction to the loss of a loved one is accompanied by a wide range of depressive symptoms. Like other people experiencing depression, Viki would do well to consider seeking professional help, for both antidepressive medications and psychotherapy might help her cope with her problem.

When should one consider seeking professional help for dysphoric reactions following romantic breakups? Here are a few thoughts. If the dysphoric reaction is accompanied by feelings of self-reproach and worthlessness, or suicidal thoughts, these are signs that the problem has gone beyond a grief reaction and warrants professional attention. Secondly, if the person becomes disabled by the situation and is unable to perform adequately on the job or at school — and this becomes a chronic problem — counseling or therapy may be useful. Finally, if the person is unable to sever the bonds to the former loved object after an extended interval of time and to open himself or herself up to the possibility of reconnection to other people, then thought, too, should be given to counseling.

How can one ease the pain of breaking up?

It would be nice to be able to offer a proven formula to end this type of distress, but unfortunately, I know of none. The best I can offer is a few observations. First, it is important to keep in mind that while breaking up can be extremely unpleasant, even agonizing, it is something that most people get over in time.[4] If you feel mired in the aftermath of a broken relationship, it may be helpful to remind yourself that this is, in all probability, a temporary stage in your life — that there will come a time in which you can reconnect with someone and once again experience the joys that come with a good relationship. Hope is the antidote for despair, and research suggests that keeping a hopeful attitude can help ward off depressive reactions.

Second, try not to indulge in endless analysis, mind games if you will, about what went wrong. This mental activity is unlikely to help anything and will keep your attention focused on the past rather than on the future. Endlessly churning over in your mind the whys and wherefores of your broken romance may well make you feel more distressed, particularly if the thoughts generate feelings of anger and self-reproach. As we discussed previously, living with chronic feelings of anger is uncomfortable and often unhealthy, and feelings of self-reproach deepen depressed moods. You probably don't need to feel any worse than you do already. If you have a tendency towards self-focusing, try to shift your attention to external things — your job, a hobby, a diverting book. While some looking backwards is inevitable, and some reexperiencing of painful emotions probably has healing value, don't make it a way of life.

Third, seek out your friends. While your friends can't offer you the special combination of sharing and intimacy that your departed lover provided, they can offer you some of these things. Your friends can provide conversation and shared activities, each in his or her own way. Friends can provide an antidote to loneliness.

Fourth, if you feel devastated, consider therapy. A therapist can provide support during periods of crisis.

Fifth, when you are ready to date again, refrain from comparing the new people you meet with your ex-partner. It probably isn't fair and it certainly isn't helpful. Comparisons can pose barriers to reconnecting. Try to think of each new person you meet as a unique human being who is special in his or her own way.

Sixth, if you are inclined to mentally reconstruct your past relationship, building it up in your mind as something wonderful, dismissing all the problems that led to the breakup, you might keep this in mind: If your previous relationship had been as ideal as you are now making it out to be, why didn't it work and why did it turn into such an unhappy experience?

Does living together improve the chances of a subsequent successful marriage?

Julie and Alex lived together for six years before they were married. Both had unhappy previous marriages ending in divorce. Neither had children. Living together was not a well thought-out decision. It just happened. They had been dating for a while, started sleeping together, began doing it routinely, and one day Julie stayed. Six years and a three-year-old daughter later, they were married in a quiet ceremony in Julie's church.

Julie and Alex's decision to live together is no longer an unusual idea. Many people are not sold on the traditional idea of marriage and shy away from it. Marriage is a formidable undertaking, entails a wide range of commitments and presents something of an obstacle course just getting in and out of it. Some people find it simpler and less intimidating just to live together. Living together has been a widespread practice for some time. In the 1970s, surveys of American college students in several universities revealed that about 20 to 30 percent of the students had had at least one experience of living with a partner of the opposite sex.[5] Sometimes moving in together was rather quick. About one-third of the students in one study began living together in less than a month after their first date. Very few of the students thought seriously of marriage when they began living together.

It is interesting that once the students began living together. They proved to be very faithful to each other. Over 90 percent of the students in one study reported that they did not date outside the relationship. Male students reported that they enjoyed both the security of a steady sexual partner and the increased intimacy of the relationship.

One can argue a case that the experience of living with a partner of the opposite sex would increase the chances of subsequent marital happiness. The argument holds that the experience would allow a person to develop realistic ideas about what to expect in a marital relationship and to develop the day-to-day skills needed to adjust to such a relationship. One learns to relate by relating, and living together is about as close to the reality of marriage as one can get.

Jeffrey Jacques and Karen Chason of Florida A&M University decided to put this idea to a test. From the files of the registrars of two southern universities, they pulled the names of married students. Then they asked these students whether they had ever lived previously with someone of the opposite sex. The students who responded "yes" were compared with those who responded "no" on a variety of measures of marital success. These measures included sexual satisfaction, the fulfillment of other important needs, openness of communication and the stability of the relationship. The results of the study can be summarized very concisely. There were no observable differences between the two groups. Living together before marriage neither improved nor detracted from the quality of the marital relationship. As a training course for marriage, this experience seems unlikely to hurt one's chances for future happiness, but is unlikely to help them either.

What are the secrets to a happy marriage?

The answers to this question seem different in some respects today from what our parents and grandparents would have said. Research suggests that the prescription for a happy marriage has changed over the years. In 1978 Michael Sporakowski and George Hughston of Virginia Polytechnic Institute interviewed couples who had recently celebrated their golden wedding anniversary.[6] (The average age of the men was 77, the women, 75.) Husbands and wives were interviewed separately. Most of the interviewees reported that their marriage had been a very positive experience.

The researchers asked both husband and wife to imagine that a couple that was considering marriage had come to them for advice. Then, the researchers asked what would be the prescription that they would give the couple for a happy marriage. The idea most often brought up by the wives was "the importance of religion." Following religion, the ideas most often cited were "love," "give-and-take," and "home, family and children." The husbands' list of ideas was somewhat different. At the top of the husbands' list was "it takes two to make a marriage work," followed by "honesty and trust," "give-and-take" and "marriage is for life." For the wives of this earlier generation, one senses the belief that a happy marriage was rooted in an institutional and moral commitment — church, home and family. For the husbands, one senses a focus on personal behaviors that will keep the marriage intact.

When we turn the clock ahead closer to the present time, we see a different emphasis in the prescriptions given for a happy marriage. Our data come from a 1985 issue of *Psychology Today*. The authors, Jeanette and Robert Lauer, reported findings from a study of couples married 15 years or longer. As was true for the previous study, most of the couples said they were happily married. The Lauers presented a list of 39 statements about marriage to their subjects, asking them to select the statements that best explained why their marriage had lasted.[7] In contrast to the earlier study, the reasons most often given by husbands and wives were nearly identical. At the top of the list for both husbands and wives, were the items, "my spouse is my best friend" and "I like my spouse as a person." As some of the subjects explained, "I feel that liking a person in marriage is as important as loving that person," and "I would want to have him as a friend even if I weren't married to him."

Following the statements that your spouse should be your best friend and you should like him or her as a person, the most frequently cited reasons for the enduring marriage were "marriage is a long-term commitment," "marriage is sacred," "we agree on aims and goals," "my spouse has grown more interesting," and "I want the relationship to succeed." Many of the people interviewed thought that the present generation took the commitment of marriage too lightly. A woman who had been married for 35 years remarked, "You can't run home to mother when the first sign of trouble appears."

So for this generation of happily married couples, the prescription for success was genuinely liking one's partner and a strong sense of commitment. It will be interesting to see whether the generation of couples marrying today will share these values or if the prescriptions for a happy marriage contain different ideas which reflect the changing American family.

Who seems to get more out of marriage — men or women?

In the 1950s there was a film made starring Cary Grant and Betsy Drake entitled *Every Girl Should Be Married*. The message implied by the title was that this was the state all girls should aspire to, and when they reached it, they would attain what they wanted most in life. Another film of that period titled *The Tender Trap* suggested that the female of the species would do whatever it took to lure a not-quite-willing male into the state of matrimony. You might also recall the lyrics of a song from that era from the Broadway musical *My Fair Lady*, where Henry Higgins talked about "anxious little hands for those wedding bands." Popular culture has been telling us for many years that marriage is an institution conceived by women for the benefit of women. And as a corollary, men are enticed into marriage and put up with its constraints in spite of their predilections to remain free and independent. This conventional wisdom may have reached the status of widely accepted dogma.

I have a couple of questions to raise: Is this commonly accepted view accurate or is it a myth? Do women get a lot out of being married and men little? The facts of the matter — insofar as research can tell us — are that both men and women tend to get a lot out of marriage. I have already cited research which indicates that marriage seems to have a protective effect on both physical and mental health.[8] Moreover, married men report that they tend to be happier than single men, and married women state that they tend to be happier than single women.[9]

It's a little difficult to assess which gender gets most out of marriage. The answer may depend on how the researcher phrases his or her questions. Wendy Wood and her colleagues reviewed many studies and concluded that when the questions dealt with life satisfaction and happiness, the edge went to women. Their conclusion was that "marriage proved to be associated with greater benefits for women than for men."[10] Marriage is a highly advertised product. When the marriage is successful, there is considerable truth in packaging.

Do spouses become more alike over the years?

You might think so. After all, two people living together a long time certainly influence each other. You would expect their values and attitudes to coalesce. You could probably expect the couple to be even more alike if they have children, for a family develops its own general standards and a shared environment in which all participate.

The findings from a study which looked at this question may come as a surprise. Between the years 1935 and 1938, E. L. Kelly carried out a study of the attitudes and personalities of 300 engaged couples living in New England. In his study he included an attitude-towards-marriage scale and a psychological test which measured six basic interests — theoretical, economic, aesthetic, social, political and religious. Approximately 20 years later, Kelly was able to locate and retest 165 of these couples using the same measuring instruments. There is a statistical technique called correlation which allows one to put a numerical value on how similar the husbands and wives were for each of the attitudinal and personality measures used in the study. A research team led by Avshalom Caspi of the University of Wisconsin at Madison made these calculations for the data that Kelly had obtained for both time periods — the 1930s and the 1950s. If the spouses had indeed become more alike, the size of the correlation coefficients should be greater for the 1950s than they were for the 1930s. This was not the case. The numbers are very similar for both time periods.[11]

Clearly, the study only looked at a small sample of the many ways men and women think, feel, believe, and behave. There may well be areas in which spouses do become more alike over the years. However, the results of this study should make us skeptical that marriage has that effect across the board.

We live in an age in which married people have multiple roles. Does conflict between these roles lead to dissatisfaction?

Carrie is a good example of a late twentieth century, highly active, multiple-role modern woman, sometimes given the appellation of "super mom." She does everything and then some. For starters, she is a wife and mother of four children, teaches math at the junior high school, and is active in her church and in community organizations. All of her children are in school. All are heavily involved in extracurricular activities. All have to be chauffeured in the family van to participate in these activities which are scattered throughout the suburban community in which they live. And Carrie is the designated driver. When she is not grading homework for her students, cooking meals for her family, running clothes to the cleaner, and taking the dog and two cats to the veterinarian, Carrie drives her oldest daughter to her ballet class, her oldest son to softball practice and piano lessons, and her younger sons to soccer matches. And these are her quiet, routine days when no one is sick and there are no special projects to do.

Carrie's husband Dennis is only of modest help in these activities. He works a ten-hour day himself as a project manager in a telecommunications firm. He does what he can on the weekend, taking the boys to their soccer practice and doing the heavy grocery shopping at the supermarket. Still, that leaves Carrie with an endless list of things to do and never enough time to do them. Too many things to do in a finite amount of time is a recipe for stress. The lifestyle also puts these various demands for time in competition with one another. If there is a need for extra time at the job, what does that do to time for the children? The modern juggling act carried by many couples can lead to unhappy compromises and a feeling that things aren't being done the way one would like. Research carried out by James Campbell and Brent Snow suggests that this situation can lead to marital strain and unhappiness.

The researchers questioned married men about the level of conflict they felt between work or school on the one hand and family relations on the other. They found that higher levels of role conflict were associated with less satisfaction with the marriage.[12] The suggestion from these findings is that too much friction between roles can sour one's attitude towards one's marriage. Couples who are experiencing this problem might well take time to reexamine what they are doing by setting priorities and cutting down on marginal activities. They might be able to diminish tensions stemming from role conflicts.

In addition to time pressures brought on by multiple roles, there are often problems in marital relationships in regard to the way these roles have been delegated — which of the partners should be doing what. One or both partners may be uncomfortable with some of the roles they have assumed in the relationship, whether it is working outside the home, child care, house cleaning, grocery shopping or managing the finances. To the extent one feels one is doing things one shouldn't be doing or isn't doing what one wants to do, a kind of tension is set us between the partners. Working at the University of Pittsburgh, Ellen Frank and her colleagues found that couples in marital therapy showed higher levels of such role strain than a control group of couples not being treated. Interestingly, this type of role strain was associated with feelings of sexual dissatisfaction. The authors commented,

> Basic to our interpretation of this finding is the belief that in order to be able to relate intimately to another individual, one must first have positive feelings about oneself. This should be especially true of a sexual relationship which is, in many respects, the most intimate of relationships. Since one aspect of how one evaluates oneself is the degree to which one is fulfilling the roles one wants to fulfill ... there is good reason to think that those individuals who are dissatisfied with the role assignments in their marriages may also experience sexual dissatisfaction. This was clearly the case in the individuals in all three groups involved in this study.[13]

A friend told me her marital relationship went downhill after her first child was born. Is that the usual pattern?

Satisfaction with marital relationships often declines during pregnancy and after childbirth. Raising children can be extremely demanding and something has to give. And it is often the relationship between the man and the woman that takes the hit. The impact that children have on a marital relationship can be pervasive, often stretching into every corner of the parents' lives. The extent to which children can become the focus of their parents' existence may not be fully appreciated until the children leave home. Norma, a dark-haired woman of 45, tells this story: "My husband was on a business trip to the Orient for six weeks. And there I was alone, really for the first time. It was a strange feeling. I didn't like it at all. My two sons are now both in college. Over the years it's always been them. My husband and I never had time for each other. Well, when he came back from his trip, it seemed like we were alone for the first time in years. And you'll never believe this — it was fantastic! We began to rediscover each other. It was something like when we first met."

Countless numbers of couples are anxious to have children. Some people spend thousands of dollars at fertility clinics in the hope of conceiving a child. The joys of parenthood are legion. Still, research suggests that the birth of a child puts a strain on many relationships. Lisa Hackel and Diane Ruble of New York University carried out research on couples as they experienced the transition to parenthood. Using questionnaires and psychological scales to obtain their data, they reported the following:

> The results of this study support previous findings showing a decline in positive feelings about the marital relationship during the transition to first parenthood. In the present study, husbands as well as wives showed this change; relative to reports during pregnancy, couples reported less satisfaction, less sexual intimacy, and greater conflict after the baby was born. ... By the postpartum phase, few men or women listed their relationship as one of the three most positive things they were experiencing and this was particularly true for women."[14]

The authors were careful to point out that the relationships had not become negative experiences, just that they had become less positive.

The decline in satisfaction for husbands often is observable during pregnancy. Hackel and Ruble suggest that men may find it stressful to give the added support their wives often need during pregnancy or that men feel threatened that they may no longer be "the center of their wives' attention."[15] When we turn to the wives, one explanation offered for their decrease in satisfaction is that many wives are led to expect before or during the pregnancy that their husbands will assume much more of the burdens of running the house and looking after the child than they actually do. It often turns out that the wives end up providing most of the child care and running the house. To the extent that these wives expected something else, it could be a downer. One is reminded of the title of the Broadway musical of years past, *Promises, Promises.*

The ease of finding adequate child care for the mother who returns to work can be an important key in maintaining her positive mental health which in turn will influence the relationship. Sociologists Catherine Ross and John Mirowsky of the University of Illinois reported that working wives with adequate child care were less depressed than working women who experienced difficulties in finding suitable child care.[17]

What if I find my marital relationship smothering?

A woman I know once told me that she got divorced because she found her marriage "smothering." She said that she needed a lot of time for herself and never got it. Smothering can mean a lot of things ranging from a squeeze on space and time to a feeling that in the multifaceted demands of marriage, one has almost disappeared as an individual. One form of smothering in marriage is a limitation on one's activities. I have heard unhappy spouses complain about all the things they "liked to do" or "used to do" that they are no longer doing. The problem can become acute when a person feels he or she has given up the interests that provided meaning and enjoyment in life and the alternative activities provided by the marriage are not satisfying. The frustrated partner may feel that he or she is trapped in a situation in which there is little personal fulfillment. His or her emotions may sour into lingering feelings of resentment.

Another form of smothering is incessant demands by family members for one's time and attention. The demands of children can bring on this reaction. So too can overly clinging spouses who are unable to give their partners the freedom they need to do the things they enjoy. Smothering can simply be a matter of not having enough personal space. You may share a small space with others. Things are just crowded. You can't find things you need; you seem to be falling over each other, and the feeling arises, "I've got to get out of here!"

Some years ago I heard a story about a couple that moved into a small one-room apartment. He was going to graduate school so they couldn't afford anything larger. Everything, including the couch which opened up into a bed and the kitchenette, was in that one room. The only other space in the apartment was a small bathroom. Now it happened that the husband had an idiosyncrasy about studying. He had to be alone. He just couldn't concentrate if anyone else was in the room. In order to accommodate him, his wife either had to get out of the apartment or spend her time sitting in the bathroom. After many a night staring at a sink and a shower, she called it quits.

Smothering may take the form of restrictions in initiative and decision making. In a family where one partner is dominant, the other may not be able to exercise his or her capabilities to formulate plans and to carry them out. The unequal relationship can stunt personal growth. Until recent times, women often found themselves in this subordinate position, as society gave license to men to take charge, and many did so in an authoritarian way. The title of Ibsen's classic play, *A Doll's House*, suggests some of the constraints that society once placed on what women could do.

These, then, are some of the ways a marital relationship can be smothering. How does one cope with such situations? I would suggest a problem-solving approach. The first task in such an approach is analysis. One has to step back and as dispassionately as possible try to figure out what is happening that has brought on these feelings of being smothered. The second step is to develop a plan of action that will change these circumstances and bring some relief. To implement the plan will probably require cooperation from one's spouse. The chances of doing this successfully are probably greater if one broaches the ideas in a way that is nonaccusatory and does not arouse defenses.

Here is an example of a success story: Sylvia had been married for six years. Her husband Jeff was an accountant who worked very long hours. Sylvia had two children, Rick and Dan, both preschoolers, both needing a lot of attention. Jeff had a widowed mother who had severe arthritis and was becoming increasingly disabled. Sylvia found herself spending more and more time shopping for and looking after Jeff's mother. In addition to these responsibilities, Sylvia worked 30 hours a week doing administrative work in a social service agency. In every area of life she felt she was giving to others and had no time for herself.

Sylvia became depressed and entered therapy. During therapy she recognized that she had let most of the activities that had once brought her pleasure — taking walks in the park, shopping in the city, singing, seeing her girlfriends — fall by the wayside. She decided to change her priorities so that there was time for her to do these things again. She began to see her friends, went on shopping trips in the city, joined a community chorus and began to take walks again, both with her husband and her children. When she began to do these things, she began to feel better about everything, including her marriage.

What are things spouses most want to change in their marital relationship?

Some years ago a team of psychologists developed a questionnaire which asks husbands and wives to point out the areas in their relationship in which they would like their spouses to "make changes." The questionnaire, appropriately named the *Areas of Change Questionnaire*, enables the researcher to identify the problem areas in a relationship. A research team led by Gayla Margolin at the University of Southern California gave the questionnaire to both "distressed" married couples and couples who had a good relationship. When they compared the groups, the investigators found that the differences in the responses to the questionnaire were very large and occurred in many areas of the relationship.[17] Both the man and the woman in the distressed relationship were much more likely to complain about nearly everything than their more happily married counterparts. For a short list of these complaints, consider the following:

- decisions about spending money
- spending time keeping the house clean
- drinking
- pay attention to my sexual needs
- helping with housework when asked
- spending time with his or her relatives
- leaving me time to myself
- agreeing to do things I like when we go out together

Note that both husbands and wives found more shortcomings in their spouses in all of these areas than their counterparts in happy couples. When things go wrong conflicts can spread throughout a relationship like a growing infection. Problems can arise even in good, stable relationships. Among the happily married couples, both parties would like to see some changes in the behavior of their partners. The U.S.C. study suggests that among the happily marrieds, it is the wife that would like to see more changes in her spouse than vice versa. Here is a list of some of the changes happily married wives would like to see in their husbands:

- start interesting conversations with me
- go out with me
- discipline the children
- spend time with the children
- help with housework when asked
- give me attention when I need it
- help in planning free time
- express his emotions clearly
- show appreciation for the things I do well
- accomplish his responsibilities promptly

For their part, the happily married husbands indicated one significant area in the relationship in which they would like to see changes in the behavior of their wives. This was sexual relations. It is the familiar theme we have encountered before. Men want more sex from their women. Women want more companionship, attention and appreciation from their men. There was another finding in this study which I found particularly interesting. The women questioned tended to overestimate the amount of change they believed the husband desired in the wives. The husbands were more satisfied with their wives than the wives imagined them to be.

Where has the divorce rate been going?

Let's look at the divorce rate historically, picking as our starting point a time just before the United States entered the Second World War. We find that the divorce rate at that time was rather low; there were 293,000 divorces and annulments in the United States in 1941 (9 per 1,000 married women).[18] The war caused a transitory bounce in the rate. Wartime marriages were quickly entered into and often quickly dissolved. After the war things began to settle down. Marriage in the 1950s, the "Ozzie and Harriet" generation, seemed very stable. Divorce rates were consistently low throughout the decade of the 1950s and remained so until about 1963. Then the situation began to change. The divorce rate began to climb. Year after year the divorce rate increased until it peaked in 1981. Between 1963 and 1981, the divorce rate more than doubled. Then, when it looked like the institution of marriage might be crumbling altogether, the rise in the divorce rate ceased, and began to fall slightly. During the peak year of 1981, there were 1,213,000 divorces and annulments in the United States. By 1991, the number had fallen to 1,187,000. So at the moment, it looks like the divorce rate may be trending downward.

What are the risk factors for divorce?

When we talk about risk factors we talk about probabilities or odds. If you happen to live in certain areas of the country or to marry at a certain age or fall into certain other social and economic categories, your chances of going through a divorce are greater than someone not in these categories. But having said the probabilities are higher, it does not mean that divorce will necessarily happen or even that it is highly likely. It simply means that for reasons not fully understood, your chances are higher than somebody else's.

Here are some facts about divorce rates. In the United States, divorce rates are highest in the South and West, lower in the Midwest and lowest in the Northeast. Leaving aside Nevada where quick divorces are an industry, some of the states in which divorce rates are highest are Arizona, Oklahoma, Arkansas and Wyoming. Among the states in which divorce rates are lowest are Massachusetts, Rhode Island, New York, Pennsylvania, and North Dakota.[19] Divorces are most likely to occur in the early years of marriage. The percent of couples divorcing peaks at about the third year of marriage then drops rather steadily the longer they are married. If you can make it past three years, you just might make it a lot longer. Second marriages, on the average, don't last as long as first marriages.[20]

Young people are the ones most likely to get divorced. Divorce rates for teenage brides are very high and decline consistently with the increasing age of the bride. Men who marry in their early twenties also have a high divorce rate which decreases consistently with age. The moral of the story is if you are very young and rushing into marriage, slow down. Studies indicate that disrupted marriages are more likely to occur among less educated people, among couples experiencing economic distress, and among persons who grew up in broken families.[21] In case you wondered, it is the wife who is most likely to sue for divorce, not the husband. Statistics gathered in 1988 indicate that 61 percent of the divorces were petitioned by the wife, 32 percent by the husband and 7 percent jointly.[22]

Women and children often take a psychological beating from divorce. Is this true for men too?

This certainly seems to be the case. Like women and children, many men find separation and divorce a stressful and unhappy experience. Writing in the *American Journal of Psychiatry*, John Jacobs cites some provocative statistics.[23] Men from broken marriages were nine times more likely to be first admissions to psychiatric hospitals than men from intact homes. Incidentally, this rate was much higher than the rate for divorced women. From six months before the divorce to six months after, automobile accidents for these men doubled. Divorced and separated men had higher rates of suicide and death from a variety of diseases. All of these statistics suggest that divorce can be a source of considerable stress for men. For some men who divorce their wives, there may be an immediate sense of freedom — a feeling of "I'm out of this mess; now I can start living again." If there are fantasies of a carefree life of being single and there is a sense of relief and exhilaration, these are likely to be short-lived. According to a study by E. Mavis Hetherington, what often happens is that men spend more time at the job and in solitary activities. Many divorced men find themselves at loose ends, falling out of touch with old friends and sometimes looking for casual sexual encounters. As time goes by, many of these men become depressed and long for a caring, stable relationship.[24]

The depressive reactions to divorce are particularly severe for men who have children and who are concerned about the loss of contact with their children. In his article, Jacobs points out that the presenting complaint of many men who seek psychiatric treatment during a divorce crisis is the threat of losing their relationship with their children. Some fathers who participated in research studies said they could not tolerate the pain of only being able to see their children intermittently. Even men who remarried talked about intense feelings of loneliness. As is the case for women and children, depressive reactions to divorce for men may persist for some time. Hetherington's data indicate by two years after the divorce, the depressive reaction had substantially decreased.

What takes place in marriage counseling?

While people have offered advice to others about how to make their marriages work better for as long as the institution of marriage has been around, the professional marriage counselor is a relatively recent development. The profession developed slowly during the 1920s and 1930s and passed a milestone in 1942 with the formation of a professional association, the American Association of Marriage Counselors. Many of the early practitioners of marriage counseling or marital therapy were heavily influenced by the theory and practice of psychoanalysis. This was a natural development, for psychoanalysis was the principal type of psychotherapy that was available at the time. Over the last few decades, many new types of individual psychotherapy have been developed (e.g., behavior therapy, cognitive therapy), and these newer ideas are being incorporated into marital therapy. When couples consider marital therapy, they are likely to find what they receive will vary considerably from one therapist to the next, depending on the training, experience and theoretical orientation of the therapist.

Most practitioners will begin the process of marital therapy by making an effort to assess the nature of the problems causing distress, and that usually means listening to both parties carefully and not taking sides. When the assessment is completed, the therapist will concentrate on helping the spouses gain better understanding of themselves and their relationship and in making needed changes in the relationship. The development of insight and the institution of changes in behavior can both be important goals in marital therapy.

I would like to discuss some of the specific techniques therapists use to help bring about changes in the behavior of the distressed spouses and in the way the spouses view each other and their marriage. In doing so, I will focus on some of the procedures that have been developed by behavioral and cognitive therapists. The behavioral oriented marital therapist typically tries to help the couple improve both problem solving and communication skills. In regard to problem solving, the therapist helps the couple identify the specific problems (often behaviors) that are generating negative reactions. Then the therapist will help the couple develop alternative proposals for changing their behaviors, decide on a mutually acceptable plan to make these changes and help the couple monitor a trial run of the plan. In improving the communication between the spouses, the therapist will work with the couple to bring about a change in the high rate of negative communications (e.g., criticism, blame) that occurs in distressed couples and ask them to substitute more positive statements. The therapist may discourage communications such as obsessing about past grievances, trying to make oneself look like the good guy, overgeneralizing about the spouse's behavior or being coercive.

One of the techniques used by behavioral oriented therapists is to get the spouses to agree to specific behavior changes. These agreements often resemble quid pro quo contracts: "I will do this, if you will do that." As an example, consider these two mundane chores not being done regularly at the Anderson house: Mr. Anderson doesn't walk the dog in the evening, and Mrs. Anderson leaves her clothes scattered about the house. Both of the Andersons are irritated by the other's behavior. In the counseling session, the therapist might help the Andersons reach an agreement that if he will walk the dog, she will pick up her clothes. If the contract is carried out, the two irritants will simultaneously vanish.

One intriguing kind of contractual agreement used by some marital therapists is the institution of love days. The idea is beautifully simple. The spouses agree that on alternate days (e.g., Saturday and Sunday), they will take turns doing something nice for each other. If nothing else, these mandated times for positive acts should break the cycle of negative behavior, providing some relief to the couple. The behavior on these days also demonstrates a better way of living together, being considerate rather than destructive.

The idea of contracts may seem a little "Mickey Mouse" for adults. It sounds like something one might try with a difficult six-year-old. Indeed, in a relationship that is working, a man and woman want to do things to help each other and are inclined to overlook the minor irritants in one another's behavior. Couples in distress, however, are so often focused on the negatives in their relationship that some quick changes may be needed to shake things up, and these "contracts" made in the presence of the therapist may induce such movement.

The idea of "contingency contracting" in romantic relationships is not a new idea. In the play *Lysistrata*, the women of Greece told their men they would withhold sex if the men didn't quit fighting. I should point out that giving or withholding sex and affection is not considered kosher bargaining chips in behavioral change agreements. One hopes that these interpersonal currencies will flow more spontaneously when the irritants in the relationship are reduced.

Another approach used by marital therapists is to help the members of distressed couples change the way they look at their interactions, at each other and at marriage itself. The idea of changing the way a person understands and interprets a situation comes primarily from a school of psychotherapy called cognitive therapy. Cognitive therapy teaches that it is possible to look at a given situation and interpret it in various ways. Some of these ways are much more destructive to one's emotional health and to relationships than others. Consider this example of interpreting a situation in a very negative way. Jack was supposed to meet Christina at a downtown restaurant for lunch. Jack was on time. In fact, he was 15 minutes early. Christina was 40 minutes late. By the time she arrived Jack was furious. He chewed her out even before she had time to explain. In his explosion he implied that she always acted this way, she was thoughtless and the incident showed that she didn't respect him. Christina became defensive and equally angry, and after the brouhaha concluded, they left the restaurant without having lunch and didn't speak to each other the rest of the day.

What Jack didn't know when he sat alone in the restaurant fuming, building up a case against his wife, was that the babysitter was late, causing Christina an unavoidable delay, and that she tried to call him in his office to let him know this, but he had already left for the restaurant and that traffic had been heavy on her trip downtown. Jack had looked at a reality (his wife was 40 minutes late) and interpreted this in a way that overgeneralized from the incident ("she always acted this way") and took it personally. In his angry outburst, he cast aspersions on his wife's character and her respect for him. Had he made other assumptions about what was happening or withheld judgment, the episode would have had a much happier ending.

In addition to helping the partners in a distressed marriage to entertain more positive assumptions about each other's behavior, the therapist can help the spouses to change some of their unrealistic ideas about what marriage is supposed to be like. An example would be Ted's complaints about Linda that she doesn't keep the house clean enough. It turns out that Ted's idea of a clean house was based on his mother's home; his mother was a compulsive house cleaner. In Ted's mother's house, the vacuum cleaner was in perpetual motion; everything had to be put away in its assigned place, and the house looked more like a museum than a home. In order to make his marriage with Linda work, Ted had to rethink his assumptions about what a home ought to look like. He had to recognize that there was a range of acceptable possibilities and that the standards maintained by his mother would be destructive to his marriage if he tried to apply them in his own home.

A marital therapist can point out assumptions people make about marital relationships which are arbitrary and unrealistic. In their book *Cognitive-Behavioral Marital Therapy*, Donald Baucom and Norman Epstein list a number of standards spouses might hold which are unrealistic.[25] Here are a few examples: Through the course of a relationship being in love will be like bells are ringing; spouses should meet all of each other's needs; spouses should support all of each other's ideas and actions; and the spouse should be a perfect sexual partner. One of the tasks of the marital therapist is to help the couple reframe such notions into standards which are more attainable, making it possible for two people to live together without feeling chronically dissatisfied and disapproved.

Who does marriage counseling?

The answer to this question is not as straightforward as one might expect. I thumbed through the yellow pages of my local phone directory and turned to marriage counselors. While there were many names listed, there was no standard degree listed after each name. There was no M.D. that you would find after a physician's name or D.D.S. after a dentist's. Some names were followed by Ph.D. which could indicate the individual is a psychologist, and some names were followed by L.C.S.W. which specifies that the person is a licensed clinical social worker. But there were many individuals listed as marriage counselors without any degrees following their names. One wonders what kind of qualifications they have to call themselves marriage counselors. In states which do not license marriage counselors, such qualifications could range from little or none to extensive training in a university. It is a case of buyer beware. It seems prudent to ask hard questions. Where was the person trained? What kind of training does he or she have?

Some states have made the process of selecting a marriage counselor less chancy by requiring licenses for people calling themselves marriage counselors. If your state does not license marriage counselors, there is another possible guideline you might want to consider. In the yellow page listings for marriage counselors, you may find people listed under the heading AAMFT — American Association for Marriage and Family Therapy. This organization requires its clinical members to hold a graduate degree which includes training in theoretical areas that are relevant to marriage counseling as well as substantial supervised experience in actually doing marital therapy.

If your preference would be to choose someone for marital therapy who is a licensed psychologist, you might look in the yellow pages under psychologists. Some psychologists who have purchased space for block advertisements will state that they do marriage counseling. Most of the listings, however, are likely to be one or two line notices and will not specify what services the psychologist provides. You would have to call the individual and ask whether he or she does marriage counseling. An alternative procedure would be to call the local or state psychological association which can often provide you with the names and phone numbers of members who do marital therapy.

If your preference would be to choose a psychiatrist or social worker for marital therapy, you would probably encounter the same difficulties that you would experience in finding a psychologist. Yellow page listings for these professionals may not specify whether the individual does marital therapy. Once again, your best bets would be to telephone the individual or check with the local or state professional association.

How effective is marriage counseling?

A fairly large number of evaluation studies have been carried out assessing the effectiveness of marital therapy. The results indicate that marital therapy usually is beneficial. Some estimates are that about 60 percent of couples treated in marital therapy are helped. Couples typically report on evaluation questionnaires that they are more satisfied with the relationship after therapy. Most of the effectiveness studies have been carried out with behavioral marital therapy. Studies show that behavior martial therapy is effective in reducing both the negative communications that characterize the exchanges between distressed spouses and the number of problem areas reported by spouses — those irritants and bones of contention that angry spouses often chew on.[26]

Couples interested in seeking marital therapy may wonder whether one approach to marital therapy (e.g., behavior marital therapy) is more effective than another (e.g., psychoanalytically oriented marital therapy). There is not yet enough evidence available to fully settle this question, but the tentative conclusion is no. Researchers using relatively pure forms of the different approaches to marital therapy in comparative outcome studies have found little differences in the effectiveness of the different types of therapy.[27] And in the realities of everyday office practice, one will often find marital therapists eclectic in their approach, drawing on the techniques from a variety of approaches to marital therapy. While a prospective client may well want to inquire about the theoretical orientation of a marital therapist, it may be more important to consider the therapist's reputation and track record.

Is marital therapy a panacea for marital problems? Far from it, but it can help many distressed couples improve the quality of their relationship. Both parties, however, should have a genuine interest in entering therapy, if the process is to have a reasonable chance of working.

How can individual psychotherapy be helpful in relationship problems?

Many of the people who have come in to see me in therapy have done so because they were feeling depressed or were having relationship problems. It has been my experience that many people who report one problem also report the other. Interestingly, researchers have reported that marital therapy may have a significant effect in diminishing symptoms of depression.[28]

Some therapists focus more on interpersonal relationships than others do. Some therapists are trained to pay major attention to "intra psychic" conflicts—the struggles that take place within oneself. Other therapists focus their attention on the removal or reduction of specific symptoms such as phobias or compulsions. There is a school of therapy which has as its primary focus interpersonal psychotherapy or IPT for short. If you are looking for help with difficulties in romantic relationships, you should look for a therapist who is sensitive to these issues. It is my belief that psychotherapy can be of value to those experiencing chronic difficulties in romantic relationships in various ways. On a very basic level, the therapist can provide emotional support while you are going through the stress engendered by a troubled relationship. There is someone in your corner who is understanding—someone with whom you can share your experiences and feelings. And what you tell the therapist is confidential—it won't come back to haunt you. This support can be very important when you are feeling troubled, distraught and depressed.

The therapist can also help you better understand both yourself as a person and the way you relate to others. Together, you and your therapist can explore your thought patterns, your behavior patterns and your past history in an attempt to better understand what you are doing and why. Understanding is often the critical beginning point for making changes in attitudes and behavior that can make relationships smoother, less conflicted and more satisfying.

Sometimes explorations in therapy will venture into the recesses of childhood experiences, for as we have seen in our discussion of attachments, relationship patterns set down early in life can have a very long reach. As an example, consider Marcella. Marcella came into therapy after experiencing a series of failed relationships. Marcella was a highly educated professional; she held a Ph.D. in economics and taught both economics and political science. Not only were Marcella's relationships unstable, she had a tendency to be attracted to men who were far outside the parameters of those who were likely to be reliable partners. She had a series of affairs with men who were high school dropouts and substance abusers. In therapy it became clear that Marcella had experienced a childhood relationship with her stepfather that, while not incestuous, was sexually charged. The romantic liaisons she entered into in her adult life had a forbidden quality to them which in many ways mirrored the unresolved feelings generated in her early relationships with her stepfather. When these connections were worked through in therapy, Marcella changed her dating patterns and met, fell in love with and married a successful lawyer. She now resides in Europe with her husband and is the mother of two girls.

Another example is Olivia. Olivia's parents were killed in an automobile accident when she was only four years old. Olivia lived with an aunt who treated her with little love and kindness. When she was 16, Olivia left her aunt's home in Iowa and moved to New York City. She found a job working in a restaurant and tried to make it on her own. It turned out to be a very difficult life. Within a year she met an older man who wanted to marry her. He was not at all the sort of person that Olivia envisioned as a husband, but she accepted his proposal and they were soon married. Olivia was unhappy from day one. In a matter of months, she separated from her husband. Depressed and confused, Olivia entered therapy where she and her therapist explored the links between her childhood experiences and her decision to marry. Olivia began to more fully understand how prolonged childhood insecurity had increased her vulnerability and had adversely affected her decision-making process. She was determined not to repeat the mistake. She is now in school trying to get the training she needs to build a better life.

A therapist may focus on contemporary behavior problems as well as childhood causes. Lisa had gone through a succession of unsatisfying relationships when she entered therapy. Her pattern of relationships was relatively easy to discern and relatively easy to "fix." Lisa's problem was that she jumped into bed very quickly with new boyfriends. For the first month there was lots of lovemaking, passion and hot and heavy romance. In the second month, there was nothing. Lisa had an empty bed, a broken heart and a sense of bewilderment. In her quick acquiescence to a sexual relationship, Lisa communicated some unintended messages, "You don't have to take me seriously," "You don't have to make any effort in the relationship," and "I don't expect anything." Her therapist gave her some motherly advice. She urged

Lisa to take things a lot slower and to add sex to the relationship only when there was a viable relationship. Lisa took the advice and now has a steady boyfriend.

When a relationship is in trouble, couples therapy is usually the approach to working out the problems. However, it is often the case that one of the partners is resistant to the idea of entering such therapy. If an individual comes into the couples therapy kicking and screaming, the sessions are not likely to be terribly useful, and the enterprise could turn out to be counterproductive. Under these circumstances, it may still be useful for the receptive partner to enter individual therapy. While such therapy is unlikely to be a panacea for one's problems, it is usually helpful.

Notes

1. Romantic Love

1. Fehr and Russell (1991), p. 427.
2. For statements of Sternberg's views, see Sternberg (1986) and (1987).
3. Davis, K.E. (1985), p. 26. The comparisons between friends and lovers are presented on pages 26 and 27.
4. See Darnay and Reddy (1994).
5. *The Face Book* (1986), p. 26.
6. *Writer's Market* (1994), p. 670.
7. Ross et al. (1990) noted that non-marrieds have higher mortality rates than marrieds—about 50 percent higher among women and 250 percent higher among men. Divorced and widowed people had higher death rates from coronary heart disease, stroke, many kinds of cancer, automobile accidents, and suicide. Non-marrieds reported more physical health problems and more psychological distress. See pp. 1001–1062.
8. Cantor et al. (1992), p. 649.
9. This Browning sonnet was taken from Thomas and Brown (1941), p. 177.
10. Shakespeare, *Romeo and Juliet*, Act II, Scene 2. In Parott (1938), pp. 179–181.

2. Childhood Influences

1. See, for example, Bowlby (1982).
2. For a discussion of research using the strange situation, see Goldsmith and Alansky (1987).
3. Hazan and Shaver (1987), Table 4, p. 516.
4. Hazan and Shaver (1987), p. 517.
5. Collins and Read (1990), p. 654.
6. Collins and Read (1990), p. 654.
7. Emery (1989), p. 324.
8. Emery (1989), p. 325.
9. Hetherington (1972).
10. See Harter et al. (1988). The survey data are reported on page 5.
11. Wyatt (forthcoming).
12. For reviews of childhood sexual abuse, see Browne and Finkelhor (1986).

13. Tsai et al. (1979), p. 416.
14. This study carried out by K. Meiselman as well as similar studies is reviewed in Browne and Finkelhor (1986), pp. 70–71.
15. See Johnson and Harlow (1992).
16. Ickes and Turner (1983), p. 218.
17. Ickes and Turner (1983), p. 218.
18. Brooks-Gunn and Furstenberg (1989), p. 250.
19. Brooks-Gunn and Furstenberg (1989), p. 250.
20. Graham (1992). The comparable figure for girls was 3 percent.
21. *A Decade of Denial.* This report was prepared in response to the AIDS crisis.

3. Physical Attractiveness

1. Feingold (1992).
2. For a review of these studies, see Feingold (1990).
3. Buss (1989), p. 10, Table 5.
4. Feingold (1990), p. 983. About one out of three male advertisers stipulated physical attractiveness versus about one of seven female advertisers.
5. Shanteau and Nagy (1979). The authors replicated these results on a second sample of women students.
6. Glenwick et al. (1978).
7. The survey results were reported by Cash et al. (April 1986), see pp. 33–34.
8. Striegel-Moore et al. (1986), p. 247.
9. Striegel-Moore et al. (1986), p. 249.
10. Striegel-Moore et al. (1986), p. 249.

4. Male and Female Expectations

1. Bergner and Bergner (1990). The paper presents an analysis rather than research findings.
2. Hendrick et al. (1984). See pages 180 and 184.
3. Davis and Oathout (1987), p. 407.
4. Eidelson and Epstein (1982), p. 716.
5. See studies by Roche (1986) and Wilson and Medora (1990).
6. Bergner and Bergner (1990), p. 465.

5. Meeting the Opposite Sex

1. The program is described in Twentyman and McFall (1975).
2. Muehlenhard et al. (1988).
3. DePaulo (1992), p. 206.
4. DePaulo (1992), p. 206.
5. Rinn (1984), p. 56
6. For a description of Moore's research see McCarthy's (1986) article in *Psychology Today.*

7. Goffman (1971).
8. DePaulo (1992), p. 207.
9. *Facts About Sexual Harassment* (January 1992), p. 1.
10. *Facts About Sexual Harassment* (January 1992), p. 1.
11. Fiske (August 1992). The study recalls Feingold's observation that an attractive person is more likely to get the benefit of the doubt in regard to other characteristics such as intelligence.
12. See Saal et al. (1989). Saal's research draws on earlier studies carried out by A. Abbey reported in *The Journal of Personality and Social Psychology* 42 (1982), 830–838.
13. Muehlenhard and Scardino (1985).
14. Shakespeare, *Henry V*, Act III, Scene I. Parott (1938), p. 451.
15. See Daly et al. (1983).

6. Rape

1. This traditional definition of rape is discussed in 1990 testimony by Mary Koss before the Senate Judiciary Committee. See Koss (1990), p. 1.
2. Koss (1990), p. 2.
3. Koss (1990), p. 2.
4. See Table 1, *National Crime Survey*, 1991, Department of Justice release, "Personal and Household Crimes Rose Less Than 2 Percent Last Year" (April 19, 1992).
5. *Rape in America* (April 1992), Paragraph 1.
6. These figures were reported by Koss for college students in an article *Rape on Campus: Facing the Facts* (forthcoming).
7. Koss, *Rape on Campus: Facing the Facts* (forthcoming).
8. See Rapaport and Burkhart (1984), Table 1, p. 219.
9. Koss and Dinero (1989), p. 249.
10. Muehlenhard and Linton (1987). The researchers reported that there were twice as many incidents of sexual aggression in the man's apartment as in the woman's apartment.
11. For a discussion of the psychological effects of rape, see Kilpatrick et al. (1979).
12. Burgess and Holmstrom (1989), p. 653.
13. Burgess and Holmstrom (1989), p. 656.
14. Burgess and Holmstrom (1989), p. 656.
15. Burgess and Holmstrom (1989), p. 654.
16. Burgess and Holmstrom (1989), p. 648.
17. This incident is mentioned briefly in Muehlenhard and Cook (1988).
18. Muehlenhard and Cook (1988), Table 2.

7. Relationships

1. See Harvey (July 1984), p. 12.
2. Buss (1989). See Table 4.

3. The mean age difference for men was 2.7 years. The mean age difference for women was 3.4 years.

4. See Bentler and Newcomb (1978), Table 2. Also, Bumpass and Sweet (1972).

5. Stark (December 1984).

6. Shorter's (1975) observation probably holds better for Europe where social class distinctions have a stronger historical basis than in the United States.

7. For a discussion of similarities in age, education, and religion and marital satisfaction, see Mott and Moore (1969). However, these trends do not always hold. For example, Bentler and Newcomb (1978) did not find more similarity in education among couples who stayed married than among couples who divorced.

8. See, for example, Surra and Longstreth (1990).

9. Surra and Longstreth (1990).

10. O'Leary and Smith (1991).

11. Bentler and Newcomb (1978), p. 1065.

12. Drigotas and Rusbult (1992). The article describes Rusbult's earlier formulations as well as the revised view.

13. Drigotas and Rusbult (1992), p. 86.

14. Gray-Little and Burks (1983), p. 531.

15. Gray-Little and Burks (1983), p. 533.

8. Understanding Your Partner

1. See Jacobson and Moore (1981).

2. Franzoi et al. (1985), p. 1592.

3. Long and Andrews (1990), p. 129.

4. These items are taken from the self-dyadic perspective-taking scale. See Long (1990).

9. Conflict Resolution

1. Koren et al. (1980), p. 464.

2. These are unpublished data.

3. Baumeister et al. (1990).

4. Freud's analysis was presented in his essay, *Mourning and Melancholia* (1953).

5. Birchler et al. (1984). The study was carried out primarily on couples seeking marital therapy.

6. Surra and Longstreth (1990).

7. Jacob and Krahn (1988), p. 77.

8. Jacob and Krahn (1988), p. 77.

9. See Wiseman (1981).

10. Robbins and Nugent (1975). See Table 1.

11. Hennigan (1989), p. 26.

12. *Violence Against Women: A Week in the Life of America* (October 1992). These estimates are given on pages ix, ii, and 1 respectively.

13. These reports may be found on pages 17, 17, 18, 18, 19, and 20 respectively in *Violence Against Women: A Week in the Life of America* (October 1992).

14. See "Violence Against Women," *The Washington Post* (Health section), September 1, 1992, for a summary of this research.

15. See Snyder and Fruchtman (1981). The five types of violence against women are described on pages 880–884.

16. These data are cited in O'Leary et al. (1989), p. 266.

17. O'Leary et al. (1989), p. 264.

18. See *Violence Against Woman: A Week in the Life of America* (October 1992), p. 33.

19. Walker (1989). Walker takes the position that violence between intimate partners always worsens even though there may be temporary respites and reversals.

20. Walker (1989), p. 697.

21. *Violence Against Women: A Week in the Life of America* (October 1992), p. 33.

22. *Violence Against Women: A Week in the Life of America* (October 1992), p. 36.

23. Hamberger and Hastings (1988).

24. Saunders (1992). The types are described on pages 270 and 271.

25. Aldarondo (1992). The quotation is from a paper presented at the annual meeting of the American Psychological Association.

26. Rosenfeld (1992). See p. 213.

27. Perog-Good and Stets (1986).

28. Rosenfeld (1992), p. 206.

29. Shakespeare, *Othello*, Act III, Scene 3, in Parott (1938), p. 750.

30. Salovey and Rodin (September 1985), p. 24.

31. Salovey and Rodin (September 1985), p. 28.

32. Robbins (1993). See Chapter 9.

33. *Diagnostic and Statistical Manual* (DSM III) (1980), p. 234.

34. Sperling (1987). The author found a negative relationship between scales measuring desperate love and ego identity.

35. Gaborit et al. (forthcoming).

36. Collins and Read (1990). These data are presented in Table 14.

10. Sexual Activity

1. Several studies indicating that people with religious affiliations tend to be less sexually permissive are cited in Story (1982), p. 737.

2. See Story (1982), p. 737.

3. Zuckerman et al. (1976), p. 18.

4. Muelenhard and Hollabaugh (1988), p. 872.

5. Muelenhard and Hollabaugh (1988), p. 874.

6. Kinsey et al. (1953), p. 614.

7. The study was carried out by Geer and Fuhr (1976).

8. Mosher and O'Grady (1979), p. 870.

9. See Campagna (1985–1986).

10. See the 1993 edition of *Writer's Market* (Cincinnati: Writer's Digest Books), for these circulation figures.

11. Malamuth and McIlwraith (1988). The authors anticipated that there would be differences between the two magazines observing that *Penthouse* was more exclusively oriented toward erotic content.

12. Kinsey et al. (1953), p. 663.

13. Kinsey et al. (1953), p. 655.

14. Kinsey et al. (1953), p. 670.

15. Moreault and Fulingstad (1978). In the instructions to the subjects, it was stated that sexual fantasies were normal, usual experiences, and this may have contributed to these results.

16. Mosher and Greenberg (1969). See pages 473 and 476.

17. Shakespeare, *Twelfth Night,* Act I, Scene I, in Parott (1938), p. 557.

18. Wallach (1960).

19. Fallon and Rozin (1985).

20. See Bozzi (1989).

21. Geer and Broussard (1990). The sexual descriptions on the cards were explicit. The researchers' observation of the potential for misunderstanding was made in the Discussion section of the paper.

11. Drugs and AIDS

1. Zimmerman (1983).

2. For a review of the effects of marijuana, see Robbins (1983).

3. Robbins (1983). See pages 30, 31 and 34.

4. Robbins and Tanck (1973).

5. See *Physician's Desk Reference* (1993) for a discussion of the beta blockers and diazepam.

6. There are some long-term survivors with AIDS and other infected people whose disease has not progressed. These people represent a small minority of AIDS infected people. The use of antiviral drugs has raised hopes that AIDS can be more effectively treated.

7. *A Decade of Denial* (May 1992), p. xxii.

8. *A Decade of Denial* (May 1992), p. xvii.

9. The results for several studies looking for changes in sexual behaviors as a response to the threat of AIDS are summarized in Roscoe and Kruger (1990).

10. See Youngstrom (October 1991).

11. Cochran and Mays (1990). See Table I.

12. Sexual Fantasies

1. Brownell et al. (1977), p. 1145.

2. Campagna (1985–1986), p. 5.

3. Campagna (1985–1986). The items for the various factors are given in Table 1.

4. Knafo and Jaffe (1984). See pp. 454–455.

5. Hariton and Singer (1974). See Table I, p. 317.

6. Meuwissen and Over (1991). Rape-like fantasies were frequent in the Hariton and Singer study, but less so in this report. This suggests the need for a study

with a larger, more representative sample, before drawing conclusions about the prevalence of such fantasies in women.

7. Knafo and Jaffe (1994), Table 2. See page 460 for interpretation.
8. Hariton and Singer (1974), p. 320.
9. See Talbot et al. (1980).
10. Hall and Van de Castle (1966). The authors present statistics for many categories of dream content.
11. Kinsey et al. (1953). See pages 212 and 196.
12. Freud's "theory of dream symbolism" is explained in his *Interpretation of Dreams* (1955).
13. Robbins, Tanck, and Houshi (1985).
14. Robbins (1988). See Chapter 12.

13. Relationships and Marriage

1. Horowitz et al. (1978), p. 557. The quotations which follow are from pages 558 and 561.
2. Simpson (1987). The findings are consistent with the ideas of Rusbult, presented earlier on page 87.
3. Harvey et al. (1986), p. 367. The quotations that follow are on pages 367 and 368.
4. The experience of an unrequited love is extremely common. Baumeister and his colleagues (1993) studied unrequited love among college students and reported that 92 percent of their subjects had loved someone who did not return their love.
5. The studies and the data cited in this section are taken from Jacques and Chason (1979).
6. See Sporakowski and Hughston (1978).
7. Lauer and Lauer (June 1985). A partial list of the statements used in the study is presented on page 24. The quotations are from pages 24 and 25.
8. See page 21.
9. Wood et al. (1989).
10. Wood et al. (1989), p. 259.
11. Caspi et al. (1992). The scale for assessing values, called "The Study of Values," was devised by P.E. Vernon and G.W. Allport.
12. Campbell and Snow (forthcoming). While the focus of stress engendered by conflicting role demands in the workplace and family has been on women, this study points out the need to also pay attention to other members of the family who may be experiencing these difficulties.
13. Frank et al. (1979), p. 1102.
14. Hackel and Ruble (1992), p. 953.
15. Hackel and Ruble (1992), p. 953.
16. Ross and Mirowsky (1983) found that the ease of finding suitable child care and the husband's participation in child care both related to the level of depression experienced by the wives.
17. Margolin et al. (1983). See Table 4 for the list of the areas of change desired by the spouses.
18. These figures were taken from the *Monthly Vital Statistics Report* (May 21, 1991), see Table 1.

19. *Monthly Vital Statistics Report* (September 30, 1992), p. 4.

20. *Monthly Vital Statistics Report* (May 21, 1991), p. 4.

21. See Mott and Moore (1979) for a review of social factors influencing marital breakups.

22. *Monthly Vital Statistics Report* (May 21, 1991), p. 4.

23. Jacobs (1982). These statistics are presented on page 1236.

24. Hetherington et al. (1976).

25. Baucom and Epstein (1990). These ideas for couples counseling are analogous to Albert Ellis's concept of irrational ideas which form the basis of rational-emotive therapy. See, for example, Ellis (1962).

26. For examples of studies evaluating marital therapy, see Baucom et al. (1989), page 36 and Snyder and Wills (1989), page 39.

27. For example, Snyder and Wills (1989) compared behavioral and insight-oriented marital therapy and found them about equally effective.

28. For a review of the efficacy of marital therapy in the treatment of depression, see Jacobson et al. (1989).

Bibliography

Ainsworth, M.D.S.; Blehar, M.C.; Waters, E.; and Wall, S. (1978). *Patterns of Attachment: A Psychological Study of the Strange Situation.* Hillsdale, N.J.: Eribaum.

Aldarondo, E. (1992). "Cessation and Persistence of Wife Assault: A Longitudinal Analysis." Paper presented at the annual meeting of the American Psychological Association. Washington, D.C.

Baucom, D.H., and Epstein, N. (1990). *Cognitive-Behavioral Marital Therapy.* New York: Brunner-Mazel.

____; ____; Sayers, S.; and Sher, T.G. (1989). "The Role of Cognitions in Marital Relationships: Definitional, Methodological, and Conceptual Issues." *Journal of Consulting and Clinical Psychology,* 57, 31–38.

Baumeister, R.F. (1990). "Victim and Perpetrator Accounts of Interpersonal Conflict: Autobiographical Narratives About Anger." *Journal of Personality and Social Psychology,* 59, 994–1005.

____; Wotman, S.R.; and Stillwell, A.M. (1993). "Unrequited Love: On Heartbreak, Anger, Guilt, Scriptlessness, and Humiliation." *Journal of Personality and Social Psychology,* 64, 377–394.

Bentler, P.M., and Newcomb, M.D. (1978). "Longitudinal Study of Marital Success and Failure." *Journal of Consulting and Clinical Psychology,* 46, 1053–1070.

Bergner, R.M., and Bergner, L.L. (1990). "Sexual Misunderstanding: A Description and Pragmatic Formulation." *Psychotherapy,* 27, 464–467.

Birchler, G.R.; Fals-Stewart, W.; and Schafer, J. (1994). "The Response to Conflict Scale: A Brief Measure of Maladaptive Marital Conflict." *The Behavior Therapist,* 17, 68–69.

Bowlby, J. (1982). "Attachment and Loss: Retrospect and Prospect." *American Journal of Orthopsychiatry,* 52, 664–678.

Bozzi, V. (1989, July–August). "Tall, Dark First Date." *Psychology Today,* p. 67.

Brooks-Gunn, J., and Furstenberg, F.F., Jr. (1989). "Adolescent Sexual Behavior." *American Psychologist,* 44, 249–257.

Browne, A., and Finkelhor, D. (1986). "Impact of Child Sexual Abuse: A Review of the Research." *Psychological Bulletin,* 99, 66–77.

Brownell, K.D.; Hayes, S.C.; and Barlow, D.H. (1977). "Patterns of Appropriate and Deviant Sexual Arousal: The Behavioral Treatment of Multiple Sexual Deviations." *Journal of Consulting and Clinical Psychology,* 45, 1144–1155.

Browning, E.B. (1941). "How Do I Love Thee?" In W. Thomas and S.G. Brown (Eds.) *Reading Poems,* p. 177. New York: Oxford University Press.

Bumpass, L., and Sweet, J.A. (1972). "Differentials in Marital Instability: 1970." *American Sociological Review,* 37, 754–766.

Burgess, A.W., and Holmstrom, L.L. (1989). "Rape: Sexual Disruption and Recovery." *American Journal of Orthopsychiatry*, 49, 648–657.

Buss, D.M. (1989). "Sex Differences in Human Mate Preferences: Evolutionary Hypotheses Tested in 37 Cultures." *Behavioral and Brain Sciences*, 12, 1–49.

Cain, J.M. (1934). *The Postman Always Rings Twice*. New York: Grosset and Dunlap.

Campagna, A.F. (1985–1986). "Fantasy and Sexual Arousal in College Men: Narrative and Functional Aspects." *Imagination, Cognition and Personality*, 5, 3–20.

Campbell, J.L., and Snow, B.M. Gender Role Conflict and Family Environment as Predictors of Men's Marital Satisfaction. (Forthcoming.)

Cantor, N.; Acker, M.; and Cook-Flannagan, C. (1992). "Conflict and Preoccupation in the Intimacy Life Task." *Journal of Personality and Social Psychology*, 63, 644–655.

Cash, T.P.; Winstead, B.A.; and Janda, L.H. (1986, April). "The Great American Shape-Up." *Psychology Today*, p. 30.

Caspi, A.; Herbener, E.S.; and Ozer, D.J. (1992). "Shared Experiences and the Similarity of Personalities: A Longitudinal Study of Married Couples." *Journal of Personality and Social Psychology*, 62, 281–291.

Cochran, S.D., and Mays, V.M. (1990). "Sex, Lies and HIV." *New England Journal of Medicine*, 329, 774–775.

Collins, N.L., and Read, S.J. (1990). "Adult Attachment, Working Models, and Relationship Quality in Dating Couples." *Journal of Personality and Social Psychology*, 58, 644–663.

Daly, J.A.; Hogg, E.; Sacks, D.; Smith, M.; and Zimring, L. (1983). "Sex and Relationship Affect Social Self-Grooming." *Journal of Nonverbal Behavior*, 7, 183–189.

Darnay, A.J., and Reddy, M.A. (eds.) (1994). *Market Share Reporter*. Detroit: Gale Research.

Davis, K.E. (1985, February). "Near and Dear: Friendship and Love Compared." *Psychology Today*, p. 22.

Davis, M.H., and Oathout, H.A. (1987). "Maintenance of Satisfaction in Romantic Relationships: Empathy and Relational Competence." *Journal of Personality and Social Psychology*, 53, 397–410.

A Decade of Denial: Teens and AIDS in America (1992, May). Report of the Select Committee on Children, Youth and Families, U.S. House of Representatives.

Department of Justice (1992, April 19). "Personal and Household Crimes Rose Less Than 2 Percent Last Year." *National Crime Survey*. Washington, D.C.: Department of Justice. BJS 202-307-0784.

DePaulo, B.M. (1992). "Nonverbal Behavior and Self-Presentation." *Psychological Bulletin*, 111, 203–243.

Diagnostic and Statistical Manual of Mental Disorders (DSM-III). (1980). Washington, D.C.: American Psychistric Association.

Drigotas, S.M., and Rusbult, C.F. (1992). "Should I State or Should I Go? A Dependence Model of Breakups." *Journal of Personality and Social Psychology*, 62, 62–87.

Edwards, A.E. (1959). *Personal Preference Schedule*. San Antonio: Psychological Corporation.

Eidelson, R.J., and Epstein, N. (1982). "Cognition and Relationship Maladjustment: Development of a Measure of Dysfunctional Relationship Beliefs." *Journal of Consulting and Clinical Psychology*, 50, 715–720.

Ellis, A. (1962). *Reason and Emotion in Psychotherapy*. New York: Lyle Stuart.
Elwood, R.W., and Jacobson, N.S. (1982). "Spouses Agreement in Reporting Their Behavioral Interactions: A Clinical Replication." *Journal of Consulting and Clinical Psychology*, 50, 783–784.
Emery, R.F. (1989). "Family Violence." *American Psychologist*, 44, 321–328.
The Face Book: The Pros and Cons of Facial Plastic Surgery. (1988). American Academy of Facial Plastic Surgery. Washington, D.C.: Acropolis.
Fallon, A.E., and Rozin, P. (1985). "Sex Differences in Perceptions of Desirable Body Shape." *Journal of Abnormal Psychology*, 94, 102–105.
Feeney, J., and Noller, P. (1990). "Attachment Style as a Predictor of Adult Romantic Relationships." *Journal of Personality and Social Psychology*, 58, 281–291.
Fehr, B., and Russell, J.A. (1991). "The Concept of Love Viewed from a Prototype Perspective." *Journal of Personality and Social Psychology*, 60, 425–438.
Feingold, A. (1990). "Gender Differences in Effects of Physical Attractiveness on Romantic Attraction: A Comparison Across Five Research Paradigms." *Journal of Personality and Social Psychology*, 59, 981–993.
____. (1992). "Good-Looking People Are Not What We Think." *Psychological Bulletin*, 111, 304–341.
Fiske, S. (1991). "Controlling Self and Others: The Impact of Power on Stereotyping." Paper presented at the Annual Convention of the American Psychological Association, Washington, D.C.
Frank, E.; Anderson, C.; and Rubinstein, D. (1979). "Marital Role Strain and Sexual Satisfaction." *Journal of Consulting and Clinical Psychology*, 47, 1096–1103.
Franzoi, S.L.; Davis, M.H.; and Young, R.D. (1985). "The Effects of Private Self-Consciousness and Perspective Taking on Satisfaction in Close Relationships." *Journal of Personality and Social Psychology*, 48, 1584–1594.
Freud, S. (1953). "Contributions to the Psychology of Love." In the *Collected Papers of Sigmund Freud, Volume IV*, 192–235. London: Hogarth Press.
____. (1955). *The Interpretation of Dreams*. New York: Basic Books.
____. (1953). "Mourning and Melancholia." In the *Collected Papers of Sigmund Freud, Volume IV*, 152–172. London: Hogarth Press.
Fromm, E. (1956). *The Art of Loving*. New York: Harper.
Gaborit, M.; O'Brien, P.E.; and O'Connor, G.T. *Codependency and Self-Monitoring*. (Forthcoming.)
Geer, J.H., and Broussard, D.B. (1990). "Scaling Heterosexual Behavior and Arousal: Consistency and Sex Differences." *Journal of Personality and Social Psychology*, 58, 664–671.
____, and Fuhr, R. (1976). "Cognitive Factors in Sexual Arousal: The Role of Distraction." *Journal of Consulting and Clinical Psychology*, 44, 238–243.
Glenwick, D.S.; Jason, L.A.; and Elman, D. (1978). "Physical Attractiveness and Social Contact in the Singles Bar." *Journal of Social Psychology*, 105, 311–312.
Goffman, E. (1971). *Relations in Public*. New York: Basic Books.
Goldsmith, H.H., and Alansky, J.A. (1987). "Maternal and Infant Temperamental Predictors of Attachment: A Meta-Analytic Review." *Journal of Consulting and Clinical Psychology*, 55, 805–816.
Graham, M.A. (1992). "The Effects of Parent-Adolescent Communication on Adolescent Sexual Behavior." Paper presented at the Annual Convention of the American Psychological Association, Washington, D.C.
Gray-Little, B., and Burks, N. (1983). "Power and Satisfaction in Marriage: A Review and Critique." *Psychological Bulletin*, 93, 513–538.

Hackel, L.S., and Ruble, D.N. (1992). "Changes in the Marital Relationship After the First Baby Is Born: Predicting the Impact of Expectancy Disconfirmation." *Journal of Personality and Social Psychology*, 62, 944–957.

Hall, C.S., and Van de Castle, R.L. (1966). *The Content Analysis of Dreams*. New York: Appleton-Century-Crofts.

Hamberger, L.K., and Hastings, J. (1988). "Characteristics of Male Spouse Abuses Consistent with Personality Disorders." *Hospital and Community Psychiatry*, 39, 763–770.

Han, S. (1952). *A Many-Splendored Thing*. Boston: Little, Brown.

Hariton, E.B., and Singer, J.L. "Women's Fantasies During Sexual Intercourse: Narrative and Theoretical Implications." *Journal of Consulting and Clinical Psychology*, 42, 313–322.

Harter, S.; Alexander, P.C.; and Neimeyer, R.A. (1988). "Long-Term Effects of Incestuous Child Abuse in College Women: Social Adjustment, Social Cognition and Family Characteristics." *Journal of Consulting and Clinical Psychology*, 56, 5–8.

Harvey, B. (1984, July). "The Second Time Around." *Psychology Today*, p. 12.

Harvey, J.H.; Flanary, R.; and Morgan, M. (1986). "Vivid Memories of Vivid Loves Gone By." *Journal of Social and Personal Relationships*, 3, 359–373.

Hazan, C., and Shaver, P. (1987). "Romantic Love Conceptualized as an Attachment Process." *Journal of Personality and Social Psychology*, 52, 511–524.

Hendrick, C.; Hendrick, S.; Foots, F.H.; and Slapion-Foote, M.J. (1984). "Do Men and Women Love Differently?" *Journal of Social and Personal Relationships*, 1, 177–195.

Hennigan, L.P. (1989). *A Conspiracy of Silence: Alcoholism*. Bethesda, MD: Gannel.

Hetherington, E.M. (1972). "Effects of Father Absence on Personality Development in Adolescent Daughters." *Development Psychology*, 7, 313–326.

____; Cox, M.; and Cox, R. (1976). "Divorced Fathers." *Family Coordinator*, 25, 417–428.

Horowitz, L.M.; Sampson, H.; Siegelman, E.Y.; Weiss, J.; and Goodfriend, S. (1978). "Cohesive and Dispersal Behaviors: Two Classes of Concomitant Change in Psychotherapy." *Journal of Counsulting and Clinical Psychology*, 46, 556–564.

Ickes, W., and Turner, M. (1983). "On the Social Advantages of Having an Older, Opposite-Sex Sibling: Birth Order Influences in Mixed-Sex Dyads." *Journal of Personality and Social Psychology*, 45, 210–222.

Jacob, T., and Krahn, G. (1988). "Marital Interactions of Alcoholic Couples: Comparison with Depressed and Nondistressed Couples." *Journal of Consulting and Clinical Psychology*, 56, 73–79.

Jacobs, J.W. (1982). "The Effect of Divorce on Fathers: An Overview of the Literature." *American Journal of Psychiatry*, 139, 1235–1241.

Jacobson, N.S., and Moore, D. (1981). "Spouses as Observers of the Events in Their Relationship." *Journal of Consulting and Clinical Psychology*, 49, 269–277.

____; Holtzworth-Monroe, A.; and Schmaling, K.B. (1989). "Marital Therapy and Spouse Involvement in the Treatment of Depression, Agoraphobia, and Alcoholism." *Journal of Consulting and Clinical Psychology*, 57, 5–10.

Jacques, J.M., and Chason, K.J. (1979). "Cohabitation: Its Impact on Marital Success." *The Family Coordinator*, 28, 35–39.

Johnson, L.W., and Harlow, L.L. (1992). "Multifaceted Perspective on Adult Problems Associated with Child Sexual Abuse." Paper presented at the Annual Convention of the American Psychological Association, Washington, D.C.

Kelly, E.L. (1955). "Consistency of the Adult Personality." *American Psychologist*, 10, 659–681.

Kilpatrick, D.G.; Veronen, L.J.; and Resick, P.A. (1979). "The Aftermath of Rape: Recent Empirical Findings." *American Journal of Orthopsychiatry*, 49, 658–669.

Kinsey, A.C.; Pomeroy, W.B.; Martin, C.E.; and Gebhard, P.H. (1953). *Sexual Behavior in the Human Female*. Philadelphia: W.B. Saunders.

Knafo, D, and Jaffe, Y. (1984). "Sexual Fantasizing in Males and Females." *Journal of Research in Personality*, 18, 451–462.

Koren, P.; Carlton, K.; and Shaw, D. (1980). "Marital Conflict: Relations Among Behaviors, Outcomes and Distress." *Journal of Consulting and Clinical Psychology*, 48, 460–468.

Koss, M.P. (1990, August 29). "Rape Incidence: A Review and Assessment of the Data." Testimony before the Senate Judiciary Committee.

____. (Forthcoming). *Rape on Campus: Facing the Facts.*

____, and Dinero, T.E. (1989). "Discriminant Analysis of Risk Factors for Sexual Victimization Among a National Sample of College Women." *Journal of Consulting and Clinical Psychology*, 57, 242–250.

____; Gidycz, C.A.; and Wisniewski, N. (1987). "The Scope of Rape: Incidence and Prevalence of Sexual Aggression and Victimization in a National Sample of Higher Education Students." *Journal of Consulting and Clinical Psychology*, 55, 162–170.

Landis, J.T. (1963). "Some Correlates of Divorce or Nondivorce Among the Unhappily Married." *Marriage and Family Living*, 25, 178–180.

Lauer, J., and Lauer, R. (1985, June). "Marriages Made to Last." *Psychology Today*, p. 22.

Long, E.C.J. (1990). "Measuring Dyadic Perspective-Taking: Two Scales for Assessing Perspective-Taking in Marriage and Similar Dyads." *Educational and Psychological Measurement*, 50, 91–103.

Long, E.J., and Andrews, D.W. (1990). "Perspective Taking as a Predictor of Marital Adjustment." *Journal of Personality and Social Psychology*, 59, 126–131.

McCarthy, P. (1986, October). "First Moves." *Psychology Today*, p. 12.

Malamuth, N.M., and McIlwraith, R.D. (1988). "Fantasies and Exposure to Sexually Explicit Magazines." *Communications Research*, 15, 753–771.

Margolin, G.; Talovic, S.; and Weinstein, C.D. (1983). "Areas of Change Questionnaire: A Practical Approach to Marital Assessment." *Journal of Consulting and Clinical Psychology*, 51, 920–931.

Meiselman, K. (1978). *Incest*. San Francisco: Josey-Bass.

Meuwissen, I., and Over, R. (1991). "Multidimensionality of the Content of Female Sexual Fantasy." *Behavior Research and Therapy*, 29, 179–189.

Mikulincer, M., and Erev, I. (Forthcoming). "Attachment Styles and the Structure of Romantic Love." *British Journal of Social Psychology*.

Moreault, D., and Follingstad, D.R. (1978). "Sexual Fantasies of Females as a Function of Sex Guilt and Experimental Response Cues." *Journal of Consulting and Clinical Psychology*, 46, 1385–1393.

Mosher, D.L., and Greenberg, I. (1969). "Females' Affective Responses to Reading Erotic Literature." *Journal of Consulting and Clinical Psychology*, 33, 472–477.

____, and O'Grady, K.E. (1979). "Homosexual Threat, Negative Attitudes Toward Masturbation, Sex Guilt, and Males' Sexual and Affective Reaction to Explicit Sexual Films." *Journal of Consulting and Clinical Psychology*, 47, 860–873.

Mott, F.L., and Moore, S.F. (1979). "The Causes of Marital Disruption Among Young American Women: An Interdisciplinary Perspective." *Journal of Marriage and the Family*, 41, 355–365.

Muehlenhard, C.L.; Baldwin, L.E.; Bourg, W.J.; and Piper, A.M. (1988). "Helping Women 'Break the Ice': A Computer Program to Help Shy Women Start and Maintain Conversations with Men." *Journal of Computer-Based Instruction*, 15, 7-13.

____, and Cook, S.W. (1988). "Men's Self-Reports of Unwanted Sexual Activity." *Journal of Sex Research*, 24, 58–72.

____, and Hollabaugh, L.C. (1988). "Do Women Sometimes Say No When They Mean Yes? The Prevalence and Correlates of Women's Token Resistance to Sex." *Journal of Personality and Social Psychology*, 54, 872–879.

____, and Linton, M.A. (1987). "Date Rape and Sexual Aggression in Dating Situations: Incidence and Risk Factors." *Journal of Counseling Psychology*, 34, 186–196.

____, and Scardino, T.J. (1985). "What Will He Think? Men's Impressions of Women Who Initiate Dates and Achieve Academically." *Journal of Counseling Psychology*, 32, 560–569.

National Center for Health Statistics. (May 21, 1991). *Monthly Vital Statistics Report*. Hyattsville, MD: Public Health Service.

National Center for Health Statistics. (September 30, 1992). *Monthly Vital Statistics Report*. Hyattsville, MD: Public Health Service.

O'Brien, P.E., and Gaborit, M. (1992). "Co-Dependency: A Disorder Separate from Chemical Dependency." *Journal of Clinical Psychology*, 48, 129–136.

O'Leary, K.D.; Barling, J.; Arias, I.; Rosenbaum, A.; Malone, J.; and Tyree, A. (1989). "Prevalence and Stability of Physical Aggression Between Spouses: A Longitudinal Analysis." *Journal of Consulting and Clinical Psychology*, 57, 263–268.

____, and Smith, D.A. (1991). "Marital Interactions." *Annual Review of Psychology*, 42, 191–212.

O'Neill, E. (1988). *Desire Under the Elms*. In *Complete Works. Volume 2*. New York: Viking.

Perog-Good, M.A., and Stets, J. (1986). "Programs for Abusers: Who Drops Out and What Can Be Done." *Response*, 2, 17–19.

Physician's Desk Reference. (1993). Mountvale, N.J.: Medical Economics Data.

Rapaport, K., and Burkhart, B.R. (1984). "Personality and Attitudinal Characteristics of Sexually Coercive College Males." *Journal of Abnormal Psychology*, 93, 216–221.

Rape in America (1992, April 23). National Victim Center.

Reik, T. (1944). *A Psychologist Looks at Love*. New York: Farrar & Rinehart.

Rinn, W.E. (1984). "The Neuropsychology of Facial Expression: A Review of the Neurological and Psychological Mechanisms for Producing Facial Expression." *Psychological Bulletin*, 95, 52–77.

Robbins, P.R. (1983). *Marijuana: A Short Course. Update for the Eighties*. Brookline Village, MA: Branden.

____ (1988). *The Psychology of Dreams*. Jefferson, N.C.: McFarland.

____ (1993). *Understanding Depression*. Jefferson, N.C.: McFarland.

____, and Nugent, J.F., III (1975). "Perceived Consequences of Addiction: A Comparison Between Alcoholics and Heroin-Addicted Patients." *Journal of Clinical Psychology*, 31, 367–369.

____, and Tanck, R.H. (1973). "Psychological Correlates of Marijuana Use: An Exploratory Study." *Psychological Reports*, 33, 703–706.

____, and ____ (1980). "Sexual Gratification and Sexual Symbolism in Dreams: Some Support for Freud's Theory." *Bulletin of the Manninger Clinic*, 44, 49–58.

____; ____; and Houshi, F. (1985). "Anxiety and Dream Symbolism." *Journal of Personality*, 53, 17–22.

Roche, J.P. (1986). "Premarital Sex: Attitudes and Behavior by Dating Stage." *Adolescence*, 21, 107–121.

Roscoe, B., and Kruger, T.L. (1990). "AIDS: Late Adolescents' Knowledge and Its Influence on Sexual Behavior." *Adolescence*, 25, 39–48.

Rosenfeld, B.D. (1992). "Court-Ordered Treatment of Spouse Abuse." *Clinical Psychology Review*, 12, 205–226.

Ross, C.E., and Mirowsky, J. (1988). "Child Care and Emotional Adjustment to Wives' Employment." *Journal of Health and Social Behavior*, 29, 127–138.

____; ____; and Goldsteen, K. (1990). "The Impact of the Family on Health: The Decade in Review." *Journal of Marriage and the Family*, 52, 1059–1078.

Runyon, D. (1976). *The Damon Runyon Omnibus*. Jackson Heights, N.Y.: American Reprint Company.

Rusbult, C.E. (1980). "Commitment and Satisfaction in Romantic Associations: A Test of the Investment Model." *Journal of Experimental Social Psychology*, 16, 172–186.

Saal, F.; Johnson, C.B.; and Weber, N. (1989). "Friendly or Sexy? It May Depend on Whom You Ask." *Psychology of Women Quarterly*, 13, 263–276.

Salovey, P., and Rodin, J. (1985, September). "The Heart of Jealousy." *Psychology Today*, 19, 22.

Sarrel, D.M., and Masters, W.H. (1982). "Sexual Molestation of Men by Women." *Archives of Sexual Behavior*, 11, 117–131.

Saunders, D.G. (1992). "A Typology of Men Who Batter: Three Types Derived from Cluster Analysis." *American Journal of Orthopsychiatry*, 62, 264–275.

Segal, E. (1970). *Love Story*. New York: Harper and Row.

Shakespeare, W. (1938). *Henry V*. In T.M. Parott (ed.), *Shakespeare: Twenty-Three Plays and the Sonnets* (pp. 438–477). New York: Scribners.

Shakespeare, W. (1938). *Othello*. In T.M. Parott (ed.), *Shakespeare: Twenty-Three Plays and the Sonnets* (pp. 730–772). New York: Scribners.

Shakespeare, W. (1938). *Romeo and Juliet*. In T.M. Parott (ed.), *Shakespeare: Twenty-Three Plays and the Sonnets* (pp. 168–207). New York: Scribners.

Shakespeare, W. (1938). *Twelfth Night*. In T.M. Parott (ed.), *Shakespeare: Twenty-Three Plays and the Sonnets* (pp. 557–587). New York: Scribners.

Shanteau, J., and Nagy, G.F. (1979). "Probability of Acceptance in Dating Choice." *Journal of Personality and Social Psychology*, 37, 522–533.

Shorter, E. (1975). *The Making of the Modern Family*. New York: Basic Books.

Simpson, J.A. (1987). "The Dissolution of Romantic Relationships: Factors Involved in Relationship Stability and Emotional Distress." *Journal of Personality and Social Psychology*, 53, 683–692.

Snyder, D.K., and Fruchtmann, L.A. (1981). "Differential Patterns of Wife Abuse: A Data-Based Typology." *Journal of Consulting and Clinical Psychology*, 49, 878–885.

____, and Wills, R.M. (1989). "Behavioral Versus Insight-Oriented Marital Therapy: Effects on Individual and Interspousal Functioning." *Journal of Consulting and Clinical Psychology*, 57, 39–46.

Sperling, M.B. (1987). "Ego Identity and Desperate Love." *Journal of Personality Assessment*, 51, 600–605.

Sporakowski, M.J., and Hughston, G.A. (1978). "Prescriptions for Happy Marriage: Adjustments and Satisfactions of Couples Married for 50 or More Years." *Family Coordinator*, 27, 321–327.

Stark, E. (1984, December). "Love Through the Ages." *Psychology Today*, p. 16.

Sternberg, R.J. (1986). "A Triangular Theory of Love." *Psychological Review*, 93, 119–135.

____ (1987). "Liking Versus Loving: A Comparative Evaluation of Theories." *Psychological Bulletin*, 102, 331–345.

Story, M.D. (1982). "A Comparison of University Student Experience with Various Sexual Outlets in 1974 and 1980." *Adolescence*, 17, 737–747.

Striegel-Moore, R.H.; Silberstein, L.R.; and Rodin, J. (1986). "Toward an Understanding of Risk Factors for Bulimia." *American Psychologist*, 41, 246–263.

Surra, C.A., and Longstreth, M. (1990). "Similarity of Outcomes, Interdependence, and Conflict in Dating Relationships." *Journal of Personality and Social Psychology*, 59, 501–516.

Sutker, P.B.; Sutker, L.W.; and Kilpatrick, D.G. (1970). "Religious Preference, Practice, and Personal Sexual Attitudes and Behaviors." *Psychological Reports*, 26, 835–841.

Talbot, R.M.R.; Beech, H.R; and Vaughan, M. (1980). "A Normative Appraisal of Erotic Fantasies in Women." *British Journal of Social and Clinical Psychology*, 19, 81–83.

Tsai, M.; Feldman-Summers, S.; and Edgar, M. (1979). "Childhood Molestation: Variables Related to Differential Impacts on Psychosocial Functioning in Adult Women." *Journal of Abnormal Psycology*, 88, 407–417.

Twentyman, C.T., and McFall, R.M. (1975). "Behavioral Training of Social Skills in Shy Males." *Journal of Consulting and Clinical Psychology*, 43, 384–395.

U.S. Equal Employment Opportunity Commission, FS/E-4. (1992, January). *Facts About Sexual Harassment*. Washington, D.C.: U.S. Equal Employment Opportunity Commission.

U.S. News and World Report. (November 8, 1993), p. 78.

Violence Against Women: A Week in the Life of America. (1992, October). Report prepared by the Majority Staff of the United States Senate Judiciary Committee.

"Violence Against Women." (1992, September). *The Washington Post* (Health section).

Walker, L.E.A. (1989). "Psychology and Violence Against Women." *American Psychologist*, 44, 695–702.

Wallach, M.A. (1960). "Two Correlates of Symbolic Sexual Arousal: Level of Anxiety and Liking for Aesthetic Material." *Journal of Abnormal and Social Psychology*, 61, 396–401.

Wilder, T. (1985). *The Matchmaker*. In *Three Plays*. New York: Harper Perennial.

____ (1985). *Our Town*. In *Three Plays*. New York: Harper Perennial.

Willingham, C. (1964). *Eternal Fire*. New York: Dell.

Wilson, S.M., and Medora, N.P. (1990). "Gender Comparisons of College Students' Attitudes Towards Sexual Behavior." *Adolescence*, 25, 615–627.

Wiseman, J. (1981). "Sober Comportment: Patterns and Perspectives on Alcohol Addiction." *Journal of Studies on Alcohol*, 42, 106–126.

Wood, W.; Rhodes, N.; and Whelan, M. (1989). "Sex Differences in Positive Well-Being: A Consideration of Emotional Style and Marital Status." *Psychological Bulletin*, 106, 249–264.

Wyatt, G.E. "The Relationship Between the Cumulative Impact of a Range of Child Sexual Abuse Experiences and Women's Psychological Well-Being. (Forthcoming). *Victimology*.

Youngstrom, N. (1991, October). "Warning: Teens at Risk for AIDS." *American Psychological Association Monitor*, 38–39.

Zimmerman, D.R. (1983). *The Essential Guide to Nonprescription Drugs.* New York: Harper and Row.

Zuckerman, M.; Tushup, R.; and Finner, S. (1976). "Sexual Attitudes and Experience: Attitude and Personality Correlates and Changes Produced by a Course in Sexuality." *Journal of Consulting and Clinical Psychology*, 44, 7–19.

Index